EFFECTIVE WRITING
Methods and Examples

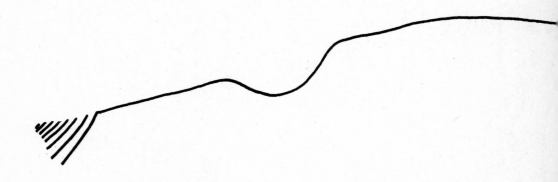

HOUGHTON MIFFLIN COMPANY BOSTON   Dallas   Geneva, Illinois   Hopewell, New Jersey
Palo Alto   London

EFFECTIVE WRITING
Methods and Examples

Kenneth R. Bindseil   *Austin Community College*
Imogene B. Dickey   *North Texas State University*

COVER AND CHAPTER-OPENING ILLUSTRATIONS BY
MICHAEL CRAWFORD

Printed in the U.S.A.

Library of Congress Catalog Card Number: 77-72907

ISBN: 0-395-24950-3

Contents

Preface

Effective Writing: Methods and Examples is a concise and realistic presentation of what most students need to know about their language in order to succeed in college and in life. The text eliminates endless pages of theory and immediately involves students in writing an acceptable college paper. It relies on clear explanations, good examples, and continued practice to move students into the realm of effective writing.

The text contains three sections. Chapters 1–13 compose the first section, which is a presentation of thirteen different methods of developing a college paper. The discussion of each method includes explanations as well as supporting examples in the form of essays and paragraphs written by students in freshman composition classes.

The second section includes twenty study units focusing on grammar, punctuation, spelling, and vocabulary. Ideal for a lab setting, these study units contain rationales, objectives, preassessments, learning activities, exercises and answers, and postassessments. They are for students who wish either to brush up on what they already know or to learn about points of grammar with which they are not yet comfortable.

The third section contains a glossary, which serves as a source of quick answers to questions that students may have in regard to writing an outline, a paragraph, or an essay. The entries—which include definitions of terms used in composition and grammar, suggestions about usage, and frequent examples—appear in alphabetical order.

All of the sample essays that constitute the "examples" of *Methods and Examples* are the work of students who have completed a course based on the text and have discovered that writing can be enjoyable. Many of the writing exercises that the text calls for involve character studies that focus on members of the class and the community. Besides serving as a means for students to get to know one another, these character studies, we have found, help to establish constructive working relationships in the classroom and reinforce for students the idea that college writing need not involve arcane subjects and difficult constructions but demands straightforward communication of information and ideas that one knows well and has found interesting.

As a further aid to learning, a list of learning objectives appears at the beginning of each chapter and study unit. The objectives relate specifically to the subject matter that follows. Every chapter includes also a list of questions that should aid students in polishing the final draft of their papers. We have tried consistently to write our explanations in sentences that are simple in construction and easy to understand. Numerous examples and the labels that appear above various parts of sentences in the study units reinforce our explanations of points of grammar and usage and should contribute to students' understanding of sentence patterns. In short, *Methods and Examples* aims at motivating students to write and getting them to write in a language whose grammar they understand and use correctly.

We wish to thank the freshman composition students in various colleges for permitting us to reprint their essays, which are an important part of the text; the graduate students of North Texas State University in classes in the teaching of college composition for offering a critical evaluation of the manuscript; Professors Jeannette McGinnes of McLennan Community College and Pat Klopp of Alvin Community College for helping us to locate samples of good student writing; and Professors Natalie West and Jeannette McGinnes of McLennan Community College for using the original manuscript in their college composition classes and making valuable suggestions for improving the text. The reviewers who commented on the text when it was in manuscript form also deserve our thanks for their helpful advice; they are Shannon Burns of the University of Arkansas, Little Rock; Betty Clement, Chairman of the Division of Communications at Paris Junior College; Kathryn Cowan of the University of California, Santa Cruz; Maury Dean of Suffolk County Community College; Tyra L. Duncan-Hall of the City College of San Francisco; William Herman of the City College of the City University of New York; and Hortense C. Parrish of the University of Tennessee, Martin.

EFFECTIVE WRITING
Methods and Examples

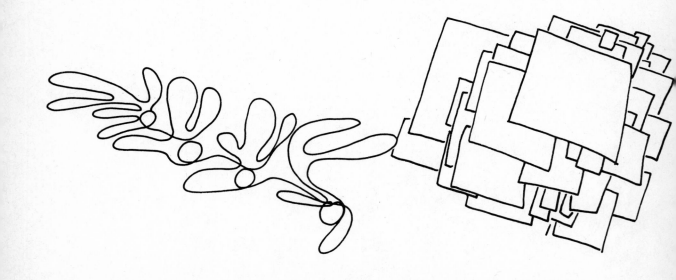

Chapter 1 □ Illustration

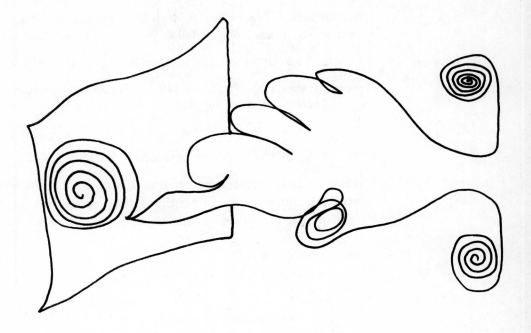

OBJECTIVES

After completing Chapter 1, you should be able to
1. write an illustration paragraph or essay
2. write and support a thesis statement
3. develop topic sentences with supporting details
4. use transitions to weave together the different parts of an essay
5. write a logical outline

You should also have gotten to know your classmates a little better.

Methods: A Formula for Illustration

Writers use illustration when they wish to clarify a statement by giving examples. A writer who is illustrating a point makes a general statement and then supports it with concrete details and examples.

General statement = concrete example + concrete example + concrete example + concrete example

A writer could use the preceding formula to illustrate the effects of inflation on college students.

Effects of inflation on college students = high tuition + high room and board fees + high cost of books and supplies + high cost of social activities

Rewritten as a sentence, this formula would read as follows:

Some of the effects of inflation on college students are high costs for tuition, room and board, books and supplies, and social activities.

Examples: Illustration in Students' Papers

Illustration can be just as effective in a paragraph or an essay as in a sentence. In the writing sample that follows, a student illustrates the statement that one of her classmates is casual, sociable, and loving.

Outline: Joanie Caruso

Topic sentence: Joanie Caruso is a casual, sociable, and loving person.
 I. Casual approach to life
    A. Clothes and hair
    B. Facial features and expressions
    C. Self-control
 II. Sociable person
    A. Ability to calm individuals
    B. Ability to win trust of others
    C. Ability to relate to people
 III. Loving character
    A. Affection for family
    B. Assistance to friends
    C. Concern for others
Conclusion: Joanie's concern for others makes her a person most people want to help.

Joanie Caruso

1, 2   Joanie Caruso is a casual, sociable, and loving person. Her long, dark hair, faded jeans, and flowing Mexican blouse emphasize her casual approach to life.
3   This casual outward appearance complements the warm smile and inner peace
4   that glow softly from her facial features. And Joanie's ability to be in control of most situations proves that her outward appearance is a true reflection of her
5, 6   inner soul. This self-control allows Joanie to be a sociable person. People enjoy

being with her, because she immediately makes them feel at ease. They often ⁷ share with her experiences that are usually saved for special friends. The ⁸ positive responses of others also encourage Joanie to relate to her friends by sharing some of her own experiences. These traits merely reinforce her loving ⁹ personality. She speaks affectionately of her parents and two brothers and ¹⁰ spends most holidays with them. Joanie's friends, likewise, benefit from her ¹¹ loving character. She never conveniently forgets someone who needs her, and ¹² she never asks for anything in return. However, Joanie's concern for others ¹³ makes her the type of person that most people just naturally want to help.

Lynne Cotton

COMMENTS ABOUT PARAGRAPH

- ☐ The title indicates the subject of the paper.

- ☐ The first sentence is the topic sentence. It informs readers that three character traits are to be illustrated: Joanie is (1) casual, (2) sociable, and (3) loving. (The topic sentence also serves as a thesis statement since it gives the main idea of the paper.)

- ☐ These character traits appear in parallel form: all three are adjectives. (Never mix parts of speech in lists.)

- ☐ The writer introduces in the second sentence the first characteristic mentioned in the topic sentence. In other words, she repeats a key word found in the topic sentence: *casual*.

- ☐ Sentences 2, 3, and 4 support this first characteristic. They are *supporting sentences*.

- ☐ Sentence 5 introduces the second characteristic.

- ☐ The writer makes a smooth transition to the second characteristic by mentioning that the first characteristic contributes to the second one.

- ☐ Sentences 6, 7, and 8 are supporting sentences for the second characteristic: *sociable*.

- ☐ Another smooth transition occurs in sentence 9 when the writer says that the third trait is reinforced by the previous characteristics.

- ☐ Sentences 10, 11, 12, and 13 support the third characteristic: *loving*.

- ☐ This whole paragraph is written in the present tense since the subject is still alive. (See page 254.)

□ Because the writer wishes to be objective by not referring to herself or her readers, she has selected the third-person point of view. (See page 241.)

Illustration works equally well in student essays.

Outline: Nick Hughes

Thesis statement: Nick Hughes is a conservative, pious, and insecure person.
I. Nick's conservative nature is obvious from his outward appearance and his personal opinions.
   A. His hair style and dress are clean-cut.
   B. He has antiliberal views about political and social issues.
   C. He has a white, conservative, middle-class background.
II. Nick's conservative attitude also accounts for his being pious.
   A. His whole life centers around the church and God.
   B. His entertainment and social activities relate directly to the church.
   C. He is totally dependent on God to make his decisions.
III. Insecurity is another of Nick's traits.
   A. He is aggressively inquisitive with people.
   B. He looks for acceptance from others.
IV. Nick's characteristics overlap.
   A. His conservative opinions influence his pious way of life.
   B. His pious way of life affects his actions among people.
   C. His most urgent need is acceptance.

Nick Hughes

1   Interviewing a stranger for a character sketch can be a difficult task, especially
2 if he has nothing to offer as a person. However, Nick Hughes has several traits
3 that make him an ideal subject. As one talks to Nick, he sees a conservative, pious, and insecure character.

1   Nick's conservative nature is very apparent from his personal opinions as well
2, 3 as from his outward appearance. His hair style and dress are clean-cut. And his antiliberal views about political and social issues reinforce his conservative
4 appearance. These views probably stem from the environment in which he lived
5 for almost thirty-one years. He spent his childhood in a small farming town in
6 South Carolina and was surrounded by white, middle-class conservatives. The first time he ever experienced a variation to this way of life was when he moved to
7 Boston only four months ago. In a man thirty-one years old, this conservative
8 attitude is naiveté. According to Nick, "There are only two kinds of people: liberals and conservatives, and I don't particularly care for the liberals."

1, 2   Nick's conservative attitude also accounts for his being a pious man. His
3 whole life centers around the church and the teachings of God. Even his enter-

tainment involves his religion as he listens only to gospel music, and all of his
social activities relate to the church. In almost everything he does, religion plays   *4*
an important part. Nick is totally dependent on God to make his decisions and   *5*
lead him through each day.

Insecurity is another one of Nick's traits, but it is not as obvious as the first two.   *1*
Nick is aggressively inquisitive with anyone who chooses to sit beside him. He is   *2, 3*
like a small puppy yearning for acceptance and in need of a friend. In his search,   *4*
he becomes pushy and persistent. But Nick is merely seeking the security of   *5*
another's acceptance, which most people need at one time or another.

As one can see, Nick's characteristics overlap somewhat. His conservative   *1, 2*
opinions influence his pious way of life, which, in return, affects his actions
among other people. The end result is a conservative and pious young man   *3*
whose most urgent need is for the security of acceptance.

Liz Cookston

COMMENTS ABOUT THE ESSAY

□ This essay is another example of illustration: the three major
    points appear in the thesis statement (sentence 3 in paragraph 1).
    Supporting examples compose the remainder of the essay. (The
    thesis statement always gives the main idea or ideas to be found in
    the paper. Every sentence that appears in the essay should expand
    upon or be logically connected to the thesis statement.)

□ The thesis statement is often the first sentence of an essay. How-
    ever, in this essay two introductory sentences precede the thesis
    statement. (Introductory paragraphs should always prepare readers
    for what is to follow and should always contain at least three
    sentences so that they do not sound incomplete or flippant.)

□ The introductory paragraph of this essay introduces the situation,
    the subject, and the subject's characteristics.

□ The word *his* relates sentence 1 of the second paragraph to the
    thesis statement. This sentence is also a topic sentence, for it states
    the topic of discussion for the second paragraph: Nick's conserva-
    tive nature.

□ Seven supporting sentences develop the topic sentence.

□ The writer alternates between *Nick* and *he* in discussing the sub-
    ject's character. This technique gives the essay variety.

□ Sentence 1 of the second paragraph introduces the first point

Illustration   7

mentioned in the thesis statement: Nick's conservative nature. The other sentences in this paragraph prove this topic sentence.

- ☐ The word *also* in sentence 1 of the third paragraph ties together the second and third paragraphs. It allows readers to glide smoothly from one paragraph to the next.

- ☐ The fourth paragraph introduces the third major point plus the transition *another*, which enables this paragraph to flow smoothly from the previous one. This last paragraph, like the other paragraphs, both begins with a topic sentence giving the main idea of the paragraph and contains relevant supporting details.

- ☐ In the last paragraph, which, like introductory paragraphs, should contain at least three sentences to avoid sounding incomplete or flippant, the writer restates the major points of the paper in a concluding and positive way.

Exercise 1-1 On a sheet of paper, record the first and last names of every member of your class. Also record nicknames and telephone numbers if your classmates wish to give them. (These names and numbers can be helpful when you need to get an assignment from a classmate.) Do not sit in your chair and wait for the class to come to you. Try to mingle with others, to learn their names.

After you have all of the names, test yourself by matching names with faces. Be prepared by the next class period to introduce every member of the class to your instructor.

Exercise 1-2 Now that you know the names of your classmates, you are ready to focus on one person.

The instructor should divide the class into pairs. As soon as you have a partner, begin interviewing by asking your partner questions that might reveal his or her personality. Ask each other questions during the class period.

If you are in doubt about what to ask, ask your partner to respond as honestly as possible to the words in the following list. Take notes so that you can use this information for your first writing assignment: an illustrative character sketch.

Words for Responses

mother	pets	money	America
father	hobbies	future	politics
brother	music	mate	presidency
sister	automobile	sex	Democrat
friendship	sports	home	Republican
life	food	major	war
death	fun	school	peace
God	clothes	vacation	communism
religion	relaxation	retirement	socialism
love	movies	Monday	men's liberation
hate	books	Wednesday	women's liberation
anger	television	Saturday	
happiness	job	Sunday	

Refer to your notes from the previous exercise as you answer the following questions in the spaces provided. Your answers will serve as an outline for the character sketch, which will be done in class. (This outline, by the way, is not intended to stifle your creativity; it is meant merely to help you prepare the first in-class assignment.) *Exercise 1-3*

1. Write the first and last names of your subject. (This information will be the title of the character sketch.)

   _____

2. In the first two spaces, write again the first and last names of your subject. In the last three spaces, write three different adjectives that describe the character of this person. (*Adjectives* are words like *kind* and *immature*; they describe persons, places, and things.)

   _____ _____ is _____, _____, and _____.

   (This sentence will serve as your topic sentence; it gives the main idea of the paragraph in one clear, concise sentence.)

3. Write the transition *for example* and continue the sentence with a statement that renames and explains the first adjective listed in the

Illustration   9

topic sentence (question 2). In other words, what did the person say or do that led you to use this adjective?

For example, _____

_____

(The transition ties together the first two sentences. Transitions weave together the different parts of a paper and allow for smooth reading.)

4. Elaborate on the sentence in question 3 by writing at least two additional statements that prove the same point. Use transitions like *also, in addition, likewise, moreover,* and *similarly,* found in the list of transitions in Exercise 1-5.

_____

_____

_____

_____

5. Write a sentence that explains why you chose the second adjective listed in the topic sentence. Begin it with one of the transitions listed in question 4. (This sentence is a *supporting sentence* because it introduces the topic of discussion for the second paragraph.)

_____

_____

6. Elaborate on the statement in question 5 by writing at least two additional sentences that prove the same point. Continue using transitions where they are needed.

_____

_____

_____

_____

_____

7. Write a sentence that explains the third adjective listed in the topic sentence. Begin it with a transition.

_____

_____

_____

8. Elaborate on the statement in question 7 by giving at least two additional sentences that prove the same point. Use transitions in the proper places.

_____

_____

_____

_____

_____

9. Restate the topic sentence in different words so that it bears a relationship to the general content of the paper and at the same time concludes it.

Illustration   11

_____

_____

_____

_____

Look at what you have written for Exercise 1-3. Notice that your sentences fall into an outline form:

Name of Subject   (question 1)

Topic sentence including three adjectives   (question 2)
   I. Renaming and explanation of first adjective   (question 3)
     A. Support of point I
     B. Additional support of point I   (question 4)
  II. Renaming and explanation of second adjective   (question 5)
     A. Support of point II
     B. Additional support of point II   (question 6)
 III. Renaming and explanation of third adjective   (question 7)
     A. Support of point III
     B. Additional support of point III   (question 8)
Conclusion: Restatement of topic sentence   (question 9)

Besides having written a logical outline, you have illustrated a person's character. As you learned earlier, illustration occurs when a statement is made and then is supported with details and examples. You made a statement and then illustrated it when you listed three dominant character traits in the topic sentence (question 2) and showed that these traits apply by giving examples for the remainder of the paper. By following a simple but useful form, you learned to write an illustration paper.

Exercise 1-4   Bring to class an outline based on the sentences you wrote in Exercise 1-3. Be prepared to use it in writing a one-paragraph character sketch of your subject. (If your classmate did not give you sufficient information, you may, instead, write a similar character sketch of a friend or relative.)

Or, if your instructor prefers an essay, be prepared to write a five-paragraph character sketch. In an introductory paragraph of at least three sentences, state the situation, subject, and subject's three main characteristics. Then devote one paragraph to each of your subject's characteristics. Be sure to add a concluding paragraph of at least three sentences. It may summarize (using other words) what has already been said, or it may draw a conclusion from previous statements. The form that follows should help you to develop an outline.

Title: _____

Paragraph I (introduction)

Background information leading to thesis statement (situation and subject):

A. _____

B. _____

Thesis statement (summary of three main characteristics):

_____

Note: The introduction should (1) have at least three sentences (so that it does not sound incomplete or flippant), (2) introduce the situation and subject, (3) provide background information leading to the thesis statement, and (4) establish very clearly the central idea of the essay (thesis statement).

Paragraph II (first major division of thesis statement)

Topic sentence (introduction of first characteristic):

_____

Illustration   13

Example A: _____

    Supporting details:

       1. _____

       2. _____

       3. _____

Example B: _____

    Supporting details:

       1. _____

       2. _____

       3. _____

Example C: _____

    Supporting details:

       1. _____

       2. _____

       3. _____

Paragraph III (second major division of thesis statement)

    Topic sentence (introduction of second characteristic):

    _____

    Example A: _____

Supporting details:

1. _____

2. _____

3. _____

Example B: _____

Supporting details:

1. _____

2. _____

3. _____

Example C: _____

Supporting details:

1. _____

2. _____

3. _____

Paragraph IV (third major division of thesis statement)

Topic sentence (introduction of third characteristic):

_____

Example A: _____

Supporting details:

1. _____

Illustration   15

2. _____

3. _____

Example B: _____

Supporting details:

1. _____

2. _____

3. _____

Example C: _____

Supporting details:

1. _____

2. _____

3. _____

Paragraph V (conclusion)

Restatement of central idea and assessment of the significance of the subject:

A. _____

B. _____

C. _____

Note: The concluding paragraph should (1) have at least three sentences (so that it does not sound incomplete or flippant), (2) restate the central idea of the essay, (3) echo previous statements, and (4) assess the significance of the subject.

Exercise 1-5

Learning the transitions in the list that follows should help you to write smoothly.

ADDITION	again, also, and, besides, equally, finally, first, further, furthermore, in addition, in the second place, last, likewise, moreover, next, nor, or, second, similar, similarly, third, too
COMPARISON	also, equally, in like manner, like, likewise, similar, similarly, too
CONTRAST	after all, although, and yet, but, conversely, despite, however, in contrast, instead, nevertheless, notwithstanding, on the contrary, on the other hand, otherwise, still, while, yet
EVIDENCE	as, as one can see, because, for, since
ILLUSTRATION	for example, for instance, for one thing, in fact, thus, to illustrate
PLACE	adjacent, beside, beyond, here, near, nearby, opposite
PURPOSE	for this purpose, for this reason, to this end, with this goal, with this idea, with this objective
RESULT	accordingly, as a result, consequently, hence, then, therefore, thereupon, thus
SUMMARY OR CONCLUSION	consequently, for example, for instance, implies that, in any event, in brief, indeed, in fact, in other words, leads one to conclude that, on the whole, proves that, therefore, thus, to be sure (Avoid *in conclusion, in summary,* and *to sum up.* These phrases insult the intelligence of your readers by suggesting that they do not realize you are concluding the essay.)

Exercise 1-6

If you wrote a paragraph, consider these questions as soon as you have completed the character sketch:

1. Does the topic sentence give the main idea (or ideas) clearly and concisely?

Illustration   17

2. Do the supporting sentences prove the topic sentence?
3. Do sufficient details and examples support the topic sentence?
4. Do transitions weave together the sentences in various parts of the paragraph?
5. Does the last sentence in the paragraph support the previous statements and does it end on a concluding note?

Exercise 1-7   If you wrote an essay, ask yourself these questions as soon as you have completed the character sketch:

1. Does the thesis statement give the main idea (or ideas) clearly and concisely?
2. Does the essay have an introductory paragraph of at least three sentences that prepares readers for what is to follow?
3. Does each of the subject's traits have a paragraph devoted to it?
4. Do all of the topic sentences prove the thesis statement?
5. Do all of the topic sentences have supporting sentences?
6. Do the supporting sentences have sufficient details and examples?
7. Do transitions weave together the paragraphs and sentences in various parts of the essay?
8. Does the concluding paragraph summarize (in other words) or bear a logical relationship to what has already been said and contain at least three sentences?

Chapter 2▫Comparison and Contrast

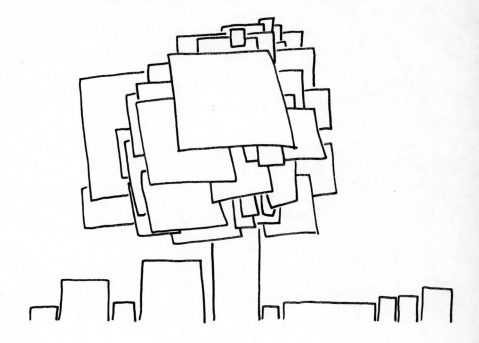

OBJECTIVES

After completing Chapter 2, you should be able to

1. write an "all A, then all B" comparison and contrast paragraph or essay
2. write an "A-B, A-B" comparison and contrast paragraph or essay
3. write a topic outline
4. write a sentence outline
5. write a paragraph outline

The "All A, Then All B" Method

Comparison and contrast is a form of illustration, because the writer of a comparison and contrast paper illustrates the similarities and differences of two or more subjects. Note that *comparison* refers to similarities and that *contrast* means differences. The best way to begin a comparison and contrast paper is to imply in the thesis statement that the subjects to be discussed are both similar and different. A writer can then organize the body of the paragraph essay in one of two ways. The simpler of these two patterns is the "all A, then all B" method. This method allows the writer to state first all the major points about subject A and then everything known about subject B in regard to these same major points. One paragraph can be devoted to each subject, or both subjects can be discussed in one paragraph. However, the writer who knows a subject well manages to gather enough material for an essay.

Examples from Students' Papers

Look at the following student paragraph that has the "all A, then all B" method of organization.

Outline: Two Instructors

Thesis statement: Mr. Richardson and Mr. Gresham reveal both similarities and differences in appearance and mannerisms.
  I. Mr. Richardson
     A. Casual and friendly East Texan
     B. Air Force appearance
     C. Informal teaching manner
     D. Textbook examinations
 II. Mr. Gresham
     A. Reserved and quiet East Texan
     B. Neat, mod appearance
     C. Systematic teaching manner
     D. Textbook examinations
Conclusion: I prefer Mr. Gresham's method of teaching.

Two Instructors

1   The two instructors whom I observed reveal both similarities and differences in
2 their appearance and mannerisms. One of these men, Mr. Richardson, a tall,
3 neatly dressed individual from East Texas, is casual and friendly. His extremely
    short hair style and conservative suits stand out as constant reminders of his
4 retired air force status. The informal manner in which he teaches, intermingled
    with constant jokes, also reflect that his students were once all-male Air Force
5, 6 personnel. However, his examinations are no joking matters. Since the material
    he presents in class is not that which is asked for on examinations, one does well
7 to study the text carefully. Like Mr. Richardson, Mr. Gresham is also a native East
8 Texan but exhibits a more reserved personality. His appearance is also neat, but

his long hair and mod style of dress strike quite a contrast in comparison to Mr. Richardson. Being a younger and less experienced teacher, Mr. Gresham is serious and systematic in his presentation of subject matter. One always knows what to expect, since Mr. Gresham follows closely the subject text matter on examinations. Even though Mr. Richardson is the more experienced of the two, I much prefer Mr. Gresham's method of teaching.

9
10
11

Paula Bloomer

COMMENTS ABOUT THE OUTLINE

- □ The writer has used a *topic outline*. Topic outlines are helpful when a writer needs only a thesis statement and a few notes for a short paper.

- □ The thesis statement gives the main idea to be found in the paragraph. (Although this outline gives the thesis statement in full, an abbreviated form is acceptable for most outlines.)

- □ With the exception of the thesis statement and the conclusion, all entries in this outline are either words or phrases. The writer has used no sentences.

- □ The major headings (I and II) are two subjects discussed in the paragraph. They are both proper nouns: Mr. Richardson and Mr. Gresham. (The major headings are equal and should always be parallel: they must all be single words, or they must all be phrases. Never list one major heading using a word and another major heading using a phrase.)

- □ The subheadings under I and II give the characteristics of the two subjects. Since all of the subheadings under a major heading are equal, they must also be parallel: they must all be words, or they must all be phrases. Notice that entries A, B, C, and D are all nouns with one or two modifiers in front of them.

- □ Unlike major headings, though, subheadings under one major heading do not have to be parallel with the subheadings under another major heading. In other words, subheadings A, B, C, and D under the first major heading do not have to be parallel with subheadings A, B, C, and D under the second major heading.

- □ Because the subheadings are details that describe the major headings, they require a slight indentation and appear underneath the first word of the major heading.

- The conclusion is a reflection on or summary of previous entries. (It is a more abbreviated version of the one used in the paragraph.)

- The outline covers the subject thoroughly.

- It also develops the subject as given in the title.

- The entries in the outline are logically arranged.

- None of the entries overlap in content.

- The outline has no single heading or subheading. (Every major heading must have at least one additional major heading, and every subheading must have at least one additional subheading. For every major heading I, there must also be a major heading II; for every subheading A, there must also be a subheading B.)

- Even though this outline has no subheadings below the first subheading level, the same rules apply to 1, 2, 3, 4, . . . ; a, b, c, d, . . . ; and (1), (2), (3), (4), . . . subheadings. These subheadings should appear underneath the first word of the previous subheading and should be slightly indented.

COMMENTS ABOUT THE PARAGRAPH

- This paragraph is an example of the comparison and contrast "all A, then all B" method. The writer tells in this paragraph everything she knows about Mr. Richardson in the first half; then she states everything she knows about Mr. Gresham in the second half.

- The topic sentence (thesis sentence) mentions that the two subjects have similarities and differences. For paragraph writing, the topic sentence and the thesis statement serve the same function: they both give the main idea or ideas to be found in the paragraph.

- The transition *one of these men* in the second sentence enables the thesis statement to flow into the body of the paper. And the transition *like* in the seventh sentence weaves together the two major subjects in this paragraph. *Like* tells readers that the two subjects have similar characteristics.

- *But* in the same sentence reminds readers that these two men also have some differences.

- The seventh sentence is also significant because it introduces a new topic of discussion: Mr. Gresham.

- The writer gives her paper variety by referring in some of her sentences to Mr. Richardson and Mr. Gresham as *he* or *his*.

- The writer compares and contrasts her subjects on the same points: appearance, mannerisms, personality, and teaching methods.

- The writer does not take her readers for granted by using *you* and *your*.

- Note the absence of contractions, which are not acceptable in formal essays.

- The writer mentions both teachers and states her preference for one of their teaching methods in the concluding statement.

Now examine a student essay with the "all A, then all B" pattern.

Outline: Riley and Mark Hathaway

Thesis statement: Although Riley and Mark are obviously different, they move, nevertheless, toward certain similarities.

I. Riley is an emotional, handsome, and intelligent eleven-year-old boy who wants to rush into maturity.
   A. His muscles reflect outdoor activities.
   B. He has a quick temper.
   C. He has a pleasant, contemporary appearance.
   D. His keen awareness and sharp mind allow him to manipulate others.
   E. He walks a tightrope between the joys of boyhood and the reality of genius.

II. Mark is an irresponsible, sensitive, fun-loving, nine-year-old boy who is reluctant to divulge his talents.
   A. He is content to be a child.
   B. His appearance suggests his fun-loving character.
   C. He plays pranks and makes his peers laugh.
   D. He is accountable for his misdeeds because of his inability to manipulate others.

Conclusion: Although each brother moves toward a recognized position in society, one is in competition with time while the other is content to enjoy each phase of life.

Riley and Mark Hathaway

Riley and Mark Hathaway are two of the most interesting boys in my neighborhood. To describe these brothers is to compare and contrast day and night with the overlapping shades of dusk and dawn. Although Riley and Mark are obviously different, they move, nevertheless, toward certain similarities.

For example, Riley is an intellectually gifted, impatient dreamer whose eleven years reflect the preteener's determination to transcend the intervening period between childhood and adulthood and to forge ahead to complete and total maturity with its imagined freedom and privileges. He is an attractive, well-proportioned youth whose muscles reflect years of outdoor activities. His blue eyes, set against an oval face, are usually loving and carefree but can become piercing and threatening when he is angry. His emotions gain further momentum when he purrs and snarls with his lips, depending on his mood. His locks are moderately long, swooping down to his brows, and fashioned in the hint of a natural wave. Riley's gifted mind, keen awareness, and sharp wit allow him to manipulate his family and friends. In spite of his skilled handling of other people, he walks a tightrope, vacillating between the immediate joys of boyhood and the reality of genius.

Mark, his nine-year-old counterpart, on the other hand, is an irresponsible, sensitive, fun-loving boy who is reluctant to divulge his talents. He is quite content to remain in the protective arms of childhood and bask in the realm of irresponsibility. Mark is a short, stocky, extremely handsome youth, whose square face has the extra adornment of platinum blond hair, gleaming green eyes that sparkle with delight, and full rosy cheeks sprinkled with freckles. He utilizes his free time in having fun, especially in playing pranks, and his eagerness to laugh makes him a welcome member of his peer group. Not without a keen intellect, his own creative genius goes unnoticed as he walks in the shadow of his brother's brilliance. Unlike his charming brother, Mark's inability to maneuver the spoken word holds him strictly accountable for his misdeeds.

The characters of Riley and Mark Hathaway, therefore, pose two interesting parallels. Although each brother moves toward a recognized position in society, one is in competition with time while the other is content to enjoy each phase of the momentous journey. That is why being their mother is a unique pleasure.

Rose Marie Davison

COMMENTS ABOUT THE OUTLINE

- ☐ The writer has developed a *sentence outline*. All of the entries are sentences. Writers who need to submit a detailed plan for an essay frequently use the sentence outline. Although the sentence outline is more detailed than the topic outline, it frees writers from the worries about parallelism that usually occur with the topic outline. It also helps writers to express their thoughts completely because, unlike a word, a sentence is a statement.

- ☐ All of the sentences are abbreviated versions of similar ones found in the essay. (The provide a skeleton for the essay.)

- ☐ The major headings are abbreviated versions of topic sentences in the essay.

- ☐ Because all of the subheadings (A, B, C, D, E) support the main headings (I, II), the writer has indented them.

- [ ] The conclusion is a restatement of the central idea, a verbal echo of the introduction, and a reflection on the significance of the topic.

COMMENTS ABOUT THE ESSAY

- [ ] In the introductory paragraph, the writer tries to interest readers in her subjects by establishing who these subjects are and why she plans to discuss them. This paragraph (which has at least three sentences) prepares readers for what is to follow.

- [ ] The introductory paragraph also gives the thesis statement: *Although Riley and Mark are obviously different, they move, nevertheless, toward certain similarities*. The whole essay proves this statement.

- [ ] All of the topic sentences—the first sentences of paragraphs 2, 3, and 4—are directly connected to the thesis statement.

- [ ] Each of these topic sentences contains a transition: *for example, on the other hand,* or *therefore*. (See Exercise 1-5.)

- [ ] In the second paragraph the writer describes Riley, and in the third paragraph she describes Mark.

- [ ] The writer uses the same points—looks, behavior, and psychology—to compare and contrast her two subjects.

- [ ] The essay has many colorful, descriptive words, including *oval, piercing, threatening, purrs, snarls, vacillating, bask, sparkle, sprinkled,* and *freckles*.

- [ ] The concluding paragraph (which contains three sentences) summarizes what has been said, reflects on previous statements, and offers a surprise in the last sentence.

- [ ] The whole essay is in the present tense (it is happening now) and the third person (it makes no direct references to readers or to the writer). (See pages 254 and 241.)

You are now ready to focus on two people. The instructor should   *Exercise 2-1*
divide the class into groups of three. You should be with two people whom you have never interviewed.

As soon as your group is complete, begin asking your partners questions that might reveal their personalities. Take turns asking questions. If you are in doubt about what to ask, look at the suggestions in Exercise 1-2. Take notes so that you can use this information for your second writing assignment: a comparison and contrast of two personalities.

Exercise 2-2   Bring to class an outline that should help you to write a one-paragraph comparison and contrast of your two subjects in Exercise 2-1. Use the "all A, then all B" method. (If your subjects did not give you sufficient information, you may, instead, write about two friends, relatives, or teachers.)

Or, if your instructor prefers an essay, be prepared to write an "all A, then all B" comparison and contrast essay. Prepare readers for your subjects by warming up with a three-sentence introduction that gives background information. Then devote one paragraph to each of your subjects. Add a concluding paragraph of at least three sentences, or add a concluding sentence to the last paragraph. If you have any difficulty, reread the examples in this chapter.

Exercise 2-3   Think about the questions that follow as soon as you have worked on the assignment discussed in Exercise 2-2.

1. Does the thesis statement give the main idea (or ideas) clearly and concisely? Remember that the topic sentence and the thesis statement serve the same purpose in the paragraph: they both give the main idea to be found in the paragraph.
2. Does the thesis statement indicate both comparison and contrast?
3. If you have written one paragraph, do all of the statements support the topic sentence?
4. If you have written an essay, do the topic sentences support the thesis statement?
5. Do the topic sentences have sufficient details and examples?
6. Does the introductory paragraph prepare readers for what is to follow?
7. Does the introductory paragraph contain at least three sentences?
8. Have you compared and contrasted your subjects on the same points?
9. Have you woven together paragraphs and sentences in various parts of the paragraph or essay by using transitions such as *also,*

however, in addition, like, likewise, moreover, on the other hand, and *similarly?* (See Exercise 1-5.)

10. Does the paragraph or essay have an adequate concluding paragraph or concluding sentence?
11. Does the concluding paragraph or concluding sentence tie in with previous statements?
12. If the essay has a concluding paragraph, does it contain at least three sentences?
13. Does every sentence in this paragraph or essay have a subject and a verb? (See page 125.)
14. Are all of the sentences punctuated correctly? (See Study Units 13, 14, and 15.)
15. Is this paragraph or essay free of contractions and the pronouns *you* and *your?*
16. Are all of the words spelled correctly? (See Study Unit 17.)

The "A-B, A-B" Pattern: Methods and Examples

The second pattern of organizing a comparison and contrast paper is the "A-B, A-B" method. This method is usually more impressive than the "all A, then all B" method because writers using it alternate between their subjects as they pinpoint similarities and differences. They always discuss both of their subjects before progressing to a new topic. The "A-B, A-B" method is especially suitable when a writer wishes to compare and contrast the attitudes and characteristics of two or more individuals. Look at the following student paragraph:

Outline: Stacy and Philip

Thesis statement: Although Stacy and Philip seem different from outward appearances, they have a surprising number of traits in common.
  I. Outdoor activities
      A. Walking and bicycling for Stacy
      B. Seasonal sports for Philip
  II. Books
      A. Science fiction for Stacy
      B. Biographies for Philip
  III. Home environments
      A. Stacy with parents
      B. Philip with mother

IV. Travel
    A. Extensive travel in United States for Stacy
    B. European travel for Philip
V. Education and future
    A. Specific career goals for Philip
    B. Uncertainty for Stacy
Conclusion: The relaxed and careless attitude of Stacy is as likable as the seriousness and maturity of Philip.

Stacy and Philip

1   Although Stacy and Philip seem different from outward appearances, they
2 have a surprising number of traits in common. One of these traits is their mutual
3 love for the outdoors. Stacy enjoys walking and bicycling, and Philip participates
4 in outdoor seasonal sports. They also spend time listening to music and reading.
5 Stacy likes novels, especially science fiction; Philip reads mainly biographies.
6, 7 Their home environments differ very much. Stacy has always lived with her family
8 and feels somewhat trapped by overprotective parents. Philip lives with his
9 mother and has to assume some responsibilities. He works after school to pay for
10 his education and to support his mother. Stacy has traveled extensively in the
11 United States. Philip, while he was stationed with the Air Force in Germany, had
12 the opportunity to see Europe. After his return from the service, he wanted to con-
13 tinue his education. He regards school as a challenge and has specific career
14, 15 goals. Stacy is still very undecided about her future. She does not feel quite
16 ready for college and would rather have time to learn what is best for her. Both
17 Stacy and Philip are interesting people. The relaxed and at times careless
attitude of one is as likable as the seriousness and maturity of the other.

Christel Scott

COMMENTS ABOUT THE OUTLINE

□ Topic outlines are usually sufficient for paragraphs and short essays.

□ The outline covers the same topics that compose the paper.

□ All the subheadings support the major headings.

□ The five major headings are parallel.

□ The conclusion is a general statement that summarizes previous entries in the outline.

COMMENTS ABOUT THE PARAGRAPH

□ This paragraph is an example of the comparison and contrast "A-B, A-B" method. The writer compares and contrasts both of her subjects on each point before she progresses to a new topic.

- The topic sentence (thesis statement) mentions that these two people have similarities and differences.

- Note the transitions *one of these traits* (in the second sentence) and *both* (in sentence 16).

- Some of the sentences mention both subjects. (Look at sentences 1, 2, 3, 4, 5, 6, and 16.)

- The writer varies her paragraph by referring in some of the sentences to Stacy as *she* and Philip as *he*. The possessive pronouns *her, his,* and *their* also add variety.

- The writer ends her paragraph with a positive comment that summarizes previous statements.

The "A-B, A-B" method is also effective in essays.

Outline: Marie and Kathy

Thesis statement: Marie and Kathy are basically conventional and religious; yet they exhibit opposite tendencies in fraternizing with peer groups, displaying ambition, and facing reality.

1. In regard to religious backgrounds, Marie and Kathy are from upper-middle-class, fairly devout families and have attended parochial schools for part of their education.
2. Even though Marie and Kathy are alike in their conventionalism, they differ in regard to peer-group relationships.
3. Marie and Kathy also display different degrees of ambition.
4. They also differ in regard to their abilities to face reality.
5. These contradictive qualities in Marie's and Kathy's peer-group relationships, lifetime ambitions, and approaches to reality are as interesting as their somewhat conventional and religious backgrounds.

Marie and Kathy

Similarities between two people are not always the foundation for friendship. For example, in the case of Marie and Kathy, both girls are best friends and seniors in high school, but they have developed different capacities to cope with life. Both girls, likewise, are conventional and religious; yet they exhibit opposite tendencies in fraternizing with peer groups, displaying ambition, and facing reality.

In regard to religious backgrounds, Marie and Kathy are from upper-middle-class, fairly devout families and have attended parochial schools for part of their education. Their religious backgrounds may account in part for their conventional attitudes. They both attend church frequently and try to adhere to their faiths. Marie and Kathy strongly oppose premarital sex and drugs. Marie is active in a drug program taught in Sunday school classes for junior high school students. Kathy does not participate in an organized program but states firmly her opinion that disobeying the teachings of the church is wrong.

Even though Marie and Kathy are alike in their conventionalism, they differ in regard to peer-group relationships. Marie is active in student, civic, and church organizations. She admits that she is popular among her peers and enjoys working with and for them. She is proud of the offices that she holds in the student council and in the band. Marie also participates occasionally in intramural sports. Kathy, however, says that she has a small group of friends and does not know many students. She is also in the band but does not play a leadership role. Kathy says that she does not care to take part in any other group program and that she does not like sports or physical education because she is not athletic.

Marie and Kathy also display different degrees of ambition. Marie is sixteen and hopes to get through high school in three years, graduating with a scholarship. She plans to get a part-time job to provide her own spending money when she graduates from high school. She says that she regards working as "necessary, but not necessarily enjoyable." Marie plans to major in special education and is looking forward to working in that field. Kathy, however, is a poor student and has no plans to work or attend college after graduation. She says that she hopes to get married soon so that she can stay at home and rear a family while her husband supports her.

Marie and Kathy also differ according to their abilities to face reality. Marie is realistic in that she has definite goals and realizes that she has to work to achieve them. She believes that life is potentially good and fulfilling, but only if one can deal with each individual and every situation as a learning experience. In contrast, Kathy's approach to life is that she must wait until she finds a husband. She apparently has no intention of confronting life actively but would rather allow life to come to her. Even though Kathy has no plans for the future, she thinks that life can be a magical fantasy in spite of her lack of effort.

The two girls, therefore, represent two different approaches to life: Marie goes out to meet the world while Kathy waits for the world to come to her. These contradictive qualities in Marie's and Kathy's peer-group relationships, lifetime ambitions, and approaches to reality are as interesting as their somewhat conventional and religious backgrounds. Regardless of their different traits, they have established the proper chemistry for a complementary friendship.

Paulette Jones

COMMENTS ABOUT THE OUTLINE

□ The writer has chosen a *paragraph outline*, which is often helpful in writing an essay or term paper of several paragraphs.

□ The paragraph outline has no major headings or subheadings. The topic sentence for each paragraph appears in the order in which it comes in the essay.

- Although the paragraph outline contains only the thesis statement and topic sentences, it is a good guide for the writer who has no difficulty remembering details.
- The topic sentences in the paragraph outline have the same wording that they have in the essay.

COMMENTS ABOUT THE ESSAY
- The title mentions the two people to be compared and contrasted in the essay.
- The thesis statement is the last sentence of the introductory paragraph.
- The introductory paragraph prepares readers by introducing the two subjects, by commenting about their relationship, and by stating the aspects of their personalities that are to be the points for comparison and contrast.
- The second paragraph, beginning with the transition *in regard to religious backgrounds,* compares and contrasts both subjects according to the first point mentioned in the thesis statement: *conventional and religious*.
- The third paragraph compares and contrasts both subjects according to the second point in the thesis statement: *fraternizing with peer groups*.
- The fourth paragraph compares and contrasts both subjects according to the third point in the thesis statement: *ambition*.
- The fifth paragraph compares and contrasts both subjects according to the fourth point in the thesis statement: *facing reality*.
- Notice that all of the paragraphs begin with a transition that connects them to previous paragraphs as well as to the thesis statement.
- The concluding paragraph summarizes in different words what has been said and offers a final comment.
- The concluding paragraph contains three sentences and summarizes the significance of previous statements.
- The writer uses the present tense because her subjects are still alive. (See page 254.)

◻ She also uses the third person because she is discussing objectively two other individuals. (See page 241.)

Exercise 2-4   Focusing on two new people, follow the directions given in Exercise 2-1.

Exercise 2-5   To prepare for an "A-B, A-B" comparison and contrast paragraph or essay, follow the directions given in Exercise 2-2.

Exercise 2-6   After you have written an "A-B, A-B" paper, review your paper. Make sure that you have compared and contrasted both subjects on each point before progressing to a new topic. Think about the questions found in Exercise 2-3.

Chapter 3 □ Analogy

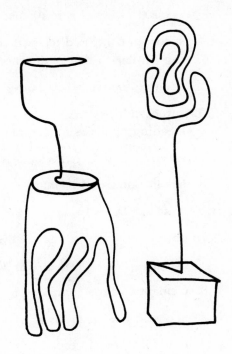

After completing Chapter 3, you should be able to
1. write an analogy
2. use different types of analogies in writing

Defining Analogy through Examples

A chapter about analogy logically follows a chapter on comparison and contrast, because an analogy allows a writer to compare two things that are essentially different except in some striking particulars. Some types and examples of analogies are as follows:

1. part related to whole

   EXAMPLE: *Bee* is to *hive* as *office worker* is to *office building*.

2. abstract compared to concrete

   EXAMPLE: *Knowledge* is to *book* as *beauty* is to *rose*.

3. effect related to cause

   EXAMPLE: *Warmth* is to *sunshine* as *happiness* is to *success*.

4. synonym compared to itself (A *synonym* is a word having a meaning similar to that of another word.)

   EXAMPLE: *Instructor* is to *teacher* as *doctor* is to *physician*.

5. antonym compared to iself (An *antonym* is a word having a meaning opposite to the meaning of another word.)

   EXAMPLE: *Light* is to *dark* as *day* is to *night*.

6. female compared to male

   EXAMPLE: *Doe* is to *buck* as *mare* is to *stallion*.

7. object compared to material of which it is made

   EXAMPLE: *Blanket* is to *wool* as *desk* is to *wood*.

8. element of time compared to another element of time

   EXAMPLE: *Hour* is to *day* as *month* is to *year*.

9. user compared to tool

   EXAMPLE: *Writer* is to *pen* as *painter* is to *brush*.

10. creator compared to creation

    EXAMPLE: *Chef* is to *meal* as *poet* is to *poem*.

11. broad category compared to narrow category

    EXAMPLE: *Rodent* is to *squirrel* as *fish* is to *flounder*.

12. person compared to characteristics

    EXAMPLE: *Weight lifter* is to *strength* as *baby* is to *helplessness*.

13. person compared to object

    EXAMPLE: *Boy* is to *sapling* as *man* is to *tree*.

14. plural compared to singular

    EXAMPLE: *We* is to *I* as *they* is to *she*.

15. symbol compared to an institution

> EXAMPLE: *Flag* is to *country* as *cross* is to *Christ*.

16. award compared to action

> EXAMPLE: *Medal* is to *bravery* as *trophy* is to *championship*.

17. object compared to object that hinders it

> EXAMPLE: *Airplane* is to *fog* as *scissors* are to *rust*.

18. something compared to a need that is satisfied

> EXAMPLE: *Water* is to *thirst* as *food* is to *hunger*.

19. family relationship compared to relative relationship

> EXAMPLE: *Mother* is to *son* as *aunt* is to *nephew*.

20. something compared to its natural medium

> EXAMPLE: *Ship* is to *water* as *airplane* is to *air*.

21. something compared to something that operates it

> EXAMPLE: *Door* is to *key* as *safe* is to *combination*.

22. virtue compared to a vice

> EXAMPLE: *Honesty* is to *dishonesty* as *bravery* is to *cowardice*.

Analogies Written by Students

The student paragraphs and essays that follow show just how unlimited the possibilities for analogies really are.

Romantic Automobiles

   Recent studies concerning human behavior and marketing point out similarities between the style of automobile and the type of woman a man finds romantic. This comparison is obvious in most automobile showrooms that display a convertible, which would be representative of the attractive, beautiful, well-groomed, and expensive woman. Both the woman and the automobile are eye-catching, but not practical choices for most men. The first automobile a man buys can be compared to his early dating experiences. The relationship with the woman is casual and not permanent, just as the first automobile a man owns may not be his first choice. As a man's experiences provide different stages of romantic adventures and comparable sports cars, there appears to be a similarity between the type of woman and the performance of the automobile he chooses. Finally, the four-door sedan, which represents the wife, proves to be the best seller. With a sedan, a man can enhance his purchase with a decorative interior, white sidewall tires, and other interesting accessories. He has an automobile that may not be perfect, but it is one he finds comfortable and enjoyable. Just as a man prefers a particular combination of accessories on the automobile he chooses, he may find an appealing combination of accessories he wishes in a woman, such as height, weight, personality traits, or ethnic preferences. These comparisons are suggestive of a way designers have found to make use of the subliminal approach in marketing automobiles.

Vivian Laverty

COMMENTS ABOUT THE PARAGRAPH

- ☐ This paragraph is an example of analogy (a person is compared to an object). The writer points out similarities between the style of automobile and the type of woman a man finds romantic.

- ☐ The title and thesis statement are original and interesting and should capture most readers' interest.

- ☐ The thesis statement tells readers what the writer is using for her analogy: *automobile* and *woman*.

- ☐ The writer compares *automobile* and *woman* on each point.

- ☐ Many of the comparisons are in one sentence.

- ☐ To give variety to this paper, the writer uses *he* and *his* in referring to man.

- ☐ The writer uses transitions, such as *this comparison, just as, finally,* and *these*. (See Exercise 1-5.)

- ☐ The writer does not take her readers for granted by using *you* and *your*. (When writers use *you* and *your*, they often erroneously project their own assumptions and values onto their readers.)

- ☐ The paragraph is free of contractions, which are not usually acceptable in formal writing.

- ☐ The paragraph ends with a concluding statement that echoes previous statements.

Now look at another student analogy developed in a paragraph.

A Study in Terror

As I sit nervously in the dentist's chair and wait for the horrors to begin, the coming ordeal reminds me of all the terrors of a roller-coaster ride. The preliminary peering and probing of the dentist recall the slow, rickety uphill grind of the coaster before the crash of the downward rush called the drill. The whirring sound lifts me, building tension onward and upward, until a precipitous drop to the nerve brings panic to the forefront. As I surge toward an empty void, and oblivion seems imminent, a sharp swerve brings me back on the track, while the dentist pauses to recoup his strength. Again, the grating hum rasps in my ears. It whirls and spins me, jerking me up and down, mouth agape and hands clenched. When I finally lurch from my seat, limp with exhaustion and exceedingly nauseated, I wonder why I paid for these thrills that afford me no enjoyment whatsoever.

Sandra Mann

COMMENTS ABOUT THE PARAGRAPH

☐ The title and thesis statement should capture readers' interest since most people have similar reactions to a visit to the dentist.

☐ The thesis statement introduces the analogy: dental appointment and roller-coaster ride.

☐ The paragraph contains strong, colorful words: *nervously, horrors, ordeal, probing, rickety, grind, crash, rush, drill, whirring, tension, onward, upward, grating, rasps, whirls, spins, jerking, clenched, lurch, limp, nauseated,* and *thrills*. These kinds of words appeal to readers' emotions. Try to use them.

☐ The paragraph ends with a punch line. The writer has taken a serious situation and developed it into an amusing analogy.

An analogy can be equally effective in an essay.

The Dating Game

Throughout history the dating game has been a subject of interest. To some observers, the game resembles a hunting expedition. There are a number of ways to go about this expedition, but two methods have proved to be the most popular among "mate hunters."

The first method, a slower and less obvious way of pursuing one's interest, is like that of a hunter who sets his trap and awaits the game. The "hunter," a single man or woman, first scouts an area to discover what prospective game it offers; then he proceeds to set the trap. In the case of a woman, she may get close enough to the "game" to observe his likes and dislikes. She then proceeds to bait the trap. The next step in the hunt takes caution and cunning. The hunter must now move in on the game and keep him just interested enough in the bait to lure him into the trap.

The second method is like a fox hunt and often proves to be useful to members of the masculine sex, since a woman's openly pursuing a man is usually considered improper. Nevertheless, some women use this method quite successfully. For example, a woman sees an attractive specimen and wastes no time in finding out his name, his address, his telephone number, his financial status, and his likes and dislikes, usually from an informant or "hound" who tells her how she can proceed to catch the prize. After becoming acquainted with the "game," the woman wastes no time in pursuing it. Some observers might refer to this part of the game as the "chase," and like many fox hunts, the "chase" rarely proceeds past this point. Although both methods require research, compromise, and perseverance, the first method provides better results.

Kim Reinking

COMMENTS ABOUT THE ESSAY

- ☐ The writer has chosen a topic that should interest most readers because most of them have dated.

- ☐ She prepares readers for what is to follow by giving some background information in the introductory paragraph. The introductory paragraph also whets readers' appetites.

- ☐ The writer also gives her thesis statement in the introductory paragraph: *To some observers the game resembles a hunting expedition.*

- ☐ She develops this thesis statement by describing two different methods of hunting a mate.

- ☐ The writer has attached to the last paragraph a concluding sentence that bears a logical relationship to previous statements. (A concluding paragraph is usually more appropriate than a concluding sentence. Regardless of which one the writer chooses, a paper should have a concluding paragraph or sentence that restates the thesis in different words or draws a conclusion from previous statements. If a concluding paragraph is used, it should have at least three sentences. Paragraphs of one or two sentences usually suggest flippant thinking or incomplete development.)

- ☐ Transitions connect the various topic sentences of the paragraphs to the thesis statement: *The first method* and *The second method.*

Exercise 3-1 Review the types of analogies exemplified at the beginning of this chapter, and think of two original subjects to compare in an analogy.

Develop your points of comparison in an outline form similar to the one that you used in the previous chapters.

Bring this outline to class and be prepared to write an analogy in either one paragraph or an essay (depending on your instructor's preference). If you have any difficulty, reread the preceding pages of this chapter, especially the sample papers.

As soon as you have completed the rough draft of your paragraph or essay, consider these questions: *Exercise 3-2*

1. Do the title and thesis statement aim to capture readers' interest? Are they original?
2. Does the thesis statement give the main idea (or ideas) clearly and concisely?
3. If you have written one paragraph, are all of the supporting sentences directly related to the topic sentence?
4. If you have written an essay, do the topic sentences support the thesis statement?
5. Have you given a sufficient number of points for comparison?
6. Have you woven together various comparisons by using transitions, such as *also, in addition, like, likewise, moreover,* and *similarly?* (See Exercise 1-5.)
7. Does the last paragraph have a concluding sentence that is connected to previous statements?
8. Does every sentence in your paragraph or essay have a subject and a verb? (See page 125.)
9. Are all of the sentences punctuated correctly? (See Study Units 13, 14, and 15.)
10. Are all of the modifiers near the words that they affect or describe? (See page 231.)
11. Is this paper free of contractions and the pronouns *you* and *your?*
12. Are all of the words spelled correctly? (See Study Unit 17.)

Chapter 4 □ Classification

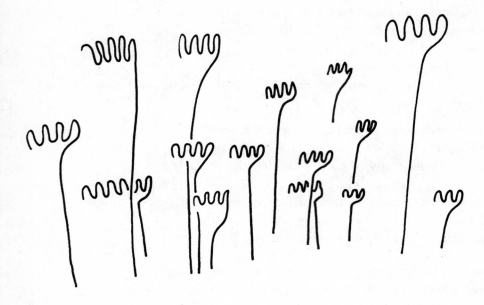

OBJECTIVES

After completing Chapter 4, you should be able to

1. write a classification paragraph or essay
2. write introductory paragraphs
3. strengthen and enliven your writing style with colorful words

The Process of Classification

Classification is the process of grouping similar experiences, ideas, persons, or things. It is a way of establishing order. For example, some people use classification when they organize the items on their grocery lists: canned goods, dairy products, fresh vegetables, meats, paper products, and soft drinks. Every time students walk into a classroom for the first time, they automatically classify their instructor according to patterns of behavior that they have observed in other instructors. In their courses, they classify writers, types of plant and animal life, forms of government, and other important subjects. In other words, the possibilities for classification are unlimited. The subjects of the student papers in the section that follows should prove this point.

Examples: Students Classify Wood, Pilots, and Spectators

Woods Used in Constructing Bows for Arrows

The most common woods for making bows are lemonwood, yew, and osage orange. Among these woods, lemonwood is the most popular one. The name of this wood comes from its creamy lemon color rather than from the tree itself. The tree is degame, and it grows around the Mediterranean and in Cuba. Although this wood is not native, it is inexpensive and appropriate for the beginning and target archer. Equally useful, the yew wood makes a very smooth shooting bow. Yew is a type of cedar which grows in the Pacific Northwest. Because of its rarity, yew is very expensive. A yew bow is especially good for target archery. The osage orange wood, unlike the other types, is not good for making a target bow. It is a hardwood, often called hedgewood, that is very coarse. In spite of its growth in areas from Indiana to Texas, osage orange is too rough and expensive for the construction of a bow. Of the three types of wood, the osage orange is definitely the least desirable in bow making.

Debbie Ingram

COMMENTS ABOUT THE PARAGRAPH

- The title gives readers an accurate idea of what is to be found in the paragraph.
- The first sentence of this paragraph is the thesis statement.
- The writer discusses the three types of wood in the order that they appear in the thesis statement.
- The writer uses transitions to introduce her discussions of the types of wood: *among, equally,* and *unlike*.
- In discussing each type of wood, the writer mentions usefulness, appearance, location, cost, and suitability.
- The concluding sentence begins with a transition phrase that connects it to previous statements.
- The writer obviously knows her subject.

□ The paragraph is written in the present tense and in the third person. (See pages 254 and 241.)

Classification is equally appropriate in an essay.

Pilot Classifications

General aviation pilots come from all walks of life. These pilots represent several distinct groups. Three of the most interesting and prominent groups are the Hangar Flyers, the Flash Gordons, and the Shaky Jakes.

Among these groups, the Hangar Flyers are usually the most obvious pilots. They congregate around flying schools, maintenance hangars, and fuel pits. Hangar Flyers do most of their flying with their mouths. They spend the better part of an afternoon in swapping flying stories, often greatly exaggerated. For their listeners' attentions, Hangar Flyers make statements like "I could barely keep the damn thing flying," "The wind was blowing twenty-five knots, ninety degrees across the runway," and "There were thunderstorms closing in from all over." They give their advice to anyone who listens. This advice stems from what they have heard from other Hangar Flyers, from what they have read in flying magazines, and occasionally from what they have experienced.

Just as interesting as the Hangar Flyers are the Flash Gordons. They may not be as noticeable as the Hangar Flyers, but they are, nevertheless, unique in appearance. The Flash Gordons wear custom-made flight suits with their names and gold wings embroidered above the left breast pockets. They also wear baseball caps with gold braid on the bills and aircraft numbers on the crowns of the caps. Protruding from the zippered pockets of their flight suits are course plotters, flight computers, pencils, pens, and pen lights. Under their arms, the Flash Gordons carry knee boards complete with stopwatches; and in their hands, they hold filled flight bags. In addition, they wear jeweled Swiss chronographs on their left wrists. They spend more time in preparation than they do in actual flight.

The Shaky Jakes are not as obvious as the Hangar Flyers and the Flash Gordons. The Shaky Jakes lack true piloting ability; yet they have licenses. Normally, they fly only when the weather conditions are ideal, and twenty degrees of crosswind is beyond their abilities. Rarely do they venture far from their home airports. Shaky Jakes' operations in the patterns are frightening, and their landings are rarely free of bounces. Of the three types of pilots, the Shaky Jakes are the most dangerous, especially in the eyes of the other two groups.

Peter Walton

COMMENTS ABOUT THE ESSAY

□ Many people consider pilots attractive and colorful people; this topic should pique their interest.

□ The essay has an introductory paragraph; the thesis statement is the last sentence of this paragraph. The first two sentences prepare readers for the thesis statement. They are background information for the thesis statement and the paragraphs that follow. (Notice that the introduction has three sentences. Two sentences are seldom enough for an introduction.)

□ The names of the three classifications are original and colorful: Hangar Flyers, Flash Gordons, and Shaky Jakes.

□ The transition *among these groups* connects the second paragraph to the first paragraph.

□ *Just as interesting as the Hangar Flyers* allows a smooth transition from the second to the third paragraph.

□ *Not as obvious as the Hangar Flyers and the Flash Gordons* provides an equally smooth transition into the fourth paragraph.

□ Dialogue in the second paragraph gives this essay variety.

□ The tongue-in-cheek style of this essay makes it light and enjoyable.

□ The writer's numerous details and examples suggest that he knows his subject well.

□ *Of the three types of pilots* in the last sentence of the essay is an effective phrase for introducing a concluding statement.

Here is another student essay that aims to catch the reader's eye with an interesting and original classification of a colorful group of people:

Horse-Racing Types

Horse races attract a multitude of people for a variety of reasons. And the reactions of the various spectators are as interesting as the actual races. These racing fans compose three main groups: the Yellers, the Whisperers, and the Mumblers.

The most conspicuous of these three goups is the Yellers. The Yellers are at the horse races to have a good time, and they work very hard to have fun. They make high wagers on the low-odds favorite, though they receive small returns on their stakes. They cheer and shout as the race begins, bellowing their horses' names, stomping their feet, and using any verbal means to speed them on their way. If their horses win, their rejoicing is something to behold! Whooping and screaming intersperse an oral replay of the gallant dash as they make a mad rush to the cashier's booth. The perennial round of drinks is ordered, and the excitement continues. If their favorites should lose, they are amazed and insulted. They bemoan their losses in high-pitched screeches and waylay every passer-by to lament their betrayals.

Though their interest is as great as that of the Yellers, the Whisperers are a completely different breed from the Yellers. They prefer betting the long odds for the big-money winners and are constantly looking for the "sure things." They scurry to and fro, whispering, murmuring, and signaling to any associate who might have the hot tip. Grasping racing forms and pencils, they check and recheck the horses' standings as they underline or cross out any significant information. The Whisperers never meet in more than two's or three's, nor do they ever look directly at each other as they mutter their advice. At the finish of the race, their seeming indifference to the results belies either their great losses or their great winnings, as they are spurred on again in search of that certain "dark horse."

The Mumblers are not as evident as the Yellers or the Whisperers. Little old ladies seem to typify this group, and they always seem to be clutching a dozen different tout sheets, racing forms, umbrellas, and change purses. As they peer nearsightedly at the racing programs, they mutter and mumble in vacillating uncertainty. These racing buffs pursue the "eeny, meeny, miny, mo" method of selection, and they use any omen for decision. An association of names, numbers, or letters is of significance and enough reason for a wager. They wait for hunches and feelings about particular horses to help remove the handicap of racing ignorance. Then, fingering their few dollars and gripping their umbrellas, they prod their ways forcefully through the crowds to take their chances. The Mumblers, more than the Yellers and the Whisperers, seem to realize the intrinsic gamble of the races; consequently, they reveal indecisiveness and fatalistic attitudes toward the outcome. Whereas the Yellers bet the obvious for fun and the Whisperers bet the odds for money, the Mumblers really have no notion as to why they bet at all.

Sandra Mann

COMMENTS ABOUT THE ESSAY

☐ The title will immediately intrigue any reader who has a notion that horse-racing people are usually exciting.

☐ The introductory paragraph, which is equally intriguing, introduces the three classifications: Yellers, Whisperers, and Mumblers. (Notice that the writer prepares readers for the thesis statement with some background information. Also note that the introduction has more than two sentences. Paragraphs with only one or two sentences usually suggest incomplete development or flippant thinking.)

☐ The classifications, as well as their supporting details and examples, are interesting and original.

- The transitions at the beginning of the second, third, and fourth paragraphs allow readers to glide smoothly from one paragraph to another.

- The writer uses words that express action and feeling: *cheer, shout, bellowing, stomping, rejoicing, whooping, screaming, dash, insulted, bemoan, screeches, lament, whispering, murmuring, signaling, grasping, mutter, spurred, clutching, peer, mumble, fingering,* and *gripping.*

- The writer mentions all three classifications again in the last paragraph.

Exercise 4-1

Think of a group of people to classify into at least three types. (If you cannot think of a subject, consider these suggestions: athletes, bartenders, clerks, cooks, dates, drivers, gamblers, ministers, movie fans, musicians, salespeople, shoppers, and waiters.) Develop your classification in an outline form similar to the one used in previous chapters.

Bring this outline to class and be prepared to write a paragraph or an essay classifying the types you have thought of. If you decide to write an essay, devote one paragraph to each type. You should also include an introductory paragraph that contains the thesis statement. The thesis statement must mention all of the types within the group to be discussed in the essay. Be sure that the introductory paragraph contains at least three sentences.

If you have any difficulty, reread the preceding pages of this chapter, especially the sample writings.

Exercise 4-2

As soon as you have completed the rough draft of your paper, review these questions:

1. Do the title, the introductory paragraph, and the thesis statement aim to capture readers' interest?
2. Does the thesis statement mention all of the types to be discussed in the paragraph or essay?
3. If there is an introductory paragraph, does it contain at least three sentences?
4. Does each of the topic sentences support the thesis statement?
5. Do the details and examples support the topic sentences?
6. Do you have a sufficient number of details and examples?

7. Do all of the new paragraphs begin with transitions? (See Exercise 1-5.)
8. Does the concluding paragraph or sentence refer to all of the types discussed in the essay?
9. Have you used words that express definite feelings or actions?
10. Does every sentence have a subject and verb? (See pages 125–126.)
11. Are all of the sentences punctuated correctly? (See Study Units 13, 14, and 15.)
12. Is this paper free of contractions and the pronouns *you* and *your*?

Chapter 5 □ Definition

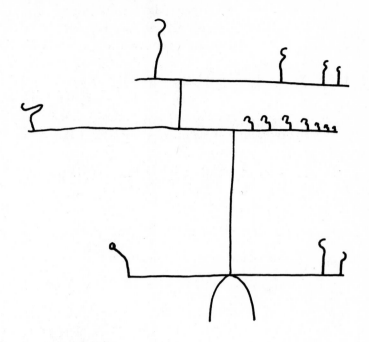

OBJECTIVES

After completing Chapter 5, you should be able to
1. write a definition paragraph or essay
2. view a word in more than one way
3. distinguish between connotation and denotation
4. set off words being defined by underlining them

Methods: A Definition of *Definition*

Definition is similar to classification because it establishes a word in a particular class before giving more specifically its various standard meanings and special meanings. For example, a study of the word *bird* reveals that it refers most generally to any member of the class Aves, any of those two-winged, warm-blooded, egg-laying creatures familiar to all of us. The "standard meanings" most of us would think of on hearing the word *bird* are the various members of the bird class—gulls, jays, and pigeons, for example. And the special meanings of the word include the following: "a bird hunted as game," "a rocket or guided missile" (aerospace slang), "a target, a clay pigeon," "the feather-tipped object used in playing badminton," "one who is odd or remarkable" (slang), "a young woman" (British slang), "a derisive sound of disapproval or derision," "to observe and identify birds in their natural surroundings," and "to trap, shoot, or catch birds."[1]

As this extended definition suggests, the writer of a definition paper begins with a general classification or meaning of a word and develops its various *denotations* (explicit meanings) and *connotations* (suggestive and associative meanings). By not limiting a discussion to one definition, writers can enlarge their vocabulary and scope of knowledge.

Examples from Students' Papers

The student papers that follow serve as good examples of definition.

What Is Establishment Today?

Although the word *establishment* means an exclusive or powerful group in control of society or a field of activity, the word has taken on another connotation today. Black power advocates and other minority groups are against the white *establishment*, the student radicals want to destroy the *establishment*, the political activists want to reform it, and the hippies want to drop out of it. Traditionally, the American *establishment* represents three power areas: political, economic, and social. The political power centers around the President, the Congress, the judicature, and the military. The economic power moves with the large companies and businesses. And the social power is in the religious groups and the national organizations. With the blacks against the whites, the poor against the rich, and the revolutionaries against all political authority, the word *establishment* has become almost meaningless. It has become a catchall word and now means anything powerful which one opposes. In modern America, the term *establishment* has become a negative term characterizing any powerful group opposing an individual's ideas.

Noureen Byrd

---

1. These meanings are taken from *The American Heritage Dictionary of the English Language*, Houghton Mifflin and the American Heritage Publishing Company, Boston, 1973.

COMMENTS ABOUT THE PARAGRAPH

▫ The writer states the formal definition (denotation) of *establishment* in the first sentence and indicates a change in connotation. (See "connotation, denotation" in the glossary.)

▫ She enlarges on these connotative definitions in other examples given throughout the paragraph.

▫ The writer views the connotative definitions through the eyes of different groups of people.

▫ The concluding sentence of the paragraph is effective because it summarizes and pulls together previous statements.

▫ Because *establishment* is the subject of this paper, the writer has given this word emphasis by underlining it. (Underlining appears as *italic* type in a printed book.) *Establishment* is also underlined (once at the beginning and twice at the end of the paper) because it is a word being referred to as a word. (See page 327.)

▫ The whole paragraph is in the present tense. (Shifting tenses is usually not a good practice. See page 260.)

Gross Is ...

The word *gross* has a number of connotations. Many people think of *gross* as including everything, total. To the businessman it means success measured by large profits; it is also an amount used in business, twelve dozen to be exact, or 144. *Gross* is, likewise, defined as "heavy or thick." Most people have seen a gross hippopotamus. Mistakes are often termed *gross*, meaning "glaring and easily seen." For example, the bank teller with a gross hairdo makes a gross mistake on my deposit. Another definition of *gross* is "coarse or vulgar," and teenagers use it as a slang word quite freely in this sense. A new series of jokes centers around the word *gross*, such as "Gross is sliding down a ten-foot razor blade into a tub of alcohol." Without a doubt, *gross* is a word with multimeanings.

Linda McKee

COMMENTS ABOUT THE PARAGRAPH

▫ The title of this paper will immediately catch the eye of many readers because the word *gross* is very popular.

▫ The first sentence serves as the thesis statement.

▫ The writer cites six different meanings of the word *gross*.

- Transitions introduce most of the definitions: *also, likewise, often, for example,* and *another*.
- The concluding sentence comments on previous sentences.

The two preceding definitions are in paragraph form. Here is a definition in a student essay:

Flamenco

Flamenco is an art originally from southern Spain. Many individuals associate the word *flamenco* with the flamenco dance and also with the flamenco guitar. The flamenco dance is one of the best-known dances in the world and the best and most popular in Spain. When the *bailadores*, or Spanish dancers, dance, they have to coordinate all body movements. They use their feet, arms, and hands, and move them according to the rhythm of flamenco music, which adapts well to either piano or guitar. These dancers have practiced this dance throughout the centuries, ever since the Romans were in Spain. The Roman emperors enjoyed the entertainment of the flamenco dancers and their wonderful style. Today, their style is still attractive, and one of the most popular dance groups performing for tourists is Los Tarantos in Barcelona.

Another aspect of flamenco is the guitar music, which parallels with the dance. Flamenco guitar playing, as well as the flamenco dance, has gained recognition all over the world. A good flamenco guitar player has to spend most of his time improving his skills because flamenco technique is very difficult. The music he makes is always very sentimental and sad; he even cries sometimes because he feels what he is doing. Flamenco guitar playing is not a strumming but a very precise and quick picking of the strings. It is often loud, not soft, because it usually accompanies dancers. Some good flamenco guitar players who perform all over the world are Andrés Segovia and Paco de Luna. Flamenco is, therefore, a twofold art of which Spaniards are very proud.

Antonio Matos

COMMENTS ABOUT THE ESSAY
- The title, thesis statement, and body of this essay are likely to capture and hold a reader's interest because most readers associate the word *flamenco* with an exotic dance.
- The thesis statement is the second sentence. The thesis statement does not always have to be the first sentence in the paragraph or essay.
- The flamenco dance is the topic of discussion in the first paragraph, and the flamenco guitar is the main topic in the second paragraph.

- ☐ The writer strengthens his definition and authority as a writer by giving some historical information in the first paragraph.
- ☐ The details in this essay indicate that the writer knows his subject well.
- ☐ The transition *another* introduces the second paragraph.
- ☐ The writer ends the essay with a strong statement, which brings back into focus the two aspects of *flamenco*.

Exercise 5-1

Think of a word that has several potentially interesting aspects or meanings. If you cannot think of one, consider these words: *bread, bum, censorship, cold-blooded, fan, fantasy, heel, juice, loose, quality, rap, skin, square,* and *token.* Develop the definitions of your word into an outline similar to the ones used in previous chapters.

Bring the outline to class and be prepared to define your chosen word in a paragraph. If your instructor prefers an essay, devote one paragraph to each aspect of the word. The thesis statement should include the word and the aspects of that word to be discussed in the paragraph or essay.

Exercise 5-2

As soon as you have completed the rough draft of your paragraph or essay, think about these questions:

1. Do the title, the thesis statement, and the body of this paragraph or essay attempt to capture readers' interest?
2. Does the thesis statement contain all of the aspects of the word to be defined?
3. Do the topic sentences support the thesis statement?
4. Do the details and examples support the topic sentences?
5. Is there a sufficient number of details and examples?
6. Do transitions introduce the various definitions of the word? (See Exercise 1-5.)
7. Does the concluding paragraph or sentence support the established definition?
8. Do all of the modifiers affect or describe other words? (For a definition of *modifier,* see the glossary.)
9. Are all of the modifiers near the words that they affect or describe?
10. Are all of the words spelled correctly? (See Study Unit 17.)

Chapter 6 □ Process

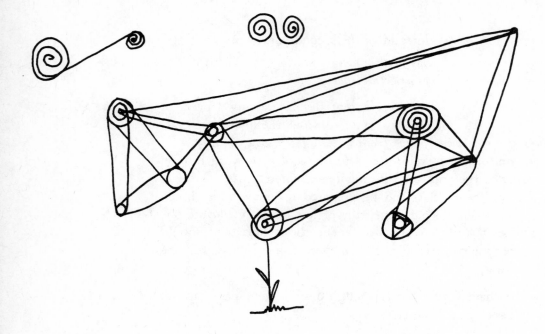

OBJECTIVES

After completing Chapter 6, you should be able to

1. write a process paragraph or essay
2. write in a logical order

Methods: Knowing a Process

A process paragraph or essay consists of a description of a series of actions, operations, or steps that lead to an end result. Writers must know their subject well because they must divide the process into steps, describe or narrate each step, and state the end result. For example, the person who washes his car carefully, dries it, rubs wax in a circular motion over every inch of the car, allows the wax to dry for one hour, and removes all of the wax with a strong but soft towel has completed a process. The end result is a clean, shining car.

Although description of a process is effective in "how-to-do-it" papers, which are the primary topic of this chapter, it can also be used to discuss an operation (by describing its different stages in chronological order), the functions of an organization (by describing the duties of the different departments), and the various causes for a known effect. (The latter subject is the basis for a causal-analysis paragraph or essay, which is the subject of the next chapter.)

Examples: Describing a Process

Look at the first student paragraph.

Good to the Last Drop!

My black-coffee-loving parents refer to the cups of instant coffee I make as "coffee-flavored milk," but the thick, bitter brew they drink is as horrible to me as mine is to them. I start with my own coffee cup. It is the smallest cup in the house, and my parents, suspecting that the secret of my foul-tasting coffee lies in the cup, refuse to touch it. I put in less than a teaspoon of Sanka, my favorite kind of coffee. I then pour a tiny bit of boiling water into the cup, just enough to dissolve the coffee grounds. After stirring the grounds, I fill the cup about two-thirds full of the boiling water. Then I fill the remaining third with milk and add about one and one-half teaspoons of sugar. This concoction may be a weak, milky, and sweet cup of coffee, but I think it is delicious.

Judy Truesdell

COMMENTS ABOUT THE PARAGRAPH
- □ The title prepares readers for the process that is to follow.
- □ The thesis statement tells readers what is to be prepared.
- □ Some of the words leave definite sensory impressions: *thick, bitter, brew, foul-tasting, boiling, weak, milky,* and *sweet*.
- □ The sentences are in chronological order, according to the process.
- □ Words such as *start, then, after,* and *remaining* indicate the progression of the process.
- □ The word *concoction* in the concluding sentence tells readers that the process has ended.
- □ The whole paragraph is in the first person (*I, me, my, mine*).
- □ The writer narrates the whole process in the present tense.

☐ The sentences are woven together skillfully and are related to the thesis sentence.

You have seen a process paragraph; now examine a process essay.

Everything You Always Wanted to Know about Chopsticks

Have you ever watched someone eating with chopsticks in a Chinese or Japanese restaurant and wished that you had the nerve to ask that person to show you how? Contrary to what you might believe, eating with chopsticks is a simple process, requiring a minimum of practice. You can hold the sticks in one hand, left or right, in a parallel position, one above the other, so that the bottom stick remains stationary, the top one moving in a downward direction toward the lower one, thereby trapping bits of food between the two pieces of wood, much like the action of tongs.

Since it is the upper stick which moves, you should practice that manipulation first. Grasp one of the sticks near the end, as you would hold a pencil, the longer end pointing away from your finger tips. Make contact with the stick and the first two fingers (held together) on one side, and the thumb, contacting the stick at a point opposite the two fingers, on the other side. Practice moving the stick up and down, keeping the wrist immobile, using as little thumb motion as possible, letting the two fingers do the job. When you can perform the up-and-down motion naturally, it is time to put your other two fingers to work.

Lay your stick down so that you can prepare your eating hand to hold the stationary piece. Fingers together, hold your hand in front of you, thumb up, palm to the side. Open your thumb and let it fall, extending naturally to the side. Separate your fingers into two pairs by moving the third and fourth fingers to the side, just as you did with your thumb. Now pick up the stick with your free hand and place it in the hand prepared for it, with one end resting on the third finger, at about the line separating the nail joint from the middle joint, and the other end resting between thumb and first finger. This position is the basic one for the stationary stick. With this item in place, you are ready to fit the two sticks together as a workable unit.

Pick up the remaining stick with your free hand, grasping it with your thumb and first two fingers, as you already know to do from previous practice. With your free hand, align the sticks, remembering to hold them even and parallel to each other. Position the bottom stick securely in the angle between the thumb and first finger and slightly forward of the middle joint of the third finger. Note that *both* sticks are secured by the thumb, the stationary one by the lower thumb and the movable one by the upper. Now that you have both sticks in place, you can begin to use them together.

Keeping as much distance between the two sticks held in your hand as you possibly can, work at moving the upper stick with the first two fingers so that it comes into contact with the lower one, held still. Practice until this motion comes consistently, using your free hand to aid in repositioning the sticks as the need arises. When you reach the point at which you make natural contact with the two sticks, you may begin the final practice, that of picking up little balls of scrap paper. With this final task mastered, you are ready to try your hand at a real Oriental meal. To the amazement of your family and friends, you can demonstrate how simple it is to eat in the Oriental fashion.

Robert P. Hallman

COMMENTS ABOUT THE ESSAY

- ☐ The title serves as an attention-getter because of its allusion to a well-known book about sex that has been parodied in the form of a movie of the same title. Most people are familiar with the title, directly or indirectly.

- ☐ A question precedes the thesis sentence, in keeping with the interest-arousing intent of the title. The writer formulates the "unutterable" question for readers.

- ☐ The thesis statement gains strength from the brief description of the process in the succeeding sentence.

- ☐ All of the topic sentences support the thesis statement.

- ☐ All of the details support the topic sentences.

- ☐ The last sentence in each paragraph cues the transitions between paragraphs. The topic sentences begin with some reference to the preceding paragraph.

- ☐ The conclusion reflects the intent of the thesis statement. It is a positive ending.

- ☐ The writer never shifts from the present tense.

- ☐ The writer has used the second person, the person being addressed, throughout this paper. The process paper is the only piece of writing in which the second person is acceptable. Directions must be given to some addressed person.

The next student essay should prove that the number of possible topics for process papers is unlimited.

Missing a Nose

Strangely enough, an embalmer's duties sometimes include building a nose. Noses, like other parts of the body, are at times missing because of accident or disease. When this situation arises, an embalmer must first determine the shape and size of the original nose. Although photographs are helpful in determining shape, simple measurements can show the size. The nose is the same length as the ear and is as wide as the eye. After the embalmer secures these measurements, he is ready to begin.

The embalmer begins building the nose by filling the cavity made by the missing nose with plaster of Paris to provide a solid base on which to model the new nose. After the base is ready, he places a piece of restorative wax, slightly larger than is needed, where the nose belongs. With fingers, modeling tools, and spatulas, the embalmer shapes and sizes the nose to look as much like the original as possible. When the molding is complete, the nose is smooth and shiny and lacks a lifelike appearance. To produce a lifelike appearance, the embalmer applies cosmetics to blend in with the natural skin color, touches the nose lightly with a medium-coarse brush to provide pores, and dusts with powder to remove the shine.

The building of a nose requires reasonable skill and infinite patience. It is not an easy task. Although the embalmer experiences many frustrations, he receives compensation from the knowledge that the death of a loved one has been made easier by his lifelike appearance.

Thomas A. Wooten

COMMENTS ABOUT THE ESSAY

□ The title and subject will attract many readers' interest because of the mystery surrounding an embalmer's work. Readers' curiosity about the subject will keep them interested as they get into the essay.

□ The writer introduces his subject in the first sentence.

□ The writer saves his thesis statement for the concluding paragraph.

□ The thesis statement bears a logical relationship to the various steps of the process: (1) filling the cavity, (2) shaping the nose, and (3) applying cosmetics.

□ The whole essay is in the third person and in the present tense. (See pages 241 and 254.)

Exercise 6-1 Think of a process that you know well. Maybe you are good at befriending a snob, concealing boredom in class, conning a car salesman, eating spaghetti in public, hustling a pool hustler, shaping a western hat, sizing up a teacher, or taming a wild animal. Develop the stages of this process into an outline form. Be prepared to write a process paragraph or essay from this outline.

If your instructor assigns an essay, the guidelines that follow should help you.

1. The title: Give careful thought to it. Do not let a dull title discourage someone from reading an otherwise good paper.
2. Paragraph 1:   This first paragraph contains the thesis statement. You might include an introductory sentence. A brief summary of the process should make it easier for you to construct the succeeding paragraphs. Try to include at least three sentences.
3. Paragraph 2 through as many paragraphs as needed: Each step in the process should be developed as a topic sentence of a paragraph. Connect all the sentences in the paragraph to both the topic sentence and the thesis sentence. There should be as many paragraphs as there are steps in the process. Be sure to include in your final paragraph a definite conclusion logically derived from your thesis statement.

Exercise 6-2

Demonstrate or describe your process to the class. You must not read your paper; however, you may glance periodically at the outline.

Exercise 6-3

As soon as you have completed the rough draft of your paragraph or essay, consider these questions:

1. Is the subject interesting and original?
2. Does the thesis statement mention the process and its stages?
3. If the thesis statement does not mention the stages, could this information strengthen it?
4. Is each stage developed or explained sufficiently?
5. Does the topic sentence of each paragraph support the thesis statement?
6. Do the sentences follow each other in a logical order?
7. Do the transitions weave together the paragraphs and sentences and show the progression of the process? (See Exercise 1-5.)
8. Does the concluding paragraph or sentence support the thesis statement and body of the paper?
9. Do the details in this paragraph or essay indicate that you know your subject well?
10. Is the whole paragraph or essay in one tense? (See page 260.)
11. Is the whole paragraph or essay in one person? (See page 244.)
12. Are all of the sentences logically connected to one another and to the thesis statement?

Chapter 7 □ Causal Analysis

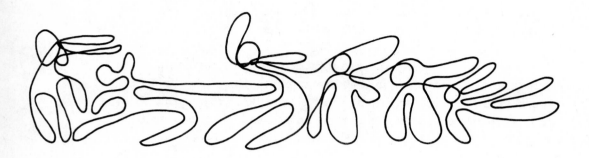

OBJECTIVES

After completing Chapter 7, you should be able to

1. write a causal-analysis paragraph or essay
2. use a narrative style in causal analysis
3. write a climactic conclusion
4. arrange events in chronological order

Methods: Cause-to-Effect Analysis

This chapter on causal analysis logically follows the chapter on process, since causal analysis requires that writers break down a process or event into its individual parts and show how these parts contribute to the whole. Writers can use causal analysis in two different instances. First, they may wish to state a *cause* in the thesis statement and to follow it with the *effects* that result from this cause. This procedure is called *cause to effect*.

Cause = effect + effect + effect

A writer could use the preceding formula to show the effects of a decrease in the supply of gasoline.

Decrease in supply of gas = higher fuel prices + increase in sales of small automobiles + increased demand for reliable public transportation

Rewritten as a sentence, this formula would read as follows:

A decrease in the supply of gasoline could lead to higher fuel prices, increased sales of small automobiles, and increased demand for reliable public transportation.

Examples from Students' Work

The paragraph that follows is an example of a causal analysis that moves from cause to effect.

A Miraculous Revival

My next-door neighbor, a man in his late fifties, was in fair condition this afternoon at Parkland Hospital's emergency room after experiencing a severe heart attack early this morning. Mr. Snapka was working in his yard when he apparently collapsed and fell. His condition went unnoticed for an undetermined period of time until a young couple, the Greens, saw him and came to his rescue. Mr. Snapka said he was experiencing chest and upper arm pains; so Mrs. Green directed a neighbor to call for an ambulance. Thereafter, Mr. Snapka's vital signs disappeared: his heart quit beating. The Greens, who had recently taken a first-aid course, knew exactly what to do. Calmly and with a systematic rhythm, this young couple administered external heart massage and mouth-to-mouth artificial respiration consisting of five external heart compressions interrupted by one forceful breath of air. Within two minutes after they initiated the revival method, the ambulance crew arrived. Without interrupting the systematic rhythm of mouth-to-mouth artificial respiration and external heart massage, the ambulance crew took over the life-reviving method. Moments later, Mr. Snapka's heart began beating, and his condition stabilized with the help of intravenous drugs. The ambulance crew then transported him to Parkland's emergency room. Since Mr. Snapka's heart had stopped beating two minutes before ambulance paramedics arrived, his survival was a miracle.

Paul W. Malone

COMMENTS ABOUT THE PARAGRAPH

☐ The writer begins the paragraph with the cause: a heart attack.

☐ He continues by describing the effects resulting from this cause.

☐ The writer's realistic presentation of these effects indicates that he really knows his subject.

- The subject should be interesting to most readers because of its drama.

- The concluding sentence reflects on the significance of the preceding sentences.

- The writer narrates the events in the third person and in the present tense. (See pages 241 and 254.)

You have seen a cause-to-effect paragraph. Here is a student essay that follows the same pattern:

Energy "Crisis"

The many problems resulting from the energy crisis have overshadowed its numerous positive aspects. One of these is that more people have become aware of the necessity of conserving our resources, which, up to now, seemed inexhaustible. Our waste of energy is slowly turning toward the saving of newspapers and cans for recycling, economizing in the use of electricity, and exploring new sources, such as solar and atomic energy.

The primary health problem of cardiovascular disease, because of lack of exercise and overweight, may also be reduced as a direct result of the limited gas supply. Many people are rediscovering the health value of walking and bicycling after having been dependent on automobiles as the only means of transportation. The proper and regular use of bicycling could greatly reduce the incidence of heart attacks and the related health problems resulting from overweight.

Of similar importance is the increased use of smaller cars. This new trend should have the added effect of not only decreasing highway congestion and air pollution but also eventually reducing the high fatality rate of accidents in larger cars.

The greatest positive result has been the rediscovery of our ability as individuals to work together in solving our problems. In a time when everything is seemingly government controlled and directed, we are discovering that the individual still makes the final decision. The person who has limited his use of gasoline and economized in his use of electricity is really responsible for the overall result. The energy situation might be the best "crisis" to come along in a long time.

Paula Bloomer

COMMENTS ABOUT THE ESSAY

- The writer states a cause in the introduction and mentions that some positive effects have resulted from this cause.

- The writer follows the thesis statement with a transition and immediately goes into the first positive effect: conservation of resources.

- ☐ Each paragraph begins with a transition that connects that paragraph to the previous one.
- ☐ The writer devotes a separate paragraph to each effect.
- ☐ The concluding sentence restates the thesis sentence in a positive tone.

Methods and Examples: Effect-to-Cause Analysis

A second use of causal analysis occurs when a writer begins a paper with a series of *effects* and concludes it with the *cause* of these effects. This diagnostic procedure is called *effect to cause*.

Effect + effect + effect = cause

This formula could be used to show the relationship between symptoms and an illness.

Chills + fever + muscle ache + headache + sore throat = flu

Rewritten as a sentence, this formula would read as follows:

If you suffer from chills, fever, muscle ache, headache, and a sore throat, you may well have the flu.

This formula can also be applied to automobile problems.

Engine vibration + heat from engine + burned smell + steam inside cab = radiator leak.

If the engine vibrates and emits heat plus a burned smell, and if there is steam inside the cab, the radiator is probably leaking.

Now look at a student paragraph that uses the effect-to-cause technique.

A Strange Awakening

I awoke from my sleep and was startled to find my bedroom filled with light more radiant than that of any summer day. The alarm clock indicated 2:30. I wondered if I had overslept. Gradually, I began to realize the similarity between this light and the electricity given off by an electrical storm. I began to feel eerie as I viewed a cloudless sky and the quiet, brightened countryside. For another five seconds, this strange sight held me in amazement; then the countryside view grew suddenly dark. Prompted by the excitement of the moment, I quickly turned on my transistor radio and expected to hear news of a nuclear war or the end of the world. An on-the-scene roving radio reporter was already reporting this happening from the far north part of town. However, he was no closer to the scene than I had been. Six meteorites had fallen from the sky, turning night into day and leaving many people confused and speechless, including me.

Mario Sandaval

COMMENTS ABOUT THE PARAGRAPH

□ The title is intriguing because most people have experienced strange awakenings.

□ The writer begins the paragraph by stating effects.

□ These effects lead to the cause, which appears in the concluding sentence.

□ The subject of this paragraph should interest many readers because of the mystery associated with outer space.

□ The writer relies on description to create his effects.

□ He chose to use the first person because *he* experienced the incident. (See page 241.)

□ The writer chose past tense because he experienced the incident in the past. (See page 254.)

□ The writer did not deviate from the first person or the past tense.

The effect-to-cause method is equally effective in essays.

Quincy's Saga

The couple bought the puppy as a pet for their young children. A puppy to feed and care for, they reasoned, would teach the children responsibility, as well as provide companionship. They did not, however, wish to spend any money on the animal, and consequently it was never examined by a veterinarian or vaccinated. The animal, soon to be named Quincy, did indeed provide entertainment for the children and was the center of entertainment for all the family members. The change in Quincy's disposition occurred, literally, overnight.

One morning Quincy awoke suffering from what was apparently a cold. He had an irritated nose and watery eyes. Food ceased to hold the great influence it once had held over him. As drastic as the changes were, the family scarcely noticed them. The children went to school, the father went to work, and the mother went about her daily chores. No one noticed Quincy's worsening condition. By early afternoon, Quincy was lying down constantly, unable to walk. By the time the children were home from school, their mother had noticed the great change in Quincy. She and the children decided to take him to the veterinarian immediately.

At the veterinarian's office, Quincy was unable to lift his head. His eyes remained in an unblinking, glazed stare, crusty with a mucous excretion. His heart and lungs were working rapidly, and his temperature was up drastically. One look was all that was necessary to tell the doctor what the trouble was. A thorough examination confirmed the diagnosis: distemper. In light of an eighty percent fatality rate at this late stage, the mother agreed that Quincy must be "put to sleep," or, in more realistic terms, killed. She and the veterinarian considered the puppy half-dead anyway. An overdose of a barbiturate, morbidly named Sleep-Away, finished the job.

When the puppy's owner had left the office, an autopsy was performed. The chest was slit from end to end with a pair of scissors, the very antithesis of surgery. All the telltale signs of distemper were there, particularly the gross abuse to the respiratory system. Quincy was placed in a plastic bag and left in the back of the hospital for the dead-animal pickup. He had been murdered by neglect!

Joe Piercy

COMMENTS ABOUT THE ESSAY

- This causal analysis is written in a *narrative* (story-telling) style.
- The thesis statement is not at the beginning of the paper because the writer is saving the cause for the end. This procedure creates a climactic effect (a series of statements in an ascending order of force or intensity).
- The writer moves swiftly from one event to another *before* he states the cause.
- The divisions of the paragraphs occur according to the major events: (1) the arrival of Quincy, (2) the change in Quincy's health, (3) the trip to veterinarian's office, (4) the autopsy.
- The writer's vivid details convey credibility (believability).
- The concluding sentence is dramatic and effective.

Place yourself in one of these situations and develop an interesting causal analysis from it: (1) the engine of your car dies, (2) you enter your front door and smell a foul odor, (3) you are taking a shower when the lights go off, (4) you are upstairs in your bedroom and hear a

Exercise 7-1

slow thump, thump, thump from downstairs. Or select another situation that interests you and develop some of the effects that resulted from this cause.

Arrange your causal analysis in outline form and be prepared to write a paragraph or essay from it. If your instructor assigns an essay, develop a paragraph on each effect. Include introductory and concluding paragraphs.

Exercise 7-2 As soon as you have completed the rough draft of your paragraph or essay, examine these questions:

1. Is the subject fresh and interesting?
2. Does the paragraph or essay have a thesis statement either at the end or the beginning?
3. Does the thesis statement give a cause?
4. Is each of the listed effects supported by details?
5. Do the topic sentences support the thesis statement?
6. Do transitions introduce the paragraphs? (See Exercise 1-5.)
7. Do the various paragraphs contain other transitions?
8. Do the details and examples indicate that you know your subject well?
9. Are all of the sentences in chronological order?
10. Are the sentences coherent and parallel? (See pages 191–193.)
11. Is the paper in one tense and in one person? (See pages 260 and 244.)
12. Are all of the modifiers near the words that they affect or describe? (See page 231.)

Chapter 8 □ General to Particular

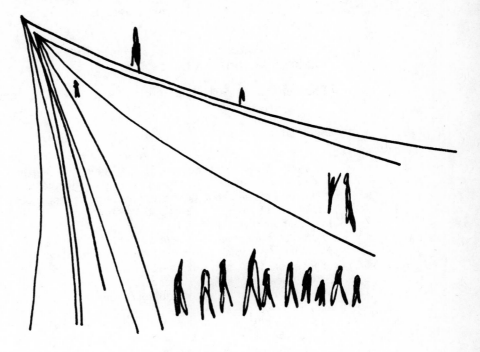

After completing Chapter 8, you should be able to
1. write a general-to-particular paragraph or essay
2. summarize a topic in a thesis statement
3. use deductive reasoning in your writing

The General Statement Plus Particular Facts

General to particular is a technique that appears in many of the previous writing exercises. It begins with a general thesis statement that summarizes the topic to be discussed. The particulars that follow must support the thesis statement. A simple outline can illustrate this procedure.

General statement: Mr. Garagiola is a commercial painter.
Supporting details:
1. He has scaffolding and buckets of paint on the back of his truck.

2. The sign on his truck reads "Acme Paint Contractors."
3. His clothing is always covered by paint splashes.
4. He has offered to paint my house for five hundred dollars.

Examples from Students' Papers

The general-to-particular method works well in paragraphs.

Investing in Stocks

Most middle-class people have reasons other than social status for investing money in stocks. The main reason for their investing in stocks is to gain an increase in the value of their investment. Many people have dreams of becoming millionaires over a short period of time because their stocks have risen to a very sizable profit, but to their disappointment the price of stocks falls, and with the loss their dreams of utopias disappear. Another objective is to earn a fairly stable and reliable income. Most investors hope to have a life filled with few worries about income shortages; so they invest in stocks. An equally important concern of investors in regard to money is protection against the loss of purchasing power because of inflation unless bankruptcy occurs within the corporation. The availability of money is an additional reason for these individuals of average means to invest in stocks. They like to pretend that their money is in a checking account. The thought that runs continuously through their minds is "How fast can I secure the money in cash?" The stock market, therefore, provides middle-class people one way to invest wisely.

Burt Burrows

COMMENTS ABOUT THE PARAGRAPH

□ The writer gives the thesis statement at the beginning of the paragraph and supports it with particular details.

□ This procedure is called *deductive reasoning:* a writer makes a general statement and leads away from it with supporting details to a particular conclusion.

□ The four major supporting details are (1) increase in the value of investment, (2) stable and reliable income, (3) protection against the loss of purchasing power, and (4) availability of money.

□ A transition introduces each major supporting detail: *main, another, equally,* and *additional.*

□ The concluding sentence comments on previous statements.

The following essays are further examples of the general-to-particular method.

The Critical Moment

The pool player moved uneasily around the pool table as he anticipated his opponent's shot and his shot that would follow. With each blast of the pool stick against the balls, his interest in the game became more intense. As he viewed his opponent, he knew that he was up against the best and that every shot counted. Any mistake could cost him the game. His concentration grew.

He had been in similar situations before, but never had he been in a match with such a consistent player. As hard as he tried to keep cool, he failed. He had never been so nervous in his life, although he knew there was reason enough for it. His hands shook, and he perspired heavily. Although he lacked calmness, his confidence never failed. He knew he was good, for he had beaten other pool players of repute. As the seconds before his turn to shoot ticked away, he told himself that he had to get himself together or there would be no way to win the game. With a few seconds remaining before his turn, he took a deep breath and told himself over and over, "I can win; I can win." He calmly grasped the pool stick and leaned over the pool table. His pool stick sent the cue ball hitting the targets he had planned. He stood up, gave a sigh of relief, and said to himself, "I am going to win."

Debbie Hennig

COMMENTS ABOUT THE ESSAY

- The writer has selected a subject with wide appeal. Most readers are familiar with the tension surrounding pool matches.

- The writer has placed the thesis statement near the end of the first paragraph: *As he viewed his opponent, he knew that he was up against the best and that every shot counted.*

- The writer uses colloquial (conversational) terminology in the thesis statement to capture the atmosphere of a poolroom. It is easy to overuse colloquial or conventional terminology such as "up against the best" or "every shot counted," but in rare situations like this one such trite phrasing can work well.

- The writer uses short sentences to build suspense. (Although this technique works well in some cases, student writers should avoid it unless they are using it with a specific purpose in mind.)

- The use of the player's actual thoughts (shown by quotation marks) contributes both reality and suspense to the situation.

- ☐ The supporting details are equally effective in building suspense.
- ☐ The suspense holds readers' interest.
- ☐ The concluding sentence appeals to readers' emotions because it relieves the tension.

Look at another general-to-particular essay.

From What to How

A curious, investigative mind led John, my three-year-old son, to new understandings about his world in a very short period of time. Driving home from church one Sunday morning, I noticed that John spied the button on the glove compartment. He realized quickly that if he depressed the button with sufficient pressure, the compartment would open. Once he secured entry to the fascinating little vault, he selected the most unusual-appearing object available, a large magnifying glass.

As John studied the magnifying glass, he discovered the loose handle. He twisted the handle one way and then another until he was able to remove it completely. Continuing to work with the detached handle and the glass, the fascinated child realized that by twisting the handle in different ways he could screw it into or unscrew it from the glass. Once he had worked through this principle, he reassembled the glass and handle.

Contemplating his plaything further, John commented with some assurance, "This is a mirror." He had seen a relationship between the design of a hand mirror and the magnifying glass; but upon reexamining the glass, he appeared to change his mind. He asked directly, "What is this thing?" At this point, he had discovered that he could not see himself in the glass, but he could see other things through it. I replied that it was a magnifying glass.

This new awareness produced several minutes of curious experimentation. Looking through the glass, John investigated my eyes, mouth, and nose. At the same time he was looking through the glass, he tried to touch the object he was observing. The inaccuracy that these attempts produced seemed to cause him some confusion, but he concluded quite correctly, "A magnifying glass makes things *look* bigger."

Knowing the name and the purpose of the object seemed to give John confidence in the use of his new toy. On arriving home, he continued to explore the world with the glass; he looked at bugs, dirt, cracks, and leaves. His exploration of this newly enlarged world led John to ask the inevitable, but always disconcerting, question: "How does a magnifying glass make things look bigger?" As I flipped through the pages of an elementary science book, I realized how far John's curiosity and investigation had taken him in the twenty minutes since he had spied the button on the glove compartment.

Carolynn L. Wartes

COMMENTS ABOUT THE ESSAY

- ☐ The writer states in the thesis statement that her son has achieved new understandings about his world.

- ☐ In the remainder of this human-interest essay, she supports this conclusion with details.

- ☐ The dialogue makes the essay lively and believable.

- ☐ The touching and effective concluding sentence enlarges the application of the thesis statement, because it suggests that the writer, too, has increased her understanding of her son and the world they both live in.

- ☐ The writer narrates in the first person: *I, my.* (If you have a choice between first and third person, use the third person. A writer who chooses the third person comments about incidents and people without taking part in the action. By not taking part in the action, the writer becomes an objective observer.)

- ☐ The whole essay is in the past tense. (If you have a choice between past and present tense, use the present tense. The present tense sounds fresh and alive.)

Exercise 8-1

Observe an athlete, barber, beautician, carpenter, clerk, farmer, instructor, janitor, minister, musician, policeman, rancher, student, trucker, waitress, or anyone else who interests you. After observing one of these people, make a general statement about the individual's personality or present situation in life. Then decide what factors led you to this conclusion.

Develop this information in outline form. Be prepared to use this outline for writing a revealing general-to-particular essay. Try to use dialogue if you can. (For punctuation, see pages 309 and 321.)

Exercise 8-2

As soon as you have completed the rough draft of your paper, think about these questions:

1. Is the subject interesting enough to attract most readers' attention?
2. Does the thesis statement summarize the topic?
3. Do the topic sentences support the thesis statement?

4. Do the details and examples support the topic sentences and flow in chronological order?
5. Do transitions introduce new paragraphs and weave together the various sentences? (See Exercise 1-5.)
6. Is the deductive-reasoning pattern obvious? (See page 66.)
7. Is the essay in one tense and in one person? (See pages 260 and 244.)
8. Do all the sentences have subjects and verbs? (See page 125.)
9. Are all of the sentences punctuated correctly? (See Study Units 13, 14, and 15.)
10. Are all of the words spelled correctly? (See Study Unit 17.)
11. Do all the modifiers have words that they affect or describe in a logical way? (See page 228.)
12. Are all of the modifiers near the words that they affect or describe?

Chapter 9▫Particular to General

OBJECTIVES

After completing Chapter 9, you should be able to

1. write a particular-to-general paragraph or essay
2. use inductive reasoning in your writing
3. observe a person effectively

Methods: The Process of Inductive Reasoning

Particular to general is just the opposite of general to particular. The writer begins with the particulars that lead to a general statement at the end of the paper:

Supporting detail + supporting detail + supporting detail = general statement

The general statement is the concluding sentence. This procedure is called *inductive reasoning*, because the writer begins with particulars (details) and leads into, or *induces*, a general statement:

Supporting details:
1. Mansue is wearing a new long dress.
2. Mansue is wearing an expensive perfume.
3. Mansue is wearing new shoes.
4. Mansue is carrying an engraved invitation.
General statement: Mansue is going to a formal party.

Inductive Reasoning in Students' Papers

The inductive method of reasoning is used in the following short paragraph:

Incident in the Library

I heard the sandaled footsteps approaching slowly across a thickly textured carpet. My eyes sighted a young man whose face was a question punctuated with knitted brows, pursed lips, and wandering eyes. He clutched a yellow legal pad decorated with a conglomeration of numbers and letters while he absent-mindedly deposited his books on one of the library tables. His free hand rose nervously on his hip while his eyes completed a swift visual scanning of the room. As he approached a stack of books, his pen seemed to drum out a rhythm on his lips, which he subsequently repeated on top of his head while he continued to scrutinize the various signs on the stacks he approached. He walked uncertainly down one aisle, reappeared, and promptly disappeared, finally surfacing like a drowning man coming up for the last time at the information desk. My fellow student was obviously lost in the library!

Sally Squibb

COMMENTS ABOUT THE PARAGRAPH

- The title holds general appeal because most readers can relate an experience in the library.
- The paragraph does not begin with a general statement.
- The general statement is the concluding sentence. This pattern of writing is called *inductive reasoning* because the writer begins with particulars and leads into (*induces*) a general statement.
- Every sentence in this paragraph contains strong, colorful words.
- The last sentence of the paragraph is a general statement that also solves the mystery.

The previous paragraph has a library for its setting. Now look at a longer paragraph that describes an incident in a park:

A Girl in the Park

A young girl sat motionless, crouched under a large oak tree beside a bubbly stream. The cool breeze blowing across the stream tousled her hair and blew it over her face. She made no attempt to shove the dangling hair out of her eyes, and it seemed as though she were almost hiding behind it. I could not see the expression on the young girl's face, but she clutched her hands tightly together and proceeded to wring them. Suddenly, the wind subsided, and I caught a quick glimpse of her face. Her forehead was wrinkled in deep thought, and the blank stare in her eyes was almost frightening. They were worried eyes set in a pale and rather lifeless face. Wondering what this young girl held in her thoughts, I began to stare curiously at her. She sensed that she was being observed and abruptly stood up. Her expression changed completely from that of concern to slight suspicion. As she rose from her shady spot, her eyes began to glance cautiously around as if she were being pursued; then she walked on, still clutching her hands tightly together. Just as I was leaving, I saw her turn back to glance at me. With pleading eyes, she took one long look and unclutched her hands long enough to release a small piece of paper, which tumbled to the ground, as she ran swiftly in the other direction. I walked toward the small piece of paper, looked curiously down at it, and began to pick it up. But my feelings of guilt were overwhelming, and I tossed it to the ground. The young girl was obviously facing an emotional crisis and had valid reasons for her feelings of turmoil, suspicion, and insecurity.

Liz Cookston

COMMENTS ABOUT THE PARAGRAPH

☐ The writer does not give a general statement at the beginning of the paragraph. Instead, she immediately gives particular details about the girl.

☐ The major sections of this paragraph are (1) first impressions of the girl, (2) more detailed impressions, (3) the girl's awareness of the observer, and (4) the girl's exit.

☐ The words in this paragraph express color, feeling, and emotion: *motionless, bubbly, cool, tousled, dangling, clutched, tightly, wring, wrinkled, pale, pleading, tumbled, guilt, turmoil, suspicion, insecurity.*

☐ The writer develops a definite conclusion about the girl based on the details she observed: *The young girl . . . obviously . . . had valid reasons for her feelings of turmoil, suspicion, and insecurity.*

□ The writer gives such a realistic presentation of her subject that she has complete control of her readers, from beginning to end.

The particular-to-general pattern is equally effective in essays:

Speech Festival "Metamorphosis"

I entered the room which was to be the setting of the high school speech festival, and a bright-eyed young man, who was the only early arrival, asked me, "Are you the poetry judge?" He was looking straight at the blank critique sheets in my hand. Obviously, I was the judge. Only a judge would be carrying critique sheets. I assumed that he was just making an awkward attempt at conversation. I replied, "Yes." Being able to talk to his judge must have been somewhat relaxing for him. Some of the tenseness went out of his shoulder muscles as he asked, "What time is it?" When I answered him, he said, "Oh, only ten minutes left," and quickly glanced down at his folder. Then he looked up as though he were addressing an audience and moved his lips silently without speaking.

As the young man practiced what he was going to read, other participants began to enter the room. "I really don't feel very confident," he told me. I was astonished. No one else seemed to have noticed his remark, which appeared to have been directed at me. Such a statement would not impress most judges, who usually look for poise and composure as well as good performance. More participants began to walk in. Most people came in with friends. Nobody sat near or talked to the young man. His face was expressionless and pale, and his body was still but no longer stiff. Only his hands, bracing against the armrests of his chair, betrayed the possibility that his professed need for reassurance was real.

As the participants began to read their selections, the young man listened with indifference. When his turn arrived, he walked to the front of the room and established a stance. His eye contact was excellent. What followed was one of the most remarkable events of the speech festival. As he began to read, the audience grew docile and responded to every emotion that rolled from his lips. For the next fifteen minutes, he completely controlled this group of people that had previously ignored him. They were *his* audience. When the young man completed the reading and walked away, his footsteps echoed in a room filled with speechless people. His metamorphosis was living proof of the old adage that a person should never judge a book by its cover.

Shane Keith Simon

COMMENTS ABOUT THE ESSAY

□ The essay does not begin with an introduction and thesis statement.

□ The writer has divided the paragraphs according to the major occurrences: (1) the judge meets the young man, (2) other participants enter the room, and (3) the other participants and the young man give readings.

□ The writer builds suspense with supporting details.

□ The writer concludes the essay with an old adage that serves as his general statement. Although it is a good idea to use original words in your writing, sometimes clichés like "you can't judge a book by its cover" can be effective. Here, using the cliché is both effective and justifiable because the entire essay proves the truth of the cliché and because the unoriginal words serve as an appropriate and immediately understandable summary.

□ The writer chose the past tense because this incident occurred in the past. (See page 254.)

□ The writer uses the past tense throughout the essay.

Exercise 9-1

Observe a person in an airport, bowling alley, country club, department store, gymnasium, health club, library, night club, park, restaurant, service station, student center, supermarket, theater, zoo, or any other place that intrigues you. After observing your subject, list in outline form and chronological order some particulars about him or her that you noticed. Then make a general statement that summarizes these particulars. Be prepared to use this list for writing a particular-to-general essay. Remember that the general statement in this method of writing appears at the end. Use details that reveal color, emotion, and feeling. You may use dialogue if you wish.

Exercise 9-2

As soon as you have completed the rough draft of your essay, review these questions:

1. Are the particulars vivid and realistic enough to hold readers' interest?
2. Do all the particulars lead toward the thesis statement?
3. Are they in a chronological order?
4. Does the concluding sentence summarize the particulars?
5. Does the essay contain words that leave definite impressions?
6. Are the words colorful?
7. Do all the sentences have a subject and a verb? (See page 125.)
8. Are the sentence elements parallel? (See pages 191–193.)
9. Do all the modifiers have words that they affect and describe in a logical way? (See page 228.)

10. Are all of the modifiers near the words that they affect or describe?
11. Is the essay in one person and in one tense? (See pages 244 and 260.)
12. Are all of the sentences punctuated correctly? (See Study Units 13, 14, and 15.)
13. Are all of the words spelled correctly? (See Study Unit 17).

Chapter 10 □ Persuasion

OBJECTIVES

After completing Chapter 10, you should be able to

1. write a persuasive essay
2. use a combination of writing patterns in one essay
3. support an argument properly
4. use examples and statistics effectively in an argument

Building a Persuasive Argument

Writers who employ persuasion attempt to convince their readers to agree with their opinions. They can use three different types of persuasion: (1) forcing their character on readers by seeming trustworthy—that is, trying to convince through sheer weight of authority and knowledge, through special access to inside information, or whatever, (2) appealing to readers' emotions, and (3) presenting a logical, believable argument supported with facts. The valid argument is, without a doubt, the best type of persuasion. It consists essentially of the writer's conclusion about a subject and the facts that support this conclusion. These facts are main premises and subpremises. Like the main headings and subheadings in an outline, the main premises support the conclusion directly, and the subpremises support it indirectly.

Because the writer is responsible for giving a valid argument for the conclusion, several of the organizational patterns from previous chapters must be employed: illustration, analogy, causal analysis, general to particular, and particular to general. These organizational patterns require either deductive or inductive reasoning. The writer who wishes to give a deductive argument gives the thesis statement in the introduction and supports it with examples in the rest of the essay:

Thesis statement

Examples and supporting details

The writer who plans to give the thesis statement in the concluding paragraph presents an inductive argument:

Examples and supporting details

Thesis statement

In other words, deductive reasoning leads away from the thesis statement, and inductive reasoning leads into the thesis statement.[1]

In addition to choosing either the deductive or inductive approach, writers must also be concerned about the following matters:

1. selecting a subject that they know well
2. limiting the subject to their own range of expertise
3. developing a clear, logical argument
4. writing objectively but not too formally
5. being fair to the opposing side
6. treating readers as equals

---

1. *Deductive* comes from the Latin *de* ("from") plus *ducere* ("to lead"); *inductive* comes from the Latin *in* ("in" or "into") plus *ducere*.

7. supporting statements with examples and statistics
8. identifying sources of information in the text or in footnotes
9. never assuming readers' acceptance of the argument

Writers deal with these concerns by learning which common argumentative fallacies (invalid methods of persuasion) distort or oversimplify the truth. Fallacies that distort the truth are as follows:

1. *Argumentum ad Hominem*   This Latin term means "attacking a person instead of an idea." The writer of the sentence that follows fell into this fallacy.

The commission's main opponent, who has been known to take bribes, continues to speak for integrity in government.

(A fair writer would have directed the argument against the opponent's views, not the opponent's character.)

2. *Begging the Question*   This fallacy occurs when writers assume that a statement they make is true without proving it. Their argument seems to move in circles, because to "prove" it they rely on the truth of the very point they are trying to prove.

Felix does not need to pay me now for typing his manuscript. As soon as a publisher buys the manuscript, Felix is going to be rich.

(The writer has no assurance of Felix's future wealth or of his chances of finding a publisher for his manuscript.)

3. *Using Extension*   "Exaggeration" is another name for this fallacy, which occurs when a writer distorts an argument by extending or exaggerating it.

My British uncle says that his American relatives have poor table manners. His comment is an insult to *all* Americans.

(The British uncle's American relatives should not be made to represent *all* Americans.)

4. *Ignoring Context*   Ignoring context is exactly what its name suggests: someone ignores the general context (content) of a statement and uses only a part of it to support an argument. Writers who resort to this fallacy read only what they want to be told.

ORIGINAL STATEMENT: The president is not as fond of baseball as he is of football.

DISTORTED VERSION: The president is not . . . fond of baseball. . . .

(The president may actually like baseball; he simply prefers football.)

5. *Name-calling* The name of this fallacy, too, suggests its meaning. Name-calling—describing people or ideas or events in loaded terms designed to arouse readers' emotions—is another indication of writers who cannot rely on the soundness of their argument to make their point and who resort, therefore, to argumentative fallacies such as name-calling as a means of attack.

My government teacher is nothing but a radical Communist: she always criticizes the American judicial system.

6. *Using a Red Herring* Just as the smell of fish attracts a cat's attention, a red herring introduces a false issue that may cause readers to lose sight of the real issue. The false issue usually contains emotional overtones.

People who refuse to attend church are the very ones who have caused apathy in this country.

(Church attendance and apathy are two completely different issues.)

In addition to the truth twisters, writers must also avoid the oversimplifiers, which encourage their readers to come to a conclusion without taking into account all relevant factors. Some of the most common oversimplifiers are as follows:

1. *Making a Hasty Generalization* Hasty generalizations are one of the most frequent abuses in writing. They occur whenever writers reach a quick, simple conclusion without presenting sufficient evidence. Indefinite pronouns like *all, anybody, anyone, everybody, everyone, nobody, none,* and *no one* often introduce hasty generalizations.

No one likes a shy person.

(Some people think that shy individuals are refreshing.)

2. *Employing Inadequate Causal Relationships* Individuals who state simple, convenient excuses (causes) for complex occurrences (effects) are using inadequate causal relationships.

My plants always die. No one in my family has a green thumb.

(The writer has not taken into account such basic factors as food, soil, sunlight, temperature, and water.)

3. *Using Stereotypes*   Stereotypes are simple, fixed mental images that people associate with certain types of individuals. For example, some people have predetermined attitudes toward lawyers, ministers, morticians, mothers-in-law, politicians, and psychiatrists.

Rowena is the typical mother-in-law: she never minds her own business.

(The writer assumes that *all* mothers-in-law never mind their own business.)

4. *Using Either-Or Fallacies*   Writers who give readers only two alternatives, when several choices are available, are oversimplifying with an either-or fallacy.

Either you are *for* the president, or you are *against* him.

(The writer does not allow for modified support or opposition.)

5. *Making Trivial Analogies*   A writer who oversimplifies an issue by using comparisons and clichés that are inadequate to the point being made has used trivial analogies. (See pages 33–35.) Comparisons and clichés can divert readers' attention from the main issue.

Romeo was attracted to Juliet as iron is attracted to a magnet.

(Love and magnetic force make an inadequate, highly oversimplified comparison.)

Think about these truth twisters and oversimplifiers as you read the essays in the section that follows.

Considering Students' Attempts at Persuasion

The Right to Die

Should an individual be legally able to determine the circumstances under which he is allowed to die in the event that he becomes hopelessly and irreversibly ill? This and other questions concerning the right to die with dignity have become increasingly urgent in the minds of many people, both within the medical profession and among victims of terminal illnesses. Currently, fifteen state legislatures are considering "death with dignity" bills, which in effect would allow a competent person to create a document stating that under certain circumstances he should have the right to die. Some individuals wonder why such a bill is necessary. These people must first consider a few facts.

For example, the dignity of human life has always permeated the teachings and practice of the medical profession and is the basis of all its ethical and legal responsibilities. From the time of Hippocrates in 400 B.C. to the present, the primary purpose of medical science has been the preservation of human life, usually at all costs. However, today, when this science has reached the ultimate in its ability to keep the hopelessly ill alive, many people are beginning to ask if it also has the wisdom to allow such a life to end.

Since 1900, the average life expectancy has increased from forty-seven to seventy years. Sociologists estimate that by 1980 the over-sixty-five group should increase to one out of every eight persons. With the disappearance of most fatal communicable diseases and the continuing development of new drugs, nearly half of the causes of death have been eliminated. Thus, with the increasing population and extended life expectancy, medical science with its medical miracles has also managed to eliminate a normal method of population equalization. Unfortunately, in its endeavor to prolong life at all costs, medicine has simultaneously established death as its natural adversary.

Today, a person stricken with a coronary, resulting in cardiac arrest, can recover if he is successfully resuscitated within a critical time period. If he exceeds this time period, causing lack of oxygen with resulting brain damage, he lives usually with the aid of a mechanical breathing machine. The same procedure prolongs the lives of victims who exist artificially for months and even years at a vegetable level. Terminal cancer patients, likewise, linger by extraordinary measures, usually prescribed by doctors who are pressured by a distraught family. It often takes weeks of heavy expense and added suffering to recognize death as a blessing.

Opponents of right-to-die legislation argue that this proposal is a form of euthanasia or mercy killing which, at present, is completely illegal as well as unethical under any circumstances. However, allowing a person to die by passive means, when he is already irreversibly dead to mental and physical function, does not include the more deliberate and positive action which euthanasia implies. Sustaining such an individual, therefore, accomplishes nothing.

Again, opposition accuses doctors of usurping the power of God by being able to pull the plug, so to speak, at their own discretion. The need for legislation in this instance is prompted by the fact that any physician can be sued for malpractice should he determine to discontinue life-support measures. This judgment is again usually left to an incapacitated, grieving relative who finds the decision overwhelming. This, the dilemma of playing God, which most individuals wish to avoid, is now effectively carried out not only by the physician but by relatives as well.

A "living will," being used by proponents of right-to-die legislation and intended to be made out by a healthy person well in advance of any illness, states in part that if there is no reasonable hope for his recovery, he should not be kept alive by artificial means.* This right should be respected and aligned with other human rights of life and liberty. If life itself is respected to the extent that men are

* Euthanasia Educational Council, *A Living Will*, 250 West 57th Street, New York, N.Y. 10019.

willing to die for the freedom to live as they choose, then that life, so preciously held, should be allowed to culminate with equal dignity and peace.

Paula Bloomer

COMMENTS ABOUT THE ESSAY

- ☐ The writer has used a particular-to-general pattern by placing the thesis statement at the end of the essay.

- ☐ She introduces her essay with a thought-provoking question. (This procedure is not usually necessary.)

- ☐ The content of the essay indicates that the writer is familiar with the medical profession and the question under discussion.

- ☐ The third-person point of view used in this paper is objective but not too formal.

- ☐ Because the writer does not use complex medical terminology or patronizingly simple words, she treats her readers as her equals.

- ☐ The writer supports her argument with examples in each paragraph.

- ☐ She uses statistics in the first and third paragraphs.

- ☐ The writer does not use words that reveal hasty generalizations: *all, always, everybody, everyone, nobody,* and *no one*.

- ☐ Her paper is free of ambiguous terms like *liberal, radical,* and *un-American*.

- ☐ The writer does not stereotype individuals. She does not present doctors, for example, either as plug-pulling villains or as unfeeling profit seekers but instead brings up ethical, legal, emotional, and practical questions that *all* people involved in the situation she is describing may face.

- ☐ Her cause-and-effect relationships are clear: the cause is stated as a question at the beginning of the essay, and the effects follow.

- ☐ The writer does not commit the "either-or" fallacy: she does not oversimplify the question by giving the reader only two alternatives.

- ☐ Her essay is free of trivial analogies. (Such comparisons and clichés cheapen the issue by oversimplifying it but often are used to sway the reader.)

□ The writer has not begged the question by shifting the burden of proof to the opposition. She gives proof throughout the essay.

□ The writer quotes accurately from a "living will." She has not changed or ignored the context.

□ Her statements are straightforward and give no evidence of being exaggerated.

□ The writer introduces no false issues to mislead readers.

□ She has not called the opposition names or used loaded terms to arouse readers' emotions.

□ The writer does not resort to attacking a person instead of an idea.

□ Throughout the essay, the writer gives attention to the opposing side's view, but in each case, she quickly points out the pitfalls of that view.

□ She never assumes reader acceptance of the argument; her essay ends on a strong note aimed at leaving readers with a convincing and provocative thesis statement.

Death, and After That, What?

Young or old, vocal or silent, countless people are deeply concerned with the thought of man's mortality and the inevitable last act in the drama of life: "Death, and after that, what?" This moot question, by its very nature, creates heated discussions as theories are expressed.

The background for most theories stems basically from what has influenced each person. The strongest of these influences is the family background. As the individual matures, either religious or nonreligious teachings are dominant. The family's religious or nonreligious imprinting gains strength by the individual's experiences from reading and from other group beliefs.

Man's immortality is a common concern. For centuries, philosophers have studied and discussed man's nature and his dependence upon a God concept, a concept which is usually structured upon his needs within his time and his environment. In *The Mansions of Philosophy*, Will Durant says, in brief, that

belief in immortality is rooted in the impulse of self-preservation.... Man longs for immortality, not because he loves life, but because he fears death, and the fear of death is the beginning of religion.... Man will always believe in God, because the idea of power united with perfection satisfies his soul, and he is pleased to be friends with omnipotence.*

* Will Durant, *The Mansions of Philosophy*, Garden City Publishing Company, Garden City, N. Y., 1929, pp. 575–576, 579.

All religions have their guidebooks; the Christian religion has the Bible. In this Bible, Christians find the basis for their concept of death and what follows it. The Bible provides, in a sense, the obituary of the leading men whom God uses throughout history; the great men of the Bible all die. David, a man after God's own heart, prays to God to lengthen his life when illness threatens death. God hears and allows him to rule Israel for forty years and to die after his full "threescore and ten." Of David's death, the Apostle Peter is inspired to say, in Acts 2:29,34, "Men and brethren, let me freely speak unto you of the patriarch David, that he is both dead and buried, and his sepulchre is with us unto this day . . . for David is not ascended unto the heavens." Peter says that Christians, after death, must wait until the appearing of Jesus Christ for resurrection and the Kingdom of God; and Peter, too, dies and is buried.

The Creator stresses the temporary qualities and uncertainties of life itself, as in James 4:14, where one reads, "Whereas ye know not what shall be on the morrow. For what is your life? It is even a vapour, that appeareth for a little time and then vanisheth away." In Genesis 3:19, God says, "For dust thou art, and unto dust shalt thou return." In Job 14:10 is a further definition of death: "But man dieth and wasteth away: Yea, man giveth up the ghost and where is he?" Job speaks of being kept in a grave and waiting there for a change to take place at the time of Christ's return.

The Apostle Paul is tested and suffers and dies. In Timothy 4:6–8, Paul says, "The time of my departure is at hand. I have fought a good fight, I have finished my course, I have kept the faith. Henceforth there is laid up for me a crown of righteousness, which the Lord, the righteous Judge, shall give me at that day." Paul cannot get his reward until the day Christ returns. The Bible stresses that resurrection must occur. The time of resurrection is man's hope and the answer to "Death, and after that, what?"

Sam Wray

QUESTIONS ABOUT THE ESSAYS

Think about the content of the two preceding essays as you answer the questions that follow. Be prepared to support your answers.

1. Which essay has a title that is directly related to the content?
2. Which essay has a more enticing introductory paragraph?
3. Do these essays differ according to location of thesis statement?
4. Do these essays use deductive or inductive development?
5. Which essay has more concrete examples and details?
6. Which essay has more documentation of statements?
7. What is the documentation for these statements?
8. Which essay has a more authoritative sound?
9. Which essay has more effective transitions?
10. Do these transitions make the sentences flow more smoothly?

11. How are the essays similar in regard to concluding paragraphs?
12. Do these essays contain fallacies in argumentation or logic?
13. What are the strong points of these essays?
14. What are some possible areas for improvement?
15. Which essay do you consider the better one?

Exercise 10-1 Select an issue that interests you and that should interest most people. (Avoid issues like abortion, drugs, premarital sex, rape, Viet Nam, and Watergate. These topics have been discussed so much in recent years that many readers are tired of them.)

If you cannot think of an issue, write an opposing argument to one of the essays in this chapter or modify one of the topics in this list:

Cults: A Threat to the American Way of Life?

Halloween: An Outdated Custom?

The Rights of Apartment Dwellers

Adoption by Single Parents

The Exemption of Single Male Parents from Jury Duty

Revision of the System for Selection of Jurors

Mandatory Neutering Laws for Pets

Closer State Supervision of Funeral-Home Technicians

Government Regulation and Supervision of Voting Polls to Protect Minorities

Government Regulation and Supervision of Campaign Expenditures

Government Control of City Traffic for Pollution Prevention

A Revision of Tax Rates for Single and Married People

Exceptions to Property Taxation for People over Sixty

Tax Exemptions for Churches

Prayer before Athletic Events

Brutality in Sports

Equal Pay for Women in Sports

The Salaries of Athletes: Too High?

Required Physical Education: A Must?

Televised Trials and the Courts

Violence on Television during Family Hours

Risqué Advertising on Television

Television Ratings and the Networks

The Academy Awards: Meaningless?

The Miss America Pageant: A Passé Event?

Take a stand on the issue and develop your stand in outline form. Include a thesis statement that summarizes the argument. Be prepared to use this outline for writing a persuasive essay.

The essay should have a thesis statement in the introductory or concluding paragraph. Devote a paragraph with examples to each point in the outline. Also use statistics where they are appropriate. Document all sources of information either in the text or in footnotes. Caution: Do not forget to mention the opposing side's views.

Your essay should be long enough to convince your readers, but not so long that it tires them. Do not use hasty generalizations, stereotypes, inadequate causal relationships, either-or fallacies, or trivial analogies. Also, do not beg the question, ignore the context, exaggerate the argument, make false issues to mislead readers, use loaded terms, or attack a person instead of an idea.

Review the information in this chapter, including the sample essays, before you begin work on your essay.

As soon as you have completed the rough draft of your essay, pretend that you are the reader and pose these questions:

Exercise 10-2

1. Does the writer know the subject well?
2. Has the writer limited the subject to his or her own range of expertise?
3. Has the writer developed a clear, logical argument?
4. Is the essay objective but not too formal?
5. Is there a definite thesis statement at the beginning or the end of the essay?
6. Does the content of the essay support the thesis statement?
7. Has the writer treated the reader as an equal?
8. Has the writer supported statements with examples and statistics?

9. Has the writer identified sources of information in the text or in footnotes?
10. Has the writer taken the reader for granted?
11. Has the writer begged the question, ignored the context, exaggerated the argument, introduced false issues to mislead the reader, used loaded terms, or attacked a person instead of an idea?
12. Has the writer made hasty generalizations or used inadequate causal relationships, either-or fallacies, and trivial analogies?
13. Does the essay have a smooth style?
14. Is the essay interesting?

Chapter 11□Interpretation

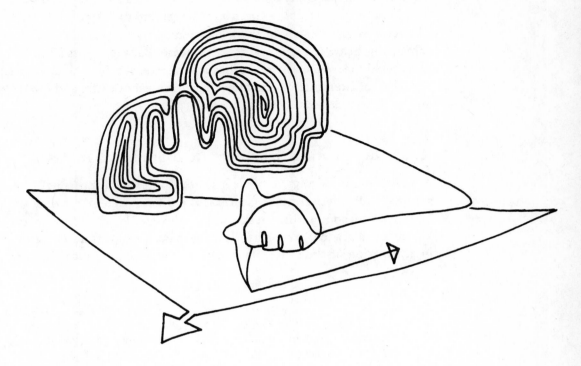

OBJECTIVES

After completing Chapter 11, you should be able to

1. write an interpretation essay, using the elements of style as a basis for interpretation
2. differentiate between plot summary and interpretation

The Elements of Interpretation

When writers tell what a work of literature or a movie means to them, they are interpreting it. They take the elements of a book or movie as a basis for discussing what that work means and what it has to say about life, according to their own views and past experiences. Some elements of style that they might use as a basis for interpretation are *characters*, the persons who carry out the action; *irony*, the author's tool for making the unexpected happen; *plot*, the plan of action; *point of view*,[1] the way an author comments about the characters and plot; *setting*, the location of the action; *structure*, the arrangement or interrelation of the different parts of a whole work of literature or a movie; *symbolism*, something in a work of literature or a movie that represents something else in real life; *theme*, the main idea that represents the action, or what the work of literature or the movie has to say about life; and *tone*, the author's attitude toward the subject.

Really Interpreting: Examples from Students' Papers

A writer should always remember that an interpretation is *not* a plot summary. The writer must interpret the different elements of a work or movie without telling readers the whole plot. To illustrate this difference, a student writer has developed both a plot summary and an interpretation of the same short story. First read the plot summary.

"The Lottery"

Shirley Jackson's "The Lottery"* is a short story with the theme that all societies need a scapegoat in one form or another. The society in this story is an imaginary village that has the age-old tradition of holding a lottery the first of every summer. Every person in the village must draw a slip from a black box. The person who draws the slip marked with a black dot is stoned to death. This ritual is supposed to insure good crops for the people who survive the lottery. The unfortunate victim in this lottery is ironically the last person to arrive on the scene. Tessie Hutchinson is a lovable, jovial person who does not take the lottery seriously at first. However, when her husband draws the slip of paper with the black dot, she insists that her husband did not have enough time to draw. She also demands that her daughter and son-in-law should be included in the final drawing. As one might expect, Tessie Hutchinson, the last person to arrive, draws the marked slip and suffers a tragic death.

Susan Hanks

* In Shirley Jackson, *Come Along with Me*, Viking Press, New York, 1968, pp. 225–233.

Now note the difference between the plot summary and the interpretation.

---

1. Point of view can be first person (the author takes a role and uses *I, me, we, us, our, ours, my,* or *mine*); second person (the author says *you* and *your*); third person (the author comments about the characters without taking a role and without going into much detail); or omniscient (the author goes into detail and comments quite freely).

"The Lottery" as a Comment on Society

Like Shirley Jackson's other short stories, "The Lottery"* is significant for its theme. In this short story, Shirley Jackson maintains that all societies need a scapegoat in one form or another. She stresses the theme through the use of a shocking plot and the actions of several very realistic characters.

The plot of "The Lottery" centers around an age-old tradition in an imaginary village. At the first of every summer, a lottery is held. Every person in the village, from the youngest child to the oldest citizen, must draw a slip of paper from a box. The unfortunate person who draws the slip marked with a black dot is stoned to death. The lottery is a ritual that the people follow to insure good crops. They consider the lottery a mark of civilization. An old man remarks, "Lottery in June, corn be heavy soon." The people of the village are quite willing to sacrifice a close neighbor or even a family member to the ritual, because the lottery is traditional and they have no desire to break with the old ways. They are shocked to hear that other villages are giving it up.

With this plot, Shirley Jackson is able to point out the need of society for a scapegoat. It is human nature to put the blame for failure on another person or on outside forces. When many humans gather in a society, this weakness multiplies. Society generally tends to select one or two persons and to lay the blame on them. The manner of selection of a scapegoat is often as random as the drawing in "The Lottery." Man is an ignorant and superstitious animal at times and can easily be swayed by the pressures of crowds and traditions.

The characters of "The Lottery" are simple and realistic. They are neighborly, slightly nervous, and concerned for each other. However, when the time comes for the stoning, they are coldhearted; even the victim's children participate. They lay all of the blame and guilt of the village upon one woman and then destroy her. This same situation of heaping guilt upon one person and then punishing her is prevalent in society today.

Shirley Jackson has used the combination of a shocking plot and simple ordinary characterization to create a vivid story. "The Lottery" points out that one of the weaknesses of society lies in its need for a scapegoat. In the case of "The Lottery," the scapegoat is Tessie Hutchinson.

Susan Hanks

* Ibid.

QUESTIONS ABOUT THE PLOT SUMMARY AND THE INTERPRETATION

1. What is the most obvious difference between the plot summary and the interpretation?
2. Which paper shows more creative effort by the writer?
3. Which paper is more impressive, and why is it impressive?
4. Why is the title of the interpretation more effective than that of the plot summary?
5. What is the thesis statement of the interpretation?

6. How does the writer support this thesis statement, and what literary elements does she use as support?
7. What is the predominant tense in the plot summary and interpretation, and why is this tense effective?
8. What point of view does the writer use in both papers, and why is this point of view effective?

The next two examples of interpretation follow the guidelines stated at the beginning of this chapter. The first one interprets a well-known short story, and the second one focuses on a popular movie.

"Barn Burning": A Story of Integrity

William Faulkner, like many other twentieth-century writers, emphasizes integrity. In his opinion, this virtue comes from within a person and becomes evident in a single gesture as the person struggles with the forces of freedom and necessity. Faulkner does not deviate from this belief in "Barn Burning,"* the story of Sarty Snopes, a ten-year-old boy who struggles against the restrictions of his family relationship and the crimes of his pyromaniac father while he longs to be free from them. When Sarty faces a colossal decision in his struggle, his integrity asserts itself; and in the gesture he makes, he finds his freedom.

The relationship of father and son, the bond of blood, is one of tradition: "like father, like son." Ab Snopes, the father in "Barn Burning," is a stiff, stubborn, unnatural, uneasy man who thinks cold, cruel thoughts and shows no warmth or kindness toward others, not even his wife and children. Sarty knows, however, that because Ab is his father, he must stand with him against their enemies. In his innocence, he does.

Sarty's struggle begins when he becomes aware of the true meaning of his father's action of deliberately soiling and later ruining Mrs. de Spain's expensive rug. For a while, Sarty is torn between loving his father because he is his father and hating him and longing to be free from him because he does wrong to others who have done no wrong to him. When he realizes his father is going to burn de Spain's barn, his terror and despair replace the blood bond. He dreams of running far away so that he should never have to see his father's face again.

Knowing that Sarty may interfere with his plan to burn de Spain's barn, Ab commands his wife to hold him. Sarty's integrity necessitates his breaking free from his mother and warning de Spain of his father's plan. This gesture does not save de Spain's barn, but it does result in Sarty's gaining his freedom from his father.

Susan Peabody

* William Faulkner, "Barn Burning," in *The Collected Short Stories of William Faulkner*, Chatto & Windus, London, 1958, II, 10–31.

COMMENTS ABOUT THE ESSAY

□ The title prepares readers for the thesis statement.

□ The thesis statement appears at the end of the introductory paragraph. (The writer prepares readers for the thesis statement by stating some background information that is relevant to the subject of this essay.)

□ The introductory paragraph contains at least three sentences and serves as an "appetizer" for what follows. (An introductory paragraph should always have at least three sentences and should whet the appetite for the rest of the paper by stating what the paper is about.)

□ The writer comments about different events in the story, but her remarks are not a summary: they are all interpretations that support the thesis statement.

□ The writer repeats in the last paragraph key words from the introduction: *integrity, gesture,* and *freedom*. (This technique unifies the different parts of the essay and reinforces the thesis statement.)

□ The last paragraph contains three sentences. (The concluding paragraph of a well-developed paper contains at least three sentences.)

□ The whole essay is in the present tense. (Always try to use present tense in writing about works of literature and movies. They are never past-tense material because every time someone reads a work or sees a movie, the action is either relived or experienced for the first time.)

□ The entire essay is in the third-person point of view. (Always try to use the third person because it allows you to be an objective observer; see comments on page 69.)

Now look at an interpretation of a popular movie.

Papillon: *A Study of Justice*

Papillon is the story of one man's relentless fight for freedom, which parallels man's unresolved struggle against the cruelty administered under the guise of "justice." The film, a true biographical account of a quest for freedom which spans fourteen years, centers about the most infamous of all prisons—Devil's

Island. This prison, located in the tropical jungles of French Guiana, was once a political prison for French criminals where men were separated from society, stripped of their identity, and reduced to subhuman existence.

The name *Papillon*, meaning *butterfly* in French, aptly describes the man who seeks to be freed from the harsh life sentence to which he has been condemned. The sentence for a murder, which Papillon denies having committed, is one which he considers unjust, and the entire story is an account of his various attempts at escape. The prison life to which Papillon and his fellow prisoners are subjected is quite harsh, and the viewer soon becomes sympathetic with the inmates of the dreaded prison. The treatment is harsh enough to cause the deaths of many prisoners.

The brutality and grimness depicted in the film are tempered to a degree by the close friendship of Papillon and Dega, a man imprisoned for counterfeiting. Both men discover a mutual need, and soon the friendship becomes a willingness to die, if necessary, for each other. Each man draws from the other the strength to keep on going after repeated attempts to escape fail. This relationship serves as the one tender and compassionate aspect of the story.

Devil's Island no longer exists, but this story should stir the consciences of present-day perpetrators of justice in their own penal practices. A good look at some of the "Devil's Islands" might reveal that too often cruelty becomes equated with punishment, thus making justice not only blind but also deaf and dumb to the dignity of man.

Paula Bloomer

COMMENTS ABOUT THE ESSAY

☐ The thesis statement appears in the first sentence of the introduction.

☐ The wording of the thesis statement prepares readers for the interpretation that follows.

☐ The writer gives readers some background information in the introduction.

☐ The two main topics of discussion are (1) the symbolism of the title and its relationship to the plot, and (2) the friendship of Papillon and Dega.

☐ In the concluding paragraph, the writer invites readers to compare the movie to present-day penal practices.

☐ The writer makes some perceptive comments about the movie and avoids giving readers a plot summary.

☐ With the exception of the last sentence in the first paragraph, the essay is in the best tense for interpretation: present tense. (See the comment on page 93.)

□ The writer has also chosen the best point of view for interpretation: third person. (See page 93.)

Choose a novel, play, short story, poem, or movie that has interested you. Outline an interpretation of it (see Exercise 11-2). Include a thesis statement in the outline.

Exercise 11-1

Be prepared to use this outline for writing an original interpretive essay. Caution: Do *not* write a plot summary. If you do not yet understand the difference between a plot summary and an interpretive essay, go back over the first two writing samples in this chapter.

Completing a form based on the one that follows should help you to develop the outline required for Exercise 11-1.

Exercise 11-2

Title: _____

Paragraph I (introduction)

   Background information leading to thesis statement:

   _____

   _____

   Thesis statement: _____

   _____

Paragraph II (first major division of thesis statement)

   Topic sentence: _____

   Example A: _____

      Supporting details (use as many as you feel are needed to make your point):

      1. _____

2. _____

3. _____

Example B:_____

Supporting details:

1. _____

2. _____

3. _____

Example C:_____

Supporting details:

1. _____

2. _____

3. _____

Paragraph III (second major division of thesis statement)

Topic sentence: _____

_____

Example A: _____

Supporting details:

1. _____

2. _____

3. _____

Example B:_____

Supporting details:

1. _____

2. _____

3. _____

Example C:_____

Supporting details:

1. _____

2. _____

3. _____

Conclusion (reflection on preceding paragraphs or restatement of thesis in different words)

_____

_____

As soon as you have completed the rough draft of your essay, consider these questions:

1. You chose to interpret a specific work of literature or movie because that work or movie interested you. What have you done

Exercise 11-3

in writing your essay to help your readers, too, become interested in your subject?

2. Does the title bear a well-thought-out relationship to the content of the essay? Does it aim to capture readers' interest?

3. Does the thesis statement prepare readers for an interpretation?

4. Does the introductory paragraph whet readers' appetites for what is to follow?

5. Does the essay actually tell what the work of literature or movie means?

6. Is this essay a plot summary rather than an interpretation?

7. Do the interpretations have clear, interesting details and examples?

8. Are the interpretations in a logical order?

9. Do these interpretations indicate that you know your subject well?

10. Are strong and colorful words present in this essay?

11. Do you use transitions throughout the essay? (See Exercise 1-5.)

12. Do you repeat key words to achieve a unified effect?

13. Do the introductory and concluding paragraphs contain at least three sentences?

14. Is the essay in the present tense and the third person? (See comments on page 93.)

15. Do all the sentences have subjects and verbs? (See page 125.)

16. Are all the modifiers in their correct places? (See Study Unit 8.)

17. Are all of the sentences punctuated correctly? (See Study Units 13, 14, and 15.)

18. Are all of the words spelled correctly? (See Study Unit 17.)

Chapter 12□Technical Analysis

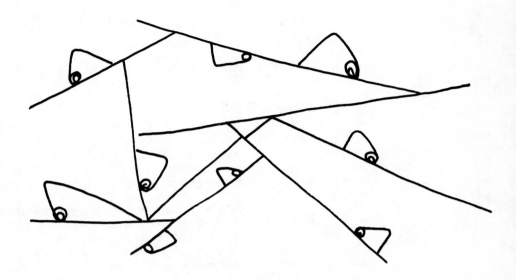

OBJECTIVES

After completing Chapter 12, you should be able to

1. write a technical-analysis essay
2. analyze carefully works of literature and movies

Analyzing Technique

Technical analysis shows *how* the characters, irony, plot, point of view, setting, structure, symbolism, themes, tone, and other elements of style in a work of literature or a movie are presented.[1] The procedure resembles that of a scientist viewing something through a microscope. The writer, similarly, makes a thorough and detailed examination of the work of literature or movie. In other words, the writer carefully

---

1. The major elements of style and their definitions appear in the introduction to Chapter 11.

analyzes the subject. Also like the scientist, the writer looks for unusual stylistic features. These features, or special effects, become the examples for the thesis statement.

Examples from Students' Papers

Here is a student essay that illustrates this technique:

Stephen Crane's Slapstick Western Saga

Slapstick need not be physically violent, as Stephen Crane ultimately proves in his story about Scratchy Wilson. The violence occurs through the use of descriptions, which are violent exaggerations. In Crane's saga of the shiftless gunslinger and the marshal, the reader faces a contradiction between imagery and reality which has humorous overtones. Overstatement and contrast produce the humor in Stephen Crane's short story "The Bride Comes to Yellow Sky."*

The author achieves this humor by the use of exaggerations. The characters tend to overreact to their situations, and the result is farcical. For instance, Marshal Potter is so imbued with his sense of duty that he feels like a traitor when he marries a young woman without the consent of the town of Yellow Sky. He believes his marriage is so important that it may be "exceeded [only] by the burning of the new hotel." It is, furthermore, an extraordinary crime. Of course, the people of Yellow Sky know nothing about Potter's marriage; so it is difficult to judge what their reaction may be. But Potter himself, musing on the prospects of their being informed about his new status, thinks that the people should meet him at the train station with a brass band. However, if Potter is such a respected citizen, Crane never supports the idea with any concrete evidence. When Potter arrives at the train depot, no one is there to greet him. The people hardly notice his absence.

Crane also uses contrasting images which reinforce the humor of his exaggerated statements. For instance, one notes the formidable image of bad guy Scratchy Wilson, contrasting it with his true image. One sees a figure in a "maroon-colored flannel shirt" carrying two "long, heavy, blue-black revolvers." He is yelling obscenities which fly over the roofs "in a volume that seems to have no relation to the ordinary vocal strength of a man." He is drunk; yet he walks "with the creeping movement of the midnight cat." Six sentences later, Crane refers to the ferocious cowboy as "the small thing in the middle of the street." One other subtle contrast is the reaction of the townspeople to Scratchy Wilson compared to his actual hell-raising activities. The barkeeper locks and bars the door to the saloon. He bars the "heavy wooden shutters." The Mexican sheepherders retreat through the back door of the saloon. "A tense, waiting hush" falls upon the six men in the saloon. The barkeeper places a Winchester on the bar.

* Stephen Crane, "The Bride Comes to Yellow Sky," in *The Complete Short Stories and Sketches of Stephen Crane*, ed. Thomas A. Gullason, Doubleday & Company, Garden City, N.Y., 1963.

But what does Scratchy Wilson do to provoke such fear? He "bellows and fumes" at the sky. He shoots at the barkeeper's dog, never hitting the animal, but simply scaring it. Scratchy shoots at a paper target nailed to the door of the saloon, and he misses. Scratchy fumes, howls, and challenges; but he never does anything more than shoot out the window and frighten a poor dog. This contrast supports the humor which Crane achieves through his use of hyperbole.

Thus, in Crane's story, the reader encounters a hero who is no hero and a bad man who is, at best, a drunken braggart. The effect is predictable. The comedy in "The Bride Comes to Yellow Sky" is a product of exaggeration and contrast.

Tom Tyler, III

COMMENTS ABOUT THE ESSAY

☐ The writer has placed his thesis statement at the end of the first paragraph.

☐ The thesis statement prepares the reader for a technical analysis: *Overstatement and contrast produce the humor in Stephen Crane's short story "The Bride Comes to Yellow Sky."*

☐ The two major examples in this essay are (1) the author's use of exaggeration, and (2) his use of contrasting images to reinforce the humor of the exaggerated statements.

☐ The writer supports each of these examples with definite details.

☐ Transitions throughout the essay weave together these details.

☐ Short quotations support the writer's statements and give the essay variety. (Try to avoid long quotations, since they bore the reader and only pad the paper.)

☐ The writer never strays from the thesis statement, even in the last sentence.

☐ The concluding paragraph contains three sentences.

☐ The essay is in the present tense and the third person. (See pages 254 and 241.)

Now examine another student essay written about a short story on a different topic.

The Use of Nature to Transmit Theme
in Sarah Orne Jewett's "A White Heron"

Sarah Orne Jewett is well schooled in transforming the familiar into the unique, the ordinary into the rare. From her opening phrases to the final paragraphs, Jewett lures the reader into a world governed by the influences of nature. The theme of "A White Heron"* comes into clear focus and gains momentum in Jewett's treatment of the intimacies of nature in relation to one young girl.

The woods, with their shadows, place the reader within the secluded realm of nature and expose the reader immediately to a dominant influence on the theme of the story. The girl, Sylvia, and her cow, "a plodding, dilatory, provoking creature," make their way home with "feet familiar with the path, and it was no matter whether their eyes could see it or not."

Within the framework of her own originality, Jewett couples her character with nature in such a way as to create a oneness. The reader sees the child as one with nature in that she listens "to the thrushes with a heart" filled with pleasure. Jewett is not content to limit such familiar descriptions to the human element of this story. She expands her command of intimate description to include the residents of the forest. The trees that so softly shade Sylvia are not inhabited by mere birds, in the eyes of Jewett, but by "birds and beasts that seemed to be wide awake, and going about their world, or else saying goodnight to each other in sleepy twitters."

At the moment of invasion, when the young ornithologist enters this soft world, he does not escape a comparison with nature. His whistle is "not a bird's whistle, which would have a sort of friendliness, but a boy's whistle, determined and somewhat aggressive." And Jewett describes Sylvia in "nature-words." Upon her alarm at her encounter with the young man, the reader learns that "it did not seem to be her fault, and she hung her head as if the stem of it were broken." Maintaining a high level of consistency, Jewett visualizes no element of nature as commonplace. She paints the sun filtering through the towering trees in terms of color and temperature as "strangely yellow and hot."

The theme, Sylvia's problem, becomes obvious again in terms of nature in one thought: "She could not understand why he [the young man] killed the very birds he seemed to like so much." During Sylvia's trek to the "stately old pine," she is "listening with a sense of comfort and companionship to the drowsy twitter of a half-awakened bird whose perch she had jarred in passing."

Throughout this short story, which can only be regarded as an interplay between acute observation and memory, Jewett achieves an intensity between the reader and the theme through a brief but intimate affair with nature. Even to the latter paragraphs of the work, the reader imagines the pine tree as "a great main-mast to the voyaging earth." This "mast" is simply a symbol of Jewett's personal relationship with nature. Continuing, Jewett says, "And the tree stood still and frowned away the winds." The choice Sylvia must make between the life of the white heron and her affection for the young ornithologist is an easy one when the reader is so overwhelmed with the appeal of nature. The familiarity and benevolence of a wood filled with "drowsy twitters" and "frowning" pines far overshadow the "aggression" of a young man's whistle.

Jewett's loyalty to nature prevails throughout "A White Heron." She maintains this theme through her abundant usage of nature images and description. The heart of the story lies not only in the destiny of the white heron but also in the

---

* Sarah Orne Jewett, *A White Heron and Other Stories*, Houghton Mifflin, Boston, 1886, pp. 1–22.

influence of a serene, benevolent, personal nature upon the spirit of a young girl. Although she is "vaguely thrilled by a dream of love," she is won by nature and its charms.

John G. Click

QUESTIONS ABOUT THE ESSAYS

As you answer the questions that follow, think about the content of the two previous essays in this chapter. Be prepared to support your answers.

1. Which essay has a more revealing title?
2. Which one has a stronger thesis statement?
3. Which essay gives better examples?
4. Which one has more supporting details?
5. Which essay has better development?
6. Which one shows more logical organization?
7. Which essay has better transitions?
8. Which one appeals more to your interest?

The previous essays analyzed the use of language in two short stories. The next essay focuses on characterization.

Dickens's Characterization of David Copperfield

In *David Copperfield*,* Charles Dickens skillfully employs characterization to present his young hero as a social outcast who develops into a morally good individual. Being an orphan, David Copperfield seems to have no chance in life at first. Evil attempts to corrupt him in his weakened state, but a natural sense for what is right saves the boy. In fact, a complete reversal of fortune occurs and enables David to join in the conflict against society's evil forces.

For example, David Copperfield suffers alone in the world during his childhood. Having never seen his real father, David must live with an unloving stepfather after his mother dies in childbirth. His lonely existence seems like death. David even imagines himself in the grave with his mother. He does, however, find companionship with Peggoty, his kindly nurse, but this relationship terminates with their separation. David's father sends him to a London counting house, where he is plunged into deeper torment as a result.

Dickens's hero is, therefore, forced to search for satisfaction and happiness in his world. He runs away from the counting house to seek the protection of Miss Betsy Trotwood, his aunt and only living blood relative. The desperateness of

---

* Charles Dickens, *David Copperfield*, Grosset & Dunlap, New York, 1898.

David's situation is evident in his having heard many unpleasant stories about his aunt from his mother. For example, he knows about Miss Betsy's angrily abandoning David's mother upon David's birth because of his not being a girl. Miss Betsy is the boy's one hope for escaping evil; therefore, David is willing to attempt a reconciliation with his aunt though reconciliation seems improbable.

After Miss Betsy adopts him and gives him the love and security he desires, David Copperfield matures into a man and joins the battle against the evil forces of society. David develops into a universal moral recorder in his new, protected environment. He passes judgment on his fellows before the reader has a chance to form an opinion, but his first impression is usually correct. For example, David describes Uriah Heep at first glance as a grotesque and evil figure. The reader later discovers this observation to be true when Uriah reveals that he intends to marry the virtuous Agnes, David's intimate confidante.

Consequently, David Copperfield functions as a force to combat evil, for Dickens uses characterization to portray society as a fusion of good and evil forces in constant conflict. Mr. Spenlow, a lawyer and the employer of David, recognizes this state of conflict and awakens his young employee to a broad understanding of it when he tells him, "Look at the world, there was good and evil in that. . . . It was all part of a system."

Jim Laney

COMMENTS ABOUT THE ESSAY

- [ ] The title gives readers an idea of what is to be found in the essay.
- [ ] The thesis statement is the first sentence of the essay.
- [ ] The introductory paragraph, which contains four sentences, prepares readers for the paragraphs that follow.
- [ ] Transitions blend the paragraphs together to form a unified essay.
- [ ] The writer uses incidents in the novel to support his examples, but he does *not* give a plot summary.
- [ ] The writer repeats in the concluding paragraph key words that he has used in the introduction: *society, evil forces,* and *conflict.* (This technique unifies the different parts of a paper.)
- [ ] The writer ends his essay with an effective quotation that reflects the content of the previous paragraphs.
- [ ] The whole essay is in the present tense and the third person. (For comments about tense and person in essays about literary works, see page 93.)

Exercise 12-1   Select a novel, play, short story, poem, or movie that interests you and that you know well. Analyze this work carefully and outline a technical analysis of it (see Exercise 12-2). Include a thesis statement in the outline.

Be prepared to use the outline for writing a technical-analysis essay. Caution: Do *not* write a plot summary. Review the sample essays in this chapter as a guide.

Completing a form based on the one that follows should help you to develop the outline required for Exercise 12-1.

Exercise 12-2

Title: _____

Paragraph I (introduction)

    Background information leading to thesis statement:

    _____

    _____

    Thesis statement: _____

    _____

Paragraph II (first major division of thesis statement)

    Topic sentence: _____

    Example A: _____

    Supporting details (use as many as you feel are needed to make your point):

    1. _____

    2. _____

    3. _____

Example B:_____

   Supporting details:

      1. _____

      2. _____

      3. _____

Example C:_____

   Supporting details:

      1. _____

      2. _____

      3. _____

Paragraph III (second major division of thesis statement)

   Topic sentence:_____

   _____

   Example A: _____

   Supporting details:

      1. _____

      2. _____

      3. _____

Example B:_____

   Supporting details:

   1. _____

   2. _____

   3. _____

Example C:_____

   Supporting details:

   1. _____

   2. _____

   3. _____

Conclusion (reflection on preceding paragraphs or restatement of thesis in different words)

_____

_____

As soon as you have completed the rough draft of your essay, think about these questions:

Exercise 12-3

1. Do the title and thesis statement aim to capture readers' interest and prepare them for a technical-analysis essay?
2. Do the topic sentences support the thesis statement?
3. Do the examples support the topic sentences?
4. Does the essay actually analyze the stylistic aspects of the subject?
5. If it does, are the descriptions of the stylistic aspects clear?

6. Does the content indicate that you really know your subject?
7. Do the introductory and concluding paragraphs contain at least three sentences?
8. Do sentences flow smoothly throughout the paper?
9. Do transitions weave together these sentences? (See Exercise 1-5.)
10. Are key words repeated to unify the different parts of the essay?
11. Do strong and colorful words strengthen this essay?
12. Do all of the sentences have subjects and verbs? (See pages 125–128.)
13. Do all of the modifiers have words to affect and describe, and are these modifiers in their correct places? (See pages 228–232.)
14. Are all of the sentences punctuated correctly? (See Study Units 13, 14, and 15.)
15. Are all of the words spelled correctly? (See Study Unit 17.)

Chapter 13 □ Judgment and Evaluation

OBJECTIVES

After completing Chapter 13, you should be able to

1. write a judgment and evaluation essay
2. support an opinion
3. evaluate works of literature and movies

Forming and Expressing an Opinion

In judgment and evaluation writing, writers give an overall opinion of the significance of a work of literature or movie by evaluating it. They often base their opinion on whether they have gained something from this literary work or movie. Although writers may rely somewhat on the methods discussed in the two preceding chapters in presenting what they have or have not gained, the content and tone of the essays *must* indicate judgment and evaluation. In fact, the thesis statement should express a writer's opinion of a subject, and the samples in the essay should support this opinion.

Examples: Students Say What They Think

Here is a student essay that utilizes the judgment and evaluation method by depicting the shortcomings of a popular movie:

The Absence of Realism in the Movie Jaws

The movie *Jaws* is one of the biggest box-office successes in history, and the film has had a great emotional impact on its viewing audiences. Recent news reports state that many people are now reluctant to swim in the ocean because of the picture. The vivid imagination of the American public is allowing a fictitious story to blind their logic. Though the movie *Jaws* is enjoying wide acclaim and popularity in the United States, the film fails to depict a realistic adventure.

For example, the fisherman who seeks to destroy the great white shark is a nineteenth-century seaman in a twentieth-century setting. He resembles the fanatic Captain Ahab of Herman Melville's *Moby-Dick*, for both men are obsessed with the need to capture a great fish at the expense of their own crew. The fisherman's British accent and seafaring manner contribute to this unbelievable image.

In addition, the mechanical sharks in the movie do not bring a sense of realism to the audience. The film viewer can easily distinguish the real great white sharks from the mechanical fish. This contrast becomes apparent when the mechanical sharks do not move with the same fluid motion that the live sharks have. And the close-ups of the mechanical sharks reveal a noticeable difference in appearance, especially in skin color and body structure.

Therefore, *Jaws* does not deserve the national attention it has achieved, for it lacks believability. Perhaps the publicity for the film is the underlying reason behind the film's great effect upon the American people. The film itself is incapable of arousing terror because it distorts reality too obviously.

Jim Laney

COMMENTS ABOUT THE ESSAY

☐ The title accurately reveals the content of the essay.

☐ The title should appeal to most readers because they have seen or heard about *Jaws*.

☐ The thesis statement appears at the end of the introductory paragraph, which contains at least three sentences.

☐ The writer leads up to the thesis statement by first discussing the film's great impact.

- The writer uses the fisherman and the mechanical sharks as his two main examples.

- Transitions introduce all supporting paragraphs.

- The essay comes to a logical conclusion that reflects the content of preceding paragraphs.

- The concluding paragraph contains at least three sentences.

- The entire essay is in the present tense and the third person. (See pages 254 and 458.)

The previous essay discussed the lack of realism in a movie. The following student essay deals with the abundance of realism in a well-known play:

The Glass Menagerie: *The Best of Tennessee Williams*

Tennessee Williams is one of the best-known literary figures on the American scene. Some critics say he is the greatest dramatist to have appeared since Eugene O'Neill. The play that won Tennessee Williams his fame is *The Glass Menagerie*.* This play is exciting because it brings realistic emotions and a new Tennessee Williams style to its audience.

For example, a person experiencing *The Glass Menagerie* becomes involved in a highly emotional situation. Williams is tremendously successful in creating realistic characters who, although living in a dream world as Amanda Wingfield and her daughter Laura do, possess realistic emotions. Tom, the son and brother, narrator of and character in the drama, is a realistic young man who finds life so empty and cruel that he runs away to escape into his own dream world. The audience shares the emotions of the three main characters, but Laura's emotions are the most moving. She is a young girl desperately trying to overcome her shyness and to touch the outside world. In *The Glass Menagerie*, the characters and the plot represent emotions which Tennessee Williams succeeds in bringing realistically to the American stage.

The play is also unique in that it illustrates a different style of Tennessee Williams. It is a modern tragedy, with little or no sensationalism and pornography, of a hero who is not a sexual specialist, but an ordinary young man. His great mistake is his choice of self instead of family. As a result of his choice, his conscience gives him no peace. In his use of Tom's narration, the flashbacks, and the interior pantomime, Tennessee Williams emphasizes his realistic characters, their realistic emotions, and the dramatic plot.

Some drama critics say that Tennessee Williams presents only a limited view

* Tennessee Williams, *The Glass Menagerie*, Random House, New York, 1945.

of life and that he lacks sufficient artistic discipline. Such criticism cannot be made of him and his work *The Glass Menagerie*. In this drama, one finds the true greatness of Williams as a playwright.

Mark Laney

QUESTIONS ABOUT THE ESSAY

Be prepared to support your answers to the questions that follow.

1. Does the title entice you to read the essay?
2. What is the thesis statement of this essay?
3. What are the main examples that support this thesis statement?
4. Do the examples have sufficient details?
5. Does the writer use effective transitions?
6. Do the sentences flow smoothly?
7. Are the sentences in logical order?
8. Does this essay stimulate your interest in the play?

Poems also make good subjects for judgment and evaluation essays, and the poem discussed in the essay that follows is no exception.

"The Road Not Taken": A Poem to Destiny

One of the best-loved American poets in modern times is Robert Frost. His work is pure lyric poetry, and his lines reflect the tone and temper of New England life. One of Frost's most famous works is "The Road Not Taken,"* and it is a poem with which almost all people can identify.

People can relate to the poem because they can understand it. Because the language of "The Road Not Taken" is simple, readers can understand it. Flowery descriptions and deep symbolism are not present to confuse the reader. Frost simply compares a fork in a road to a decision in life. He presents what could have been a complicated philosophy in an analogy that the common man understands.

People can also identify with "The Road Not Taken" because it deals with a problem that all people inevitably face in their lives. Most individuals have at one time or another come to that fork in the road and wondered which way to turn. Frost tells his reader that once when he was traveling alone, he stood at a fork in the road and was undecided about which path to take. Finally, the poet says, he chose one because it seemed a little less frequented, though actually there was no such difference. All people make decisions and later wonder about the consequences.

---

* Robert Frost, *The Poems of Robert Frost*, Random House, New York, 1946, p. 117.

The words of Robert Frost in "The Road Not Taken" are unforgettable. Most readers look back and remember difficult past decisions as they think about the words of the poem. Their memories are of dreams and destinies. Some readers look back in triumph, and others look back in grief. Each person sees his own life and a decision that eternity can never change.

Mark Laney

QUESTIONS ABOUT THE ESSAY

Be prepared to support your answers to the questions that follow.

1. Does the writer's choice of poem interest you?
2. What reasons does the writer give for appreciating this poem?
3. Why does the writer repeat the word *people* at the beginning of paragraph 1 and paragraph 2?
4. Does the last sentence of this paper end on a concluding note and bear a logical relationship to statements in preceding paragraphs?
5. Can you think of additional reasons for appreciating "The Road Not Taken"?

The preceding essays in this chapter have been about a poem, a play, and a movie. The next essay evaluates a novel that depicts one writer's view of life in the South.

The Violent Bear It Away

The works of Flannery O'Connor are unique for their presentation of southern realism. *The Violent Bear It Away* * is also an achievement in realism which lives up fully to the obligation of realistic fiction to present a plausible and revealing imitation of reality. Although many of her characters are usually grotesque, O'Connor adheres so consistently to the patterns she creates for her characters that the reader must judge them on levels that transcend idiosyncracies and regional flavor and apply to the whole of humanity.

Though the novel deals largely with the specific guilt inherent in southern Christian religion, it reveals the consistent result of all guilt: violence to one's self and to others. As the three main characters—young Tarwater, his great-uncle, and the schoolteacher—turn to one another for relief from self-hatred, they realize that there can be no relief because each is infected with the same disease, guilt, and the capacity for forgiveness appears to be hereditarily replaced with the capacity for violence. The direction of the novel becomes

---

* Flannery O'Connor, *The Violent Bear It Away*, Farrar, Straus & Cudahy, New York, 1960.

painfully clear in light of this violent force that is working on the minds of the characters, but O'Connor creates a set of contrasting circumstances which keep the reader in anticipation of a solution to the characters' problems. As the extent to which the old man has warped the boy's thinking becomes apparent, it also becomes apparent that the old man has a greater hold over the boy in death than he had in life. Like the last act of a mad dog, the old man dooms another to suffer the madness of his beliefs.

Young Tarwater's battle against his upbringing and against himself is a conflict which all men face in their quest for self-understanding, and the South has no exclusive claim on the elements of ignorance and violence that finally separate Tarwater from reality. *The Violent Bear It Away* is a novel set in the South, but it has implications that apply to all men who try to rebel against their backgrounds. Some readers call O'Connor a regionalist, and some people would like to confine the ugly, the ignorant, the grotesque, and the helpless to a distant and definable limbo. It is only with some discomfort that the reader recognizes the universality of O'Connor's characters.

David Barrow

COMMENTS ABOUT THE ESSAY

- ☐ The writer gives his general opinion of the novel in the second sentence of the first paragraph. (This sentence is the thesis statement.)

- ☐ The first paragraph contains three sentences: (1) an introductory comment, (2) a thesis statement, and (3) a supporting comment.

- ☐ The second and last paragraphs develop the thesis statement.

- ☐ Each paragraph begins with a strong topic sentence that summarizes the content of the paragraph.

- ☐ All of the topic sentences support the thesis statement.

- ☐ The concluding paragraph restates the central idea (thesis statement), summarizes previous statements, and offers some philosophical insights.

The last evaluation in this group of student essays comments on closely observed feelings and emotions.

"Roman Fever": An Emotionally Moving Story

Edith Wharton is famous for her emotionally moving novels and short stories. Her short story "Roman Fever"* is no exception. By portraying feelings known to

---

* In Edith Wharton, *The Best Short Stories of Edith Wharton*, ed. Wayne Andrews, Charles Scribner's Sons, New York, 1958, pp. 3–15.

every reader and weaving them into a suspenseful tale, Edith Wharton has created a stirring and memorable piece of literature.

Wharton successfully elicits feeling from the reader by displaying a panorama of readily empathized emotions in the characterizations of Grace Ansley and Alida Slade. When the two women discuss the "new system" under which their daughters have freedom of movement and contrast it with their own strict adolescent guidelines, a feeling of melancholy is transmitted to the reader. This melancholy accents through the women's realization that the new system has given them a good deal of time to kill, and the reader feels pity toward two women who have the mistaken assumption that they have outlived their usefulness.

Melancholy dissolves into a strong sense of jealousy that Mrs. Slade harbors toward her friend. Even as she mentally compares their daughters, Mrs. Slade realizes that her attempt to destroy Grace Ansley created a situation that returned to hurt herself. The ominous power of this "Roman Fever," or deathly jealousy, completely jars the reader with the unforgettable final scene.

The strong love for the same man that caused the jealousy serves as an overwhelming stimulus for sympathy and understanding toward both victims in the story. As Mrs. Slade detects a note of emphasis in Grace Ansley's voice during their discussion of Roman memories, the author plants the seed of suspense, which eventually leads to the revelation and irony that the two women are lamenting the loss of the same lover.

The reader vicariously experiences these strong emotions of love, jealousy, and melancholy as he interprets the riddle of Rome in the women's lives. The author's use of portentous pauses in dialogue between the two women draws out the investigatory instincts in the reader. The result of this intellectual and sensorial stimulation is that a simple story turns into an unforgettable drama.

Linda East

COMMENTS ABOUT THE ESSAY

□ The writer uses a three-sentence introduction moving from the general to the specific, sometimes called focusing or narrowing to the thesis.

□ The thesis appears in the last sentence of the first paragraph after the author has led readers to it.

□ The essay uses three major examples to support the thesis: (1) melancholy, (2) jealousy, and (3) love.

□ The writer devotes one major paragraph to each example.

□ The writer refers to various incidents to support her opinion of the novel.

□ The last sentence of each paragraph prepares readers for the next paragraph.

□ The paper is in the third person and the present tense (with the exception of several allusions to Grace Ansley's and Alida Slade's early years). (See pages 458 and 254.)

☐ The sentences vary in length and structure.

☐ The conclusion contains three sentences that relate to the thesis and the three supporting examples.

Exercise 13-1 Think of a novel, play, short story, poem, or movie that interests you and about which you have a definite opinion. Decide what characteristics of the work or movie have influenced your opinion and might appeal to others. Write an outline using your opinion as the thesis statement and these characteristics as examples (see Exercise 13-2).

Be prepared to use this outline for writing a judgment and evaluation essay. Caution: Do *not* write a plot summary. Review the sample essays in this chapter for use as a guide.

Exercise 13-2 Completing a form based on the one that follows should help you to develop the outline required for Exercise 13-1.

Title: _____

Paragraph I (introduction)

    Background information leading to thesis statement:

    _____

    _____

    Thesis statement: _____

    _____

Paragraph II (first major division of thesis statement)

    Topic sentence: _____

    Example A: _____

Supporting details (use as many as you feel are needed to make your point):

1. _____

2. _____

3. _____

Example B:_____

Supporting details:

1. _____

2. _____

3. _____

Example C:_____

Supporting details:

1. _____

2. _____

3. _____

Paragraph III (second major division of thesis statement)

Topic sentence:_____

_____

Example A: _____

Supporting details:

1. _____

2. _____

3. _____

Example B: _____

Supporting details:

1. _____

2. _____

3. _____

Example C: _____

Supporting details:

1. _____

2. _____

3. _____

Conclusion (reflection on preceding paragraphs or restatement of thesis in different words)

_____

_____

_____

As soon as you have completed the rough draft of your essay, review   *Exercise 13-3*
these questions:

1. Does the thesis statement express your own opinion?
2. Do the topic sentences support this opinion?
3. Do the examples support the topic sentences?
4. Do the examples indicate that you have a valid opinion?
5. Are all of the sentences coherent?
6. Do the sentences flow smoothly?
7. Do transitions unify the sentences and paragraphs? (See Exercise 1-5.)
8. Do the introductory and concluding paragraphs contain at least three sentences?
9. Do all of the sentences have subjects and verbs? (See pages 125–128.)
10. Do all of the sentences have modifiers in their correct places? (See pages 128 and 228–232.)
11. Are all of the sentences punctuated correctly? (See Study Units 13, 14, and 15.)
12. Are all of the words spelled correctly? (See Study Unit 17.)

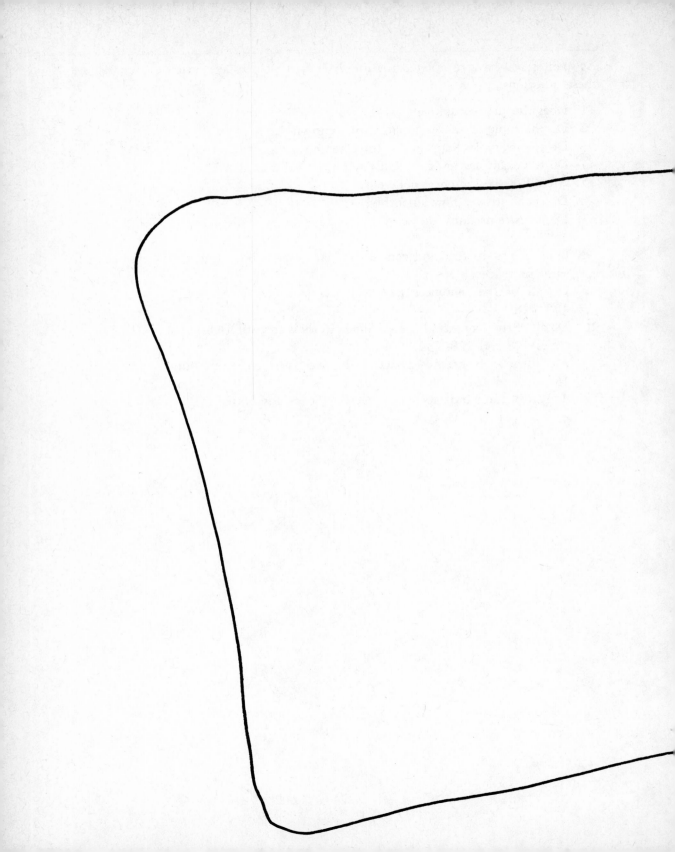

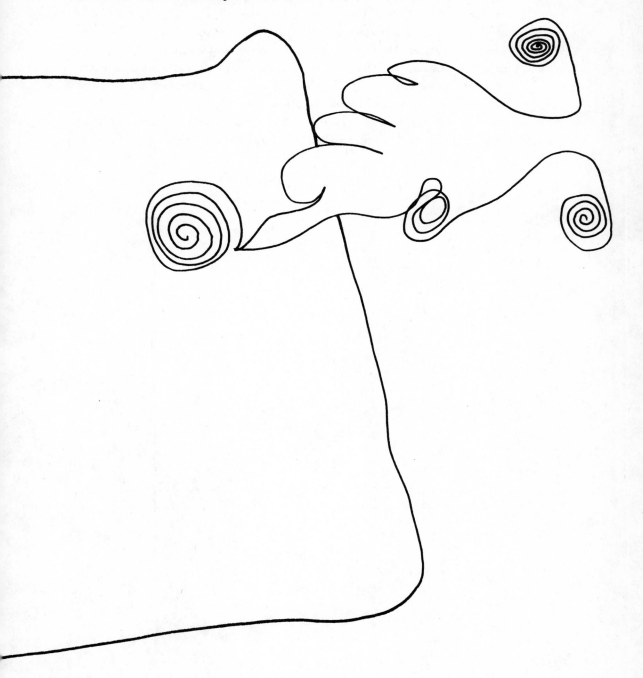

The study units that follow begin with preassessment questions that determine just how much brushing up you need to do. A preassessment score of 90 percent or more indicates that you already know most of the material in a particular unit and that you are ready to move on to another unit. A score below 90 indicates that you need to study the explanations and exercises of the learning activities in the unit. To save you time, an answer section follows each exercise. Postassessment questions at the end of each unit allow you to check your comprehension of the material: a score of 90 or more means that you have mastered the unit; a score below 90 indicates that you need to review the material.

Study Unit 1 □ The Elements of Sentences

RATIONALE

This unit should give you a basic knowledge of sentence patterns. By breaking sentences into their components, you can learn to identify these components according to their names and functions within the sentences. In addition, you can gain a thorough knowledge of the total sentence structure.

OBJECTIVES

After completing Study Unit 1, you should be able to distinguish among these sentence elements:
1. subject
2. predicate
3. subject complement
4. direct object
5. indirect object

Preassessment

Identify the *italicized* word or words in each of the sentences that follow by marking S for subjects, P for predicates or verbs, C for subject complements, D for direct objects, and I for indirect objects.

_____ 1. Christmas *is* an enjoyable season.

_____ 2. In fact, it is a real *treat* for me.

_____ 3. I am a different *person* at Christmas.

_____ 4. My friends and I feel *happy*.

_____ 5. We also *think* of other people.

_____ 6. Although we buy *gifts* for each other, we also give money to charities.

_____ 7. Giving money to charities *is* gratifying for us.

_____ 8. It also gives less fortunate *people* hope for the future.

_____ 9. In every city *are* to be found many worthy charities.

_____ 10. My *friends* and *I* include homes for the aged in our Christmas visitations.

_____ 11. Many of the people in these homes are not *joyful* during the Christmas season.

_____ 12. In their rooms are no *cards* or *gifts*.

_____ 13. My friends and I give *them* cookies and fruit.

_____ 14. We are their only *link* with the outside world.

_____ 15. Therefore, we spend several *hours* with them.

_____ 16. Watching their faces brighten with smiles *is*, indeed, a reward for us.

_____ 17. However, I always feel *sad* when I have to leave them.

_____ 18. Their *faces* reveal disappointment at our having to leave.

_____ 19. We remind them that we *plan* to return.

_____ 20. However, I always wonder if *we* are going to get that opportunity.

1. P	6. D	11. C	16. P
2. C	7. P	12. S	17. C
3. C	8. I	13. I	18. S
4. C	9. P	14. C	19. P
5. P	10. S	15. D	20. S

Learning Activities

SUBJECTS AND PREDICATES

Many writing errors, such as sentence fragments and run-on sentences, result from an inadequate knowledge of sentence components. The two most important sentence elements are subjects and predicates. (Sometimes, predicates are referred to as verbs. For the purposes of this study unit, you may use either term.)[1]

Every normal sentence contains at least one subject and one predicate. The subject and predicate can be either expressed or implied. The *subject* is what the sentence is about. It is the person, thing, or idea talked about. The *predicate* (verb) expresses the action of the sentence. It tells what the subject does or is.

To find the subject and predicate of a sentence, first ask yourself, "*What* action is happening in this sentence?" The answer to this question is the predicate. Then ask yourself, "*Who* or *what* is doing this action?" The answer to this question is the subject. In the sentences that follow, the subjects are underlined once, and the verbs are underlined twice.

Dogs bark.

(*What* is happening? Dogs *bark*. *Who* or *what* is doing this barking? *Dogs* are.)

The squirrel ran up the tree.

(*What* happened? The squirrel *ran* up the tree. *Who* or *what* ran? The *squirrel* did.)

---

1. Strictly speaking, a *verb*, like a noun, is really a part of speech, whereas a *predicate*, like a subject, is a grammatical part of a sentence.

Often, several words join to form either the subject or the predicate. When this happens, the subject or predicate is called a *compound subject* or *compound predicate*.

Kurt, Max, and Ronald went to school.
Wendy wrote letters and stamped envelopes.

Exercise 1 *Identifying Subjects and Predicates*

In each of the following sentences, draw *one* line under every subject and *two* lines under every predicate.

1. A man and his son went to a movie.

2. The man enjoyed the movie, but his son was bored.

3. Abraham and Moe are our guests.

4. They lived and studied in England for two years.

5. Mary Weinstein visited her aunt, who teaches at a university.

6. Elmer gave Bonnie a party when she was in New York.

7. Neither Janie nor Toby knows the answer.

8. As time passed, Mr. Talley began to relax.

9. The lambs showed signs of being easily trained.

10. They learned very quickly but proved to be expensive pets.

11. The members of Aaron's church are sponsoring a carnival.

12. Realizing that he could not disappoint his friends, Joey attended the party.

13. He had a good time and enjoyed seeing some former acquaintances.

14. The couple celebrated their first wedding anniversary by going to an expensive restaurant.

15. A group of wandering musicians played the couple's favorite song.

ANSWERS TO EXERCISE 1

1. man, son went
2. man enjoyed; son was
3. Abraham, Moe are
4. They lived, studied
5. Mary Weinstein visited; who teaches
6. Elmer gave; she was
7. Janie, Toby knows
8. time passed; Mr. Talley began
9. lambs showed
10. They learned, proved
11. members are sponsoring
12. he could disappoint; Joey attended
13. He had, enjoyed
14. couple celebrated
15. group played

If you completed Exercise 1 successfully with at least thirteen correct answers, proceed to the next learning activity. If you had difficulty with this exercise, review the rules and examples and consult with your instructor.

INVERTED ORDER AND OTHER COMPLICATIONS

In most sentences, the subject comes before the predicate. However, in some sentences, the subject follows the predicate or a part of the predicate. This arrangement is called *inverted order*.

Across the highway was a boarded-up gas station.
Where did you go to college?
On his desk lay a picture.
There are many guests here today.

Notice the word *there* in the last sentence. This word is an *expletive*. Its function is to get the sentence started; it has no other function or meaning in the sentence. Never mistake *there* for the subject of a sentence. Look at these sentences:

expl.
There is one student in the room.

expl.
There are two students in the room.

Modifiers (words that describe) or other words may separate the parts of a predicate.

mod.
We had often written to each other.

mod.
Sue Eagle would not take my advice.

Do not confuse subjects of sentences with the objects of prepositions. (A *preposition* is a word that shows the relationship between a noun or pronoun that follows and some other word in the sentence.)

obj. of
prep.   prep.
One of my friends is going to Europe.

obj. of
prep.   prep.
The pages of the book should not be torn.

(*Friends* and *book* are not subjects but objects of the preposition *of.*)
In commands, the subject *you* is implied or understood.

v.   subj.   v.
Go to town.   (You) go to town.

v.   subj.   v.
Come to see me.   (You) come to see me.

VOICE
All verbs have either *active* or *passive* voice. A verb is in active voice when the subject does the acting.

Noriko is writing a letter.

Laura watches too much television.

A verb is in passive voice when the subject receives the action.

The audience was observed.

The candidates were screened.

   Passive verbs are always various forms of the verb *be* (*am, are, is, was, were, been*). Most writers use the passive voice sparingly because it often gives a sentence a dead effect. The active voice, by contrast, suggests energy and activity.

Regular to Inverted Order   *Exercise 2*
The following sentences are written in regular order. Rewrite them, using inverted order.

1. The fox ran up the hill like a flash.

   _____

2. A man sat at the top of the hill.

   _____

3. He was shocked to see the fox.

   _____

4. The fox snarled at the man.

   _____

5. The man ran down the hill like a flash.

   _____

ANSWERS TO EXERCISE 2
1. Up the hill like a flash ran the fox.
2. At the top of the hill sat a man.

3. Shocked to see the fox was he. Or: Was he shocked to see the fox!
4. At the man snarled the fox.
5. Down the hill like a flash ran the man.

If you completed Exercise 2 successfully with at least four correct answers, proceed to the next exercise. If you had difficulty with this exercise, review the rules and examples and consult with your instructor.

Exercise 3 *Inverted to Regular Order*
The following sentences appear in inverted order. Rewrite them in regular order.

1. Did you go with Shane and Sam?

   _____

2. Have you received a letter from Lana?

   _____

3. Shall we go into the other room?

   _____

4. Had you gone to another theater?

   _____

5. Has Jack Lightfoot been accepted by his colleagues?

   _____

ANSWERS TO EXERCISE 3
Notice that each of the preceding sentences changes from a question to a statement.

1. You did go with Shane and Sam.
2. You have received a letter from Lana.

3. We shall go into the other room.
4. You had gone to another theater.
5. Jack Lightfoot has been accepted by his colleagues.

If you completed Exercise 3 successfully with at least four correct answers, proceed to the learning activity that follows. If you had difficulty with this exercise, review the rules and examples and consult with your instructor.

COMPLEMENTS AND OBJECTS

You may have noticed as you looked at the sentences in the previous exercises that some sentences are complete with only a subject and a verb: "Dogs bark." However, other sentences are not complete with just a subject and a verb.

$$\text{Rosa is}$$

<small>subj. v.</small>

To make this sentence fragment complete, you must add something to the verb.

$$\text{Rosa is president.}$$

<small>subj. v. subj. comp.</small>

The additional word in this sentence is *president,* which is the *subject complement. President* is a subject complement because it completes (complements) the meaning of the verb *is* by renaming the subject.

Subject complements are always nouns, pronouns, or adjectives, and they always follow linking verbs (verbs such as *appear, become, feel, smell, taste,* and the various forms of the verb *be,* which relate subjects to subject complements). Nouns and pronouns functioning as subject complements are called *predicate nouns* and *predicate pronouns.* They have these two characteristics:

1. They always follow linking verbs.
2. They refer to (or rename) the subject.

Adjectives serving as subject complements are called *predicate adjectives.* They, too, follow linking verbs. But rather than renaming the subject as predicate nouns and pronouns do, they *describe* the subject. Here are some examples of the various types of subject complements.

PREDICATE ADJECTIVE: Holly became <u>ill</u>. (*Ill* describes *Holly*.)

The children felt <u>happy</u>. (*Happy* describes *children*.)

Jason looked <u>strange</u>. (*Strange* describes *Jason*.)

PREDICATE NOUN: Cary is my <u>friend</u>. (*Friend* renames *Cary*.)

Green is my favorite <u>color</u>. (*Color* renames *green*.)

PREDICATE PRONOUN: Was it <u>they</u>? (*They* renames *it*.)

The culprit was <u>he</u>. (*He* renames *culprit*.)

Two other commonly used sentence elements are *objects:* direct objects and indirect objects. A *direct object* receives the action of a *transitive* verb (a verb that always affects someone or something). Look at these examples of direct objects.

```
subj.   v.        d.o.
```
Pepe shot the <u>deer</u>.

```
subj.   v.      d.o.
```
Luke hit the <u>ball</u> into left field.

```
subj.   v.       d.o.
```
Carver saw his <u>wife</u>.

```
d.o.    pred. subj. pred.
```
<u>Whom</u> did you visit?

```
subj.   v.          d.o.
```
Zack painted his <u>car</u> bright yellow.

One way to locate direct objects is to place the pronoun *whom* or *what* after the verb (predicate). For example, in the first sentence ask yourself, "Pepe shot *what?*" The answer, of course, is *deer.* In the third example, ask yourself, "Carver saw *whom?*" He saw his *wife.*

The *indirect object* is the person or thing to whom the action is directed or for whom the action is performed. Some verbs have both a direct and an indirect object. Look at the indirect and direct objects in these sentences.

```
            i.o.      d.o.
```
Ira gave his <u>mother</u> a watch.

(Ira performed the action for *mother*, since he bought the watch for his *mother*.)

i.o.   d.o.
Give <u>me</u> a dollar.

(The action is directed toward *me*, since I am requesting that a dollar be given to *me*.)

Be aware of words that are within a prepositional phrase: they cannot function as direct objects or indirect objects. For example, in the sentence "I gave a book to him," *him* cannot be the direct or indirect object because it is the object of the preposition *to*.

On the pages that follow are some exercises that will give you an opportunity to demonstrate your ability to recognize and identify subject complements, direct objects, and indirect objects. You may refer to the rules as you do the exercises.

Subject Complements   *Exercise 4*

Write six sentences (in your own words) in which the subject complement is a noun, a pronoun, or an adjective.

1. a noun _____

_____

2. two nouns _____

_____

3. a pronoun _____

_____

4. two pronouns _____

_____

5. an adjective _____

_____

6. two adjectives _____

_____

Write four sentences (in your own words) that contain these elements:

7. a noun as the direct object; no indirect object _____

_____

8. a pronoun as the indirect object and a noun as the direct object

_____

9. a noun as an indirect object with another noun as the direct object

_____

10. a compound direct object (two direct objects; use either nouns or

pronouns); no indirect object _____

_____

ANSWERS TO EXERCISE 4
Responses will vary. Your instructor will grade the exercise and give you further instructions.

Exercise 5   *More Subject Complements*
In the spaces provided, mark A if the *italicized* subject complement is an adjective, N if it is a noun, and P if it is a pronoun.

_____ 1. Paul Chutkow is a *chemist*.

_____ 2. Betty is a beautiful *person*.

_____ 3. Mark is very *intelligent*.

_____ 4. Irene can be quite *charming*.

_____ 5. Ector is my best *friend*.

_____ 6. Susan is a good *teacher*.

_____ 7. Beau is an affectionate *person*.

_____ 8. Is Trinidad still *alive*?

_____ 9. The winner is *he*.

_____ 10. The students were *quiet* in class.

_____ 11. I am that *person*.

_____ 12. The culprit was *I*.

ANSWERS TO EXERCISE 5

1.	N	7.	N
2.	N	8.	A
3.	A	9.	P
4.	A	10.	A
5.	N	11.	N
6.	N	12.	P

If you completed Exercise 5 successfully with eleven correct answers, proceed to the next exercise. If you had difficulty with this exercise, review the discussion and particularly the examples on pages 131 and 132 and consult with your instructor.

Exercise 6 *Various Sentence Elements*

In the first blank opposite each *italicized* word, mark D if the word is a direct object and I if it is an indirect object. In the second blank, mark N if the word is a noun and P if it is a pronoun.

1. ____ ____ Give *me* the book.

2. ____ ____ She gave *him* a lecture.

3. ____ ____ Leo sent *me* a telegram.

4. ____ ____ Reuben gave his telephone *number* to the reporter.

5. ____ ____ *Whom* are you seeing every night?

6. ____ ____ Do you like *Tess* and *Bernadine*?

7. ____ ____ Beth types a hundred *pages*.

8. ____ ____ Don saved his *dollars* for a European trip.

9. ____ ____ Larry gave *Ruby* a birthday gift.

10. ____ ____ She threw *it* into the river.

ANSWERS TO EXERCISE 6

1. I, P	6. D, N
2. I, P	7. D, N
3. I, P	8. D, N
4. D, N	9. I, N
5. D, P	10. D, P

If you completed Exercise 6 successfully with at least nine correct answers, proceed to the next exercise. If you had difficulty with this exercise, review the rules and examples and consult with your instructor.

In the spaces provided, mark C if the *italicized* word is a subject complement, D if it is a direct object, and I if it is an indirect object.

_____ 1. Roosevelt placed the *book* on Bridget's desk.

_____ 2. Abraham saw the beautiful blue figurine and decided to buy *it*.

_____ 3. Rudolph painted the ceramic *vase*.

_____ 4. The dog surprised the *visitor*.

_____ 5. It bit his *leg*.

_____ 6. Joey gave the *tickets* to his mother-in-law.

_____ 7. His mother-in-law sent *him* a book as her gift of appreciation.

_____ 8. The parade of homes was *interesting*.

_____ 9. Traveling can be *expensive*.

_____ 10. Sidney and Randy are *alike* in one way: they pay for their luxuries.

ANSWERS TO EXERCISE 7

1. D	6. D
2. D	7. I
3. D	8. C
4. D	9. C
5. D	10. C

If you completed Exercise 7 successfully with at least nine correct answers, proceed to the next exercise. If you had difficulty with this exercise, review the rules and examples and see your instructor.

Exercise 8   *A Review of Sentence Elements*

Identify the *italicized* word or words in each of the following sentences by marking S for subjects, P for predicates or verbs, C for subject complements, D for direct objects, and I for indirect objects.

_____ 1. *Albert* did not go to the concert.

_____ 2. Did you give *Ike* a copy of your new book?

_____ 3. *Whom* are you going to visit in Magnolia?

_____ 4. While we *were* in Florida, our home was destroyed.

_____ 5. *Are* you *going* to enroll for the spring semester?

_____ 6. I saw *Rita* and *Erik* in Wilmington.

_____ 7. Ramon was my best *friend* in college.

_____ 8. He gave *me* good advice when I had problems.

_____ 9. I have not seen *him* since we were roommates.

_____ 10. *Each* of us will deliver a speech.

_____ 11. Robert Finnigan will be the second *speaker*.

_____ 12. My speech *contains* some valuable information.

_____ 13. The valley behind our home is *beautiful* in the spring.

_____ 14. Paul gave *Abe* a dollar during the football game.

_____ 15. Jim did not want *it*.

_____ 16. However, he finally *consented*.

_____ 17. Ted was *surprised* when Jay gave Lucy the antique doll.

_____ 18. Lucy is Jay's favorite *sister*.

_____ 19. I hope that this *exercise* will satisfy you.

_____ 20. As you know, it *serves* a valuable purpose in this course.

ANSWERS TO EXERCISE 8

1. S	6. D	11. C	16. P
2. I	7. C	12. P	17. C
3. D	8. I	13. C	18. C
4. P	9. D	14. I	19. S
5. P	10. S	15. D	20. P

If you completed Exercise 8 successfully with at least eighteen correct answers, proceed to the postassessment. If you had difficulty with this exercise, review the rules and examples and consult with your instructor.

Postassessment

Identify the *italicized* word or words in each of the following sentences by marking S for subjects, P for predicates or verbs, C for subject complements, D for direct objects, and I for indirect objects.

_____ 1. As I *entered* the room, I saw the picture.

_____ 2. It was a strange *sight* to behold.

_____ 3. The dominant colors were *blue* and *green*.

_____ 4. The picture was indeed very *beautiful*.

_____ 5. The room became *dark* as the hours progressed.

_____ 6. During my silent moments in the room, I found a *book* on one of the tables.

_____ 7. My uncle *had written* it.

_____ 8. He had given my *parents* the book during one of his visits to their home.

_____ 9. Inside the book cover *were* several newspaper articles.

_____ 10. The articles described him when *he* was in Europe.

_____ 11. The room became more *interesting* as I continued my slow, thought-filled tour.

_____ 12. At the foot of the bed sat an old *chest*.

_____ 13. A pirate gave my *uncle* that chest in 1890.

_____ 14. It was my uncle's most precious *possession*.

_____ 15. My uncle would not let anyone touch *it*.

_____ 16. *Had* he *given* me the opportunity, I would not have refused it.

_____ 17. As I walked to the door, my eyes felt *moist*.

_____ 18. The memories that this *room* offered were too much for me.

_____ 19. I *will* never *go* back again.

_____ 20. As you might have guessed, *memories* make me sentimental.

ANSWERS TO POSTASSESSMENT

1. P	6. D	11. C	16. P
2. C	7. P	12. S	17. C
3. C	8. I	13. I	18. S
4. C	9. P	14. C	19. P
5. C	10. S	15. D	20. S

Study Unit 2 □ Kinds of Sentences

RATIONALE

Although you have studied and used sentences since you were in elementary school, you are probably aware that your sentences can be improved. One of the ways to improve them is to learn the characteristics of a well-constructed sentence and to be sure your sentences have these characteristics. Another way is to learn about and to use different kinds of sentences in order to avoid monotony in your writing. Well-constructed, varied sentences characterize all effective written communication.

OBJECTIVES

After completing Study Unit 2, you should be able to
1. write better sentences
2. recognize faulty sentences
3. vary your sentences

Preassessment

In the space provided, write G for each well-constructed sentence and F for each faulty sentence.

_____ 1. If I had all the money in the world.

_____ 2. Punting is when you kick a football you drop before it hits the ground.

_____ 3. Ina Cantu took us to the game, and we stopped at a café, and we bought some candy, and we ate it during the game.

_____ 4. Rose Ann never made a low grade during the four years that she was at the university.

_____ 5. The coat was new, and she had bought her hat in London.

_____ 6. The reason I want to go is because I like football.

_____ 7. The reason I failed was that I did not study.

_____ 8. This paper has, although you would not believe it, been corrected three times.

_____ 9. I am going home you may stay if you wish.

_____ 10. I am going home, but you may stay if you wish.

_____ 11. Never hand in your test before thoroughly checking.

_____ 12. I do not think he is wrong.

_____ 13. Thea read the book; she found it interesting; she gave me a copy; she asked me to review it for her club.

_____ 14. Being very expensive, she did not buy the picture.

_____ 15. Because the picture was very expensive, she did not buy it.

Categorize each sentence as simple, compound, or complex by writing the correct word in the space provided.

_____ 16. You had better study more, or you will fail all your subjects.

_____ 17. When Clay Weniska studies, he learns.

_____ 18. English is Jeannette McGinnes's favorite subject.

_____ 19. Every person stood when Kate Kowaski entered the room.

_____ 20. We will go in my car, and we will arrive in Minneapolis within three hours.

ANSWERS TO PREASSESSMENT

1. F	6. F	11. F	16. compound
2. F	7. G	12. F	17. complex
3. F	8. G	13. F	18. simple
4. G	9. F	14. F	19. complex
5. F	10. G	15. G	20. compound

Learning Activities

If you had difficulty distinguishing between a good sentence and a faulty sentence, perhaps you should be sure you understand the definition of a sentence. A _sentence_ is a group of words with a subject (noun or pronoun) and a predicate (or verb) that expresses one complete thought or one or more closely related thoughts.

CHARACTERISTICS OF A GOOD SENTENCE

One way to recognize and to write good sentences is to know the three characteristics of all good sentences.

1. _Completeness_   The thought of a sentence should be complete. No part of the thought should be missing.

WRONG: When I begin to worry about taking a test.

CORRECTED: When I begin to worry about taking a test, I know that I must do some extra studying.

2. _Unity_   All the words in the sentence should express one single, complete thought or a group of closely related thoughts. In other words, a good sentence has oneness.

WRONG: We have an excellent English teacher, but we do not know how to communicate effectively, and we are learning.

CORRECTED: Although we have an excellent English teacher, we have not yet learned to communicate effectively; however, we have learned some of the fundamentals of communication.

3. *Clearness* The clear sentence is stated so that it is easily and quickly understood. A sentence that lacks completeness and unity is not clear. However, a sentence may be complete and unified and still not be clear if the grammar is incorrect, the word order is wrong, or the construction is faulty.

WRONG: Has the bell rang?

CORRECTED: Has the bell rung?

WRONG: She only won one prize.

CORRECTED: She won only one prize.

WRONG: Any student who can learn English, most teachers would look upon him with approval.

CORRECTED: Any student who can learn English should have the approval of his teachers.

Exercise 1 **Characteristics of a Good Sentence**
In the space provided, write C before each sentence that is complete, unified, and clear. If the sentence is faulty because it lacks completeness, unity, or clarity, write F before it.

_____ 1. Miss Rietz bought a new coat, and she had a good time at the coffee.

_____ 2. Pete wrote all his themes in a hurry. Twenty minutes for each.

_____ 3. Lewis Williams is so tired.

_____ 4. I picked up the hat and put it on my head which I had bought in San Francisco.

_____ 5. Cindy Rowinski is so sleepy she is nodding.

_____ 6. Although Lester Morehead likes to swim.

_____ 7. Are you really sorry?

_____ 8. I have an interest in and a love for you.

_____ 9. Tom Ryberg has a new car and it has a stick shift and there are two horns.

_____ 10. His only weakness is his carelessness.

ANSWERS TO EXERCISE 1

1. F	6. F
2. F	7. C
3. F	8. C
4. F	9. F
5. C	10. C

KINDS OF SENTENCES ACCORDING TO FORM

There are several ways of classifying sentences. In this learning activity, you will be looking at sentences classified according to their form—that is, according to the grammatical patterns that the words of the sentences fall into. Three sentence forms are described: the simple sentence, the compound sentence, and the complex sentence.

1. A *simple sentence* has one subject and one predicate (or verb) and expresses one complete thought.

subj.   pred.
The house is burning.

subj.   pred.
Christmas comes but once a year.

2. A *compound sentence* consists of two or more independent clauses joined by a coordinating conjunction (*and, but, or, for, nor*), by a semicolon alone (;), or by a conjunctive adverb (such as *therefore*).

indep. cl.   indep. cl.
Nita played the piano , and Henry sang two songs.

indep. cl.   indep. cl.
An adjective modifies a noun or pronoun ; an adverb modifies a verb, an adjective, or another adverb.

Note: An *independent clause* is like a sentence in structure: it has a subject and a predicate and makes complete sense. But an independent clause in a compound sentence does not both begin with a capital and end with a period as a sentence does. The first independent clause in the first example above ends with a comma, and the first independent clause in the second example ends with a semicolon. Differently punctuated, however, these independent clauses would be sentences.

A comma should be used before the coordinating conjunctions *and, or, nor, but*, and *for* when they join two independent clauses to make a compound sentence, and a semicolon should appear before *still, yet, then, however, otherwise*, and other conjunctive adverbs when they join two independent clauses. A comma follows the long conjunctive adverbs (conjunctive adverbs of more than one syllable) when they join clauses.

| | coor. | |
| indep. cl. | conj. | indep. cl. |

I did my best at the speech tournament , but I did not win.

| indep. cl. | conj. adv. | indep. cl. |

This class is interesting ; however , there should be more class discussion.

3. A *complex sentence* consists of one independent clause and one or more dependent clauses.

| indep. cl. | dep. cl. |

I thought that you were studying.

| dep. cl. | indep. cl. |

If I were you , I would play this afternoon and study tonight.

Note: A *dependent clause* has a subject and a predicate, but it does not make complete sense. The dependent clause is usually obvious because it begins with a key word such as *if, as, when, while, after, until, though*, or *although*.

When a dependent clause comes at the beginning of a sentence, a comma follows it.

dep. cl.

When I heard the bell , I ran to class.

dep. cl.

While I checked the spelling in Mary Ann's theme , she checked the sentence structure in mine.

Classify each of the following sentences according to form by writing *simple, complex,* or *compound* in the space provided.

_____ 1. When you go to New York this fall, will you see many plays?

_____ 2. The committee left the room, for it had completed its assignment.

_____ 3. Diane read some of Shakespeare's sonnets; then she began *Hamlet*.

_____ 4. I am sorry that you cannot go with us.

_____ 5. Lincoln was a compassionate human being.

_____ 6. Otto speaks Spanish, but he has never studied German.

_____ 7. Dogs and cats are the only animals that I like.

_____ 8. We waited an hour before Fay Ojeda came.

_____ 9. We are worried about what Fred Cattani might select for a major.

_____ 10. Neil Plunkett is a serious student.

ANSWERS TO EXERCISE 2

1. complex   6. compound
2. compound   7. complex
3. compound   8. complex
4. complex   9. complex
5. simple   10. simple

KINDS OF SENTENCES ACCORDING TO MEANING

1. A *declarative sentence* states a fact.

I see you.

2. An *interrogative sentence* asks a question.

Did you see me?

3. An *imperative sentence* issues a request or a command.

Please help me. (request)
Sit down and be quiet. (command)

4. An *exclamatory sentence* expresses strong feeling.

Oh, if this trial would only end!

Exercise 3 **Sentences According to Meaning**
Classify each of the following sentences according to meaning by writing *declarative, interrogative, imperative*, or *exclamatory* in the space provided.

_____ 1. What is our assignment for Monday?

_____ 2. Look! There's a fire!

_____ 3. I am glad I am able to vary my sentence structure.

_____ 4. Please explain to me the differences among complex, compound, and simple sentences.

_____ 5. This cake is really good.

_____ 6. Try to remember to say different *from*, not different *than*.

_____ 7. There is only one way to spell *all right*.

_____ 8. Are you really discouraged?

———————————— 9. Do not try to sell that food to me.

———————————— 10. Hurry! He's badly hurt!

ANSWERS TO EXERCISE 3
1. interrogative
2. exclamatory
3. declarative
4. imperative
5. declarative or exclamatory (If the cake is very good indeed, the person who speaks this sentence would probably make it an exclamation: "... *really* good!")
6. imperative
7. declarative
8. interrogative
9. imperative
10. exclamatory

Postassessment

In the space provided before each sentence, write C if the sentence is complete, unified, and clear. If the sentence is faulty because it lacks completeness, unity, or clarity, write F before it and rewrite the sentence correctly in the space provided.

——— 1. Although I am very sorry for him and much concerned about him.

————————————————————————

————————————————————————

————————————————————————

——— 2. Because Maria is one of the most intelligent and most honest people I have known, I am going to vote for her.

————————————————————————

————————————————————————

————————————————————————

_____ 3. Troy is a great quarterback, but I never played that.

_____

_____

_____

_____ 4. Trying to act grownup in her speech and manner.

_____

_____

_____

_____ 5. Everyone at the Brookhouse School for Girls should do their best.

_____

_____

_____

_____ 6. Judy's mother received her degree from college when she was sixteen years old.

_____

_____

_____

_____ 7. Grandfather was not interested in our vacation plans however he tried to act as though the trip were a good idea and he wanted to go.

_____

_____

_____

_____ 8. Waking up that morning, I saw that it was snowing and I knew that the track meet would be canceled and I would stay at home and I would work all day.

_____

_____

_____

_____ 9. Composition must be studied carefully to learn to write well.

_____

_____

_____

_____ 10. Playing games and telling stories, the slumber party was a big success.

_____

_____

_____

_____ 11. Two friends and myself did the work.

_____

_____

_____

_____ 12. Whom were you with last night?

_____

_____

_____

Categorize each of the following sentences as simple, compound, or complex by writing the correct word in the space provided.

_____ 13. Ashley and Melissa will be arriving by plane this evening.

_____ 14. Joyce and Lynn are going to Denmark this summer, but they plan to be home in time to enroll for the fall semester.

_____ 15. If you need to borrow my radio, please ask for it.

_____ 16. Although Sid Garneski may not know much about the mechanics of singing, his voice is beautiful.

_____ 17. Getting tickets for the concert Saturday night is impossible; however, tickets are available for the Sunday afternoon performance.

_____ 18. Everyone admires Kate Swan's courage and poise during these difficult days.

In the space provided, categorize each sentence as declarative, interrogative, imperative, or exclamatory by writing the appropriate word.

_____ 19. I am glad that you are here with us.

_____ 20. Whom did he marry?

_____ 21. Look! There's a fire!

_____ 22. Try to attend to your own business.

_____ 23. Everyone in the class did the assignment.

_____ 24. Be more careful with that package.

_____ 25. "Help! Help!" he cried.

ANSWERS TO POSTASSESSMENT

Sentences 2 and 12 are correct. You may need help from your instructor in checking the faulty sentences you have rewritten. Here are some possible answers for sentences 1 through 12:

1. Although I am very sorry for him and much concerned about him, I do not know how to help him.
2. C
3. Troy is a great quarterback, but I never played that position.
4. Trying to act grownup in her speech and manner, Erin seemed immature and insincere.
5. Everyone at the Brookhouse School for Girls should do her best.
6. When Judy was sixteen years old, her mother received her degree from college.
7. Grandfather was not interested in our vacation plans; however, he

tried to act as though the trip were a good idea, and he said he wanted to go.

8. Waking up that snowy morning, I knew there would be no track meet and I would work all day at home.
9. To learn to write well, a student must study composition.
10. Playing games and telling stories, we had a good time at the slumber party.
11. Two friends and I did the work.
12. C
13. simple
14. compound
15. complex
16. complex
17. compound
18. simple
19. declarative
20. interrogative
21. exclamatory
22. imperative
23. declarative
24. imperative
25. declarative (Did you write *exclamatory*? What he said—the words in quotation marks—*is* exclamatory, but what the sentence says is not. The sentence merely states that he said something.)

Study Unit 3▫Sentence Fragments

RATIONALE

Incomplete sentences, called sentence fragments, pose problems for many writers. They indicate incomplete and rushed thoughts. This unit should help you to avoid writing fragments.

OBJECTIVES

After completing Study Unit 3, you should be able to

1. write complete sentences
2. recognize sentence fragments
3. change sentence fragments into complete sentences

Preassessment

In the spaces provided, develop every sentence fragment into a complete sentence. If the example is already a complete sentence, write C in the space.

1. Looking at the new car.

   _____

   _____

2. Bernard is my friend.

   _____

   _____

3. Run!

_____

_____

4. Manuel, stop!

_____

_____

5. Riding our bicycles.

_____

_____

6. We fished.

_____

_____

7. Picnics are relaxing.

_____

_____

8. People are funny.

_____

_____

9. After we drove to the lake.

_____

_____

10. He was a most important person.

_____

_____

11. Give me an apple.

_____

_____

12. Given a new automobile when he was only seventeen.

_____

_____

13. Ms. Goldberg to go to New York.

_____

_____

14. The house that was destroyed.

_____

_____

15. To receive an excellent education in a small university.

_____

_____

_____

16. The man who gave the speech.

_____

_____

17. Developing a set of personal goals.

_____

_____

18. The home that I liked.

_____

_____

19. Because we love you.

_____

_____

20. Roberta, my best friend in college.

_____

_____

21. While we were in Colorado.

_____

_____

22. Leo Mehrhoff spoke quickly.

_____

_____

23. Whether Susan Duran wants to go.

_____

_____

24. If Don Quintero can help you.

_____

_____

25. In a great hurry!

_____

_____

ANSWERS TO PREASSESSMENT
Numbers 2, 3, 4, 6, 7, 8, 10, 11, and 22 are correct. Answers will differ for the rest and should be looked over by your instructor.

Learning Activities

FRAGMENTS CAUSED BY MISSING VERBS

A *sentence fragment* is just what the name suggests. It is a part, or fragment, of a sentence written and punctuated as if it were a complete sentence. A fragment may be a word, a group of words, a phrase, or a dependent clause (a group of words that has a subject and a predicate but cannot stand alone as a sentence because it does not make sense). (For discussion of the elements of sentences, see Study Unit 1.)

Fragments often result because of a missing predicate (or verb). A *verb*, as you remember, expresses action, existence, or occurrence. A good way to determine whether a particular word might be a verb is to try to put it into the past tense.

Present Tense	**Past Tense**
Today I play.	Yesterday I played.
Today we sing.	Yesterday we sang.
Today they work.	Yesterday they worked.

Certain words ending in *-ing* and having verbal roots look like verbs; however, they are not verbs for two reasons:

1. They are without helping verbs and cannot be in the past tense unless helping verbs are added.

FRAGMENT: Isaac playing his flute.

CORRECTED: Isaac was playing his flute.

2. Without helping verbs, these words resemble adjectives in that they describe other words.

FRAGMENT: Nadine doing her homework.

CORRECTED: Nadine is doing her homework.

Infinitives also look like verbs but serve a different function. An *infinitive* is the word *to* plus a verb: *to go, to see*. An infinitive can never take the place of a verb in a sentence.

FRAGMENT: Bertha to go to Chicago.

CORRECTED: Bertha is to go to Chicago.

FRAGMENT: Reuben to take an examination.

CORRECTED: Reuben is to take an examination.

Here are some examples of sentences lacking verbs. Be sure you can identify the verb in the corrected versions. If you are not certain whether a word is a verb, look it up in a dictionary. The abbreviation *v.* or *vb.* that accompanies the definition identifies the word as a verb.

FRAGMENT: Such as collecting guns, designing homes, and making candles.

CORRECTED: Mitchell enjoys a number of hobbies, such as collecting guns, designing homes, and making candles.

FRAGMENT: For example, baseball, golf, and tennis.

CORRECTED: Nicole plays baseball, golf, and tennis.

Stop at this point and check your understanding of sentence fragments by completing Exercise 1.

Adding Verbs

Exercise 1

Correct each of the following fragments by adding a verb and forming a complete sentence. Underline the subject *once* and the verb *twice* in your corrected sentences.

1. Lorraine Mosier writing a letter

   _____

2. Rufus to give a speech

   _____

3. Such as grammar, punctuation, and spelling

   _____

   _____

   _____

4. Most men making some mistakes

_____

_____

5. For example, a beautiful view, a large back yard, and a new coat of paint

_____

_____

FRAGMENTS CAUSED BY MISSING SUBJECTS

The *subject* of a sentence is a noun, pronoun, infinitive, or gerund about which something is said. (*Gerunds* are verbal forms that end in *-ing* and function as nouns.) To find the subject of a sentence, first locate the predicate or verb (the word that expresses action). Then ask yourself, "*Who* or *what* is doing this action?" Look at this sentence:

Moses saw the deer.

Ask yourself, "Who saw?" The answer, of course, is *Moses*.

The only sentences that you might find troublesome even after applying the rule are commands.

Give me the book.

Give looks like the verb here. Ask yourself, "Who or what is to be doing this giving?" The answer is the individual to whom the person making the command is speaking—namely, *you*. *You* is the implied subject; the verb is *give*.

Watch the broken glass!

Again, *you* is the implied subject. The verb is *watch*.

Notice also that word groups can serve as subjects of sentences:

subj.   pred.
<u>Going to sleep</u> <u>can be</u> difficult.

Ask yourself, *"What* can be difficult?" *Going to sleep* can be difficult.
(By the way, *going to sleep* is a gerund.)

One additional example of word groups that serve as subjects is the infinitive phrase.

inf. phrase (subj.)   v.
<u>To be a good athlete</u> <u>was</u> her goal in life.

Ask yourself, *"What* was her goal in life?" *To be a good athlete* was her goal in life. *To be a good athlete* is an infinitive phrase. Infinitive phrases always contain the word *to* plus a verb, such as the verb *be* in our example: *to + be.* They also include objects, or complements, and their modifiers: *a good athlete. Athlete* completes the infinitive by telling who receives the action of the infinitive. *A* and *good* describe, or modify, *athlete.*

Always remember that every sentence must have its own subject. Even when two sentences are closely related in thought, each sentence must have a separate subject.

FRAGMENT: Frank was very happy. Had won a scholarship.

CORRECTED: Frank was very happy. He had won a scholarship.

OR: Frank was very happy because he had won a scholarship.

FRAGMENT: The professor surprised her students. Dismissed them early.

CORRECTED: The professor surprised her students. She dismissed them early.

OR: The professor surprised her students when she dismissed them early.

Adding Subjects

Exercise 2

Correct each of the following fragments by adding a subject and forming a complete sentence. Underline the subject *once* and the verb *twice* in your corrected sentences.

1. Gave a speech in New York

2. Enjoyed her enthusiastic audience

_____

3. Talked well and had no distracting mannerisms

_____

_____

4. For example, read two books and wrote two reports

_____

_____

5. Knew how to work with his hands

_____

_____

ANSWERS TO EXERCISE 2
Answers will vary and should be checked by your instructor. Here are some possible suggestions:

1. Pablo gave a speech in New York.
2. Louise enjoyed her enthusiastic audience.
3. Enrika talked well and had no distracting mannerisms.
4. Jafus was very busy. For example, he read two books and wrote two reports.
5. Mr. Ling knew how to work with his hands.

FRAGMENTS INTRODUCED BY KEY WORDS
Dependent clauses (clauses that cannot stand alone as complete sentences) are sentence fragments because they do not express complete thoughts. All dependent clauses have these four characteristics:

1. They have subjects and predicates (or verbs).
2. They depend on the rest of the sentence for their meaning.
3. They cannot stand alone as complete sentences.
4. They begin with *key words*.

Here is a list of the key words that most commonly introduce dependent clauses:

RELATIVE PRONOUNS   that, what, whatever, which, who, whoever, whom, whomever

SUBORDINATING CONJUNCTIONS   after, although (though), as (if), because (for), before, if, since, so that, unless, until, when, where, whereas, whether, while, why

Some writers have difficulties with dependent clauses introduced by the key words known as *subordinating conjunctions*. When they try to let these dependent clauses stand as sentences, they write fragments rather than sentences. You can spot these writers' fragments readily once you are familiar with the common subordinating conjunctions given in the preceding list.

FRAGMENT: <u>Before</u> I knocked

FRAGMENT: <u>While</u> Sam was in Atlanta

FRAGMENT: <u>After</u> we saw the movie

Notice that each of these expressions is incomplete. After reading each expression, you probably wish to ask, "What happened?" For example: *What happened* before I knocked?

CORRECTED: The dog barked before I knocked.

Or: *What happened* while Sam was in Atlanta?

CORRECTED: The children arrived while Sam was in Atlanta.

Or: *What happened* after we saw the movie?

CORRECTED: After we saw the movie, we took a long drive.

Aside from helping you to identify dependent clauses and to avoid dependent-clause fragments, subordinating conjunctions also link dependent and independent clauses.

indep. cl.   dep. cl.

Mark Bernstein wants to visit friends while he is in London.

(*While he is in London* refers to *visit*. The dependent clause adds a detail to the sentence. It specifies *when* Mark wants to visit friends.)

indep. cl.   dep. cl.

Winston Grimsley wrote a book after he retired from his job.

(*After he retired from his job* refers to *wrote*. The dependent clause specifies *when* Winston wrote the book.)

dep. cl.   indep. cl.

When the speaker completed the joke, the audience laughed.

(*When the speaker completed the joke* relates to *laughed*. Again, the dependent clause adds a "when" detail. It specifies when the laughter occurred.)

Relative pronouns (especially *who, which,* and *what*) are another category of key words that frequently introduce dependent clauses. They appear between subjects of *sentences* and verbs of *dependent clauses*. This combination often results in sentence fragments. (Remember that a dependent clause has a subject and a predicate; but in a sentence that contains a dependent clause, the subject and the predicate of the *sentence* are always in the *in*dependent clause.) In the examples that follow, the subject of a potential sentence is underlined once, and the verb of the clause is underlined twice.

FRAGMENT: The lady who left her package

FRAGMENT: The room that was once mine

FRAGMENT: The record that won the award

Notice that none of these fragments tell you what happened. All of them express incomplete thoughts. However, they can become complete thoughts with the insertion of predicates.

dep. cl.

The lady who left her package returned later.

dep. cl.

The room that was once mine became a study.

dep. cl.

The record that won the award sold over a million copies.

Relative pronouns also link dependent and independent clauses.

indep. cl.   dep. cl.

Mr. Zing is the man who called today.

(*Who* refers or relates back to *man*; consequently, *who* ties these two clauses together.)

indep. cl.   dep. cl.

Ms. Roundtree is the instructor whom we saw.

(*Whom* relates back to *instructor* and ties these two clauses together.)

As you can see, key words work effectively in complex sentences that express complete thoughts. Stop here and try writing some complete sentences with the use of key words.

Using Key Words in Complete Sentences   *Exercise 3*

Use each of the following key words in a complete sentence. Underline your subject *once* and your verb *twice*.

1. who _____

_____

2. whoever _____

_____

3. whom _____

_____

4. whomever _____

_____

5. what _____

_____

6. whatever _____

_____

7. which _____

_____

8. that _____

_____

9. after _____

_____

10. although (though) _____

_____

11. as (if) _____

_____

12. because (for) _____

_____

13. before _____

_____

14. whereas _____

_____

15. if _____

_____

16. since _____

_____

17. so that _____

_____

18. unless _____

_____

19. until _____

_____

20. when _____

_____

21. where _____

_____

22. whether _____

_____

23. while _____

_____

24. why _____

_____

ANSWERS TO EXERCISE 3

Every person who does this exercise will think of different answers. Before asking your instructor to check your sentences, be sure that your use of *who, whoever, whom,* and *whomever* is correct. Can you substitute *he* for *who* and *whoever*, and *him* for *whom* and *whomever*? If you can, your sentence is correct. If you cannot, make the necessary corrections.

Exercise 4   **Review of Sentence Fragments**

1a. Write a fragment that results from a missing verb.

_____

1b. Make a complete sentence from the fragment that you wrote in 1a.

_____

_____

2a. Write a fragment that results from a missing subject.

_____

2b. Make a complete sentence from the fragment that you wrote in 2a.

_____

_____

3a. Write a fragment that uses a relative pronoun.

_____

3b. Make a complete sentence from the fragment that your wrote in 3a.

_____

_____

4a. Write a fragment that uses a subordinating conjunction.

_____

4b. Make a complete sentence from the fragment that you wrote in 4a.

_____

_____

ANSWERS TO EXERCISE 4
Answers will differ and should be checked by your instructor.

Postassessment

Rewrite as complete sentences any fragments that appear in the list that follows. Write C after each sentence that is already complete.

1. After Ramiro fell asleep.

_____

_____

2. Mr. Booker laughed.

_____

3. Tiko saw Mary.

_____

_____

4. Children who are in business.

_____

_____

5. Riley McShane starting a daily routine.

_____

_____

6. The people laughing and cheering.

_____

_____

7. Keith Odishaw to appear in a Broadway musical.

_____

_____

_____

8. To be a great American scholar.

_____

_____

9. When we gave Ingrid Sorenson the gift.

_____

_____

_____

10. Mike Kopetski applauded.

_____

_____

11. While Ms. Soo was in South Dakota.

_____

_____

12. While Leotis wants to live in Iowa.

_____

_____

13. Whoever enters my front door.

_____

_____

14. Whomever we select.

_____

_____

15. Which of these beautiful homes?

_____

_____

16. Why me?

_____

_____

17. That I saw.

_____

_____

18. Because Fay Lund won.

_____

_____

19. So that Mr. DeSalvo can see.

_____

_____

20. Until Mr. Gonzales arrived.

_____

_____

21. Unless Selso studies.

_____

_____

22. If I give you five dollars.

_____

_____

23. Before the rain began.

_____

_____

24. As if Toby Obar knew.

_____

_____

25. Sit down!

_____

_____

ANSWERS TO POSTASSESSMENT

Numbers 2, 3, 10, and 25 are correct. Your instructor will need to check all other answers.

Study Unit 4□Run-on Sentences and Comma Splices

RATIONALE

Learning to communicate effectively is one of the first steps in becoming a good writer. Run-on sentences obstruct communication because they usually are confusing to readers. They also indicate that the writer does not know when one sentence ends and another begins. Consequently, they represent poor writing.

OBJECTIVES

After completing Study Unit 4, you should be able to

1. avoid writing run-on sentences
2. avoid writing comma splices
3. communicate more effectively with your readers

Preassessment

Mark in the space beside each sentence R for a run-on sentence, S for a comma splice, and C for a correct sentence.

_____ 1. The party was over the guests had left.

_____ 2. The kitten was happy, she loved her master.

_____ 3. Maria resigned her position; furthermore, she left the country.

_____ 4. Murray won the award, and his parents were happy.

_____ 5. The parade began early it lasted three hours.

_____ 6. Henry drove for two hours he then stopped for lunch.

_____ 7. Although Melba is an athlete, she enjoys creative writing.

_____ 8. Paul Moyer is my friend he is also my minister.

_____ 9. Fernando is not interested in politics he is too busy with his medical practice.

_____ 10. The candle was beautiful as it glowed on the table.

_____ 11. The room had five chairs two of them were antique.

_____ 12. The convention drew a small crowd, the weather was cold.

_____ 13. Spring is usually an enjoyable season however it causes some people to suffer from hay fever.

_____ 14. Connie Lee has always been kind to me, therefore I am going to help her.

_____ 15. The children are asleep, and their toys have been gathered.

_____ 16. Mark Bradshaw can accept this scholarship, or he can wait for a better one.

_____ 17. Since the semester began, the professor has been absent twice.

_____ 18. The book is interesting, an expert wrote it.

_____ 19. The table looks new, the O'Rileys have hardly used it.

_____ 20. After the family moved, their home showed neglect.

ANSWERS TO PREASSESSMENT

1. R	6. R	11. R	16. C
2. S	7. C	12. S	17. C
3. C	8. R	13. R	18. S
4. C	9. R	14. S	19. S
5. R	10. C	15. C	20. C

Learning Activities

RUN-ON SENTENCES

Run-on sentences are just what the name implies: two or more sentences that run head-on into each other with no punctuation separating them.

RUN-ON: Oak trees grow slowly they provide maximum shade.

CORRECTED: Oak trees grow slowly. They provide maximum shade.

Notice that when you read this example, your voice falls with the word *slowly* because it ends a complete thought: *Oak trees grow slowly.* Also notice that the pronoun *they* begins another complete thought: *They provide maximum shade.* A pronoun that begins a new complete thought is a good indication that a sentence needs punctuation. As you go through this learning activity to find out how to correct run-on sentences, you will need to remember that a group of words having a subject and a verb and expressing a complete thought is an *independent clause.*

Run-on sentences can be corrected in a number of ways.

1. Use a period between two complete thoughts and begin the first word of each thought with a capital letter.

RUN-ON: Wilbert finally completed the portrait his subject was very pleased.

CORRECTED: Wilbert finally completed the portrait. His subject was very pleased.

2. Use a colon to separate two independent clauses if the second independent clause explains or illustrates the first.

RUN-ON: The answer to the question is quite simple additional funds must come from the members.

CORRECTED: ⌐——————————— indep. cl. ——————————¬   ⌐————— indep. cl.
The answer to the question is quite simple : additional funds

⌐————————————————————————¬
must come from the members.

(Notice that by joining these two independent clauses with a colon, you can form a compound sentence and avoid using two choppy sentences separated by a period.)

3. Use a semicolon between two independent clauses.

RUN-ON: The dog barked he heard a noise.

CORRECTED: ⌐—— indep. cl. ——¬   ⌐—— indep. cl. ——¬
The dog barked ; he heard a noise.

(The semicolon in this compound sentence indicates that the two independent clauses are closely related. Compound sentences contain two or more independent clauses and are more effective than short, choppy sentences, which are often caused by the substitution of periods for semicolons.)

RUN-ON: Many people have applied for the position consequently an examination will be given.

CORRECTED: ⌐——————————— indep. cl. ——————————¬   ⌐—
Many people have applied for the position ; consequently, an

indep. cl. ——————————¬
examination will be given.

(The semicolon appears before the conjunctive adverb *consequently,* which joins two independent clauses that are closely related. A *conjunctive adverb* is an adverb that functions as a conjunction. In the above sentence, *consequently* indicates the relationship between *have applied* and *should be given.* Because *consequently* joins two independent clauses, it provides the structure for a compound sentence.)

4. Use a comma and a coordinating conjunction (*and, or, nor, but, for*) to join two independent clauses.

RUN-ON: Two people have resigned others are to follow.

CORRECTED: Two people have resigned , and others are to follow.

(By joining two independent clauses with a comma and a coordinating conjunction, you can form a compound sentence and avoid using two choppy sentences separated by a period.)

5. Change one of the independent clauses to a phrase or to a dependent clause. (Dependent clauses depend on independent clauses to complete the thoughts.)

RUN-ON: Elmo had lunch in Waco he then drove to Dallas.

CORRECTED: Elmo had lunch in Waco before driving to Dallas.

(Condensing the second independent clause to a prepositional phrase creates one well-developed simple sentence and eliminates two choppy sentences.)

RUN-ON: The weather is warm we should have a picnic.

CORRECTED: Since the weather is warm, we should have a picnic.

(Changing the first independent clause to a dependent clause eliminates two choppy sentences and creates a smooth complex sentence. A *complex sentence* contains one independent clause and two or more dependent clauses.)

Check your understanding of these suggestions by working through Exercise 1.

***Exercise 1* Run-on Sentences**
Supply correct punctuation and capitalization in any run-on sentences. If a sentence is correct, write C in the space provided.

_____   1. The pianist played no one heard him.

_____ 2. The speaker told jokes her audience responded.

_____ 3. The man spoke he did not know me.

_____ 4. The policeman stopped the driver he had been speeding.

_____ 5. The weather was sunny the birds were singing.

_____ 6. The students gave their reports and participated in a discussion.

_____ 7. The children played two games of checkers then they had lunch.

_____ 8. The parking lot was almost empty only two cars were left.

_____ 9. The food was delicious the entertainment was enjoyable.

_____ 10. The football tickets were expensive therefore we did not buy them.

_____ 11. The guests laughed and talked throughout the party.

_____ 12. The books were not lost Ollie found them in the attic.

_____ 13. The room was beautiful the hostess waited for her guests.

_____ 14. The writer arranged the events in chronological inductive order.

_____ 15. The candidates gave their speeches then they answered questions from the audience.

ANSWERS TO EXERCISE 1
Numbers 6, 11, and 14 are correct. Answers to all the others will vary, so your instructor should check them.

COMMA SPLICES

A *comma splice* is the use of only a comma to separate two or more independent clauses. In other words, a comma splice is the splicing together of sentences by a comma instead of a period or semicolon. Consequently, the rules for correcting run-on sentences also apply to correcting comma splices.

1. Use a period between two independent clauses.

COMMA SPLICE: Summers in Texas are quite hot, many Texans go to cooler states for their vacations.

CORRECTED: Summers in Texas are quite hot . Many Texans go to cooler states for their vacations.

2. Use a semicolon between two independent clauses.

COMMA SPLICE: Mr. Collins is my teacher, he is also my friend.

CORRECTED: Mr. Collins is my teacher ; he is also my friend.

COMMA SPLICE: Hilda was tired, therefore she went to bed.

CORRECTED: Hilda was tired ; therefore, she went to bed.

Note: *Therefore* in the preceding example is a conjunctive adverb (an adverb that serves as a conjunction). Other common conjunctive adverbs are:

accordingly	however	otherwise
besides	in fact	then
consequently	moreover	thus
hence	nevertheless	yet

A conjunctive adverb alone cannot be substituted for a semicolon or period. For example, "Hilda was tired therefore she went to bed" is not only difficult to read but also incorrect, because the writer has tried to let the conjunctive adverb *therefore* take the place of a semicolon or a period.

Conjunctive adverbs containing two or more syllables and separating two independent clauses should be preceded by a semicolon and followed by a comma.

```
           _____ indep. cl. _____        conj.          _____ indep. cl.
                                                      adv.
The baseball team went to San Francisco ; therefore , the manager sched-
uled no game in this city.
```

A comma does not follow one-syllable conjunctive adverbs.

Mario read one chapter; then he went to bed.

In some cases, conjunctive adverbs do not separate two complete thoughts but serve only as interrupters.

Jamie will , nevertheless , attend the meeting

Notice that commas set off interrupters.

3. Use a comma and a coordinating conjunction (*and, or, nor, but, for*) to join two independent clauses.

COMMA SPLICE: The letter arrived yesterday, I have not had an opportunity to read it.

```
                  _____ indep. cl. _____   conj.   _____ indep. cl.
CORRECTED:        The letter arrived yesterday, but I have not had an oppor-
                  tunity to read it.
```

4. Change one of the independent clauses to a phrase or a dependent clause.

COMMA SPLICE: Jill called me, then she left for Boston.

```
                            _____ phrase _____
CORRECTED:      Jill called me before leaving for Boston.
```

COMMA SPLICE: My guests should be arriving in two hours, I need to prepare the refreshments.

```
                _____ dep. cl. _____        _____
CORRECTED:      Because my guests should be arriving in two hours , I need
                indep. cl. _____
                to prepare the refreshments.
```

Keep these suggestions for correcting comma splices in mind as you work through Exercise 2.

Improve the following sentences by correcting all comma splices. Write the revised sentences in the spaces provides.

1. Magazine writers often glamorize apartment living, however these articles are often misleading.

   _____

   _____

2. The pictures in these articles show tenants enjoying parties, unfortunately most tenants in an apartment complex know very few of their neighbors.

   _____

   _____

3. Apartment people tend to be mobile, therefore they place little emphasis on knowing their neighbors.

   _____

   _____

4. Noise is a problem in most apartments, privacy is another problem.

   _____

   _____

5. Apartments are usually of poor construction, within three years they begin to deteriorate quickly.

   _____

   _____

6. The fireplaces usually reveal poor construction, in many cases they are fire hazards.

_____

_____

7. Many apartment dwellers complain about inadequate space, they need larger rooms and more closets.

_____

_____

8. Swimming pools in most complexes are either crowded or unsanitary, they also encourage late-evening noise.

_____

_____

9. Laundry facilities are small, they often need repair.

_____

_____

10. Apartments have certain advantages, these advantages do not exceed the disadvantages.

_____

_____

ANSWERS TO EXERCISE 2
The varying responses should be checked by your instructor.

Exercise 3   **A Review of Run-ons and Comma Splices**

Mark in the space beside each sentence R for a run-on sentence, S for a comma splice, and C for a correct sentence.

_____ 1. The rains did not come, the crops failed.

_____ 2. The child dropped his toy, he knew that his mother would pick it up.

_____ 3. The door opened no one walked into the room.

_____ 4. The mysteries of the night affect Mr. Trevino's imagination he often hears strange noises.

_____ 5. The cowboy took off his hat and spoke softly.

_____ 6. Eating out is fun it is also expensive.

_____ 7. Cooking well is an art it is also a form of relaxation.

_____ 8. The man in the portrait looked stern, he was one of Leonard's ancestors.

_____ 9. The chairs were empty the audience had left.

_____ 10. The desk drawer contained papers, pencils, and pens.

ANSWERS TO EXERCISE 3

1. S	6. R
2. S	7. R
3. R	8. S
4. R	9. R
5. C	10. C

Postassessment

Mark in the space beside each sentence R for a run-on sentence, S for a comma splice, and C for a correct sentence.

_____ 1. Mr. Urbanski is an informed person he reads a newspaper every day.

_____ 2. Jasper had an accident, the road was wet.

_____ 3. The picnic was in the park, twenty people attended.

_____ 4. Mississippi has some interesting historical homes. Many of them are open to the public.

_____ 5. Austin, Texas, is a desirable place to live, it is clean and beautiful.

_____ 6. The chest was old, it contained jewelry.

_____ 7. The flag was raised Beryl Omahoney watched.

_____ 8. Tabitha plans to drive her car to Denver, she then wants to fly to San Francisco.

_____ 9. The reporter edited the story too much, consequently he distorted the facts.

_____ 10. Troy Touchstone read the letter to the large audience.

_____ 11. Trees provide shade they also provide beauty.

_____ 12. Because Lucas Groundwater is my friend, I plan to give him the book.

_____ 13. The congregation stood as the choir entered the church.

_____ 14. Many people have expressed opinions, few people have listened.

_____ 15. If you answered this question incorrectly, you might as well review this unit from the beginning.

ANSWERS TO POSTASSESSMENT

1. R	6. S	11. R
2. S	7. R	12. C
3. S	8. S	13. C
4. C	9. S	14. S
5. S	10. C	15. C

Study Unit 5□Parallel Sentences

RATIONALE

The word *parallel* suggests two like things going along together. This same idea is the general principle behind parallel sentences: *Always express two or more parallel ideas in parallel grammatical form.* Parallel sentences have not only balance but also clarity and rhythm. Consequently, they eliminate confusion, increase understanding, and flow smoothly—all characteristics of good writing.

OBJECTIVES

After completing Study Unit 5, you should be able to write in parallel form two or more
1. words
2. phrases
3. clauses
4. sentences

Preassessment

In the spaces provided, write C for each parallel sentence and W for each sentence that is not parallel.

_____ 1. The colors on the wall were red, blue, and white.

_____ 2. Either mow the grass or feed the chickens.

_____ 3. Alice Weaver is majoring not only in biology but also in history.

_____ 4. Virgil Lomax told me that the Walton farm is for sale and that the Walton home is for rent.

_____ 5. Wilton Vega is the fireman who saved the boy's life and received a gold medal.

_____ 6. Jason Berryhill wants to buy five acres of farmland from his father, and he wants to raise corn on this land.

_____ 7. Elizabeth Waltrip has lived in Boston, Dallas, and San Francisco.

_____ 8. Ben Gipe bought apples, cheese, and meat.

_____ 9. John Salmon enjoys English, history, and journalism.

_____ 10. Rick Walkup hunts and fishes.

_____ 11. Either use this instrument or return it to the store.

_____ 12. Neither the Weinbergers nor the Hamptons moved to a different neighborhood.

_____ 13. If you are ever in New York and if you have no place to stay, please let me know.

_____ 14. Marjorie Stein told me that she is interested in the job and that she plans to apply for it.

_____ 15. Reg's friends are interested in all kinds of art, especially modern sculpture.

ANSWERS TO PREASSESSMENT
All of the sentences are correct.

Learning Activities

PARALLEL STRUCTURE

The sentences that follow illustrate parallel structure.

WORDS IN A SERIES: Adele has served as secretary, treasurer, and president.

(Notice that all of the words in the series are *nouns*, the names of persons, places, or things.)

WORDS IN A SERIES: The children worked, sang, and played.

(All of the words in the series are *verbs*, words that express action.)

WORDS IN A SERIES: Armando is kind, sensitive, and trustful.

(All of the words in the series are *adjectives*, words that describe nouns or pronouns.)

PHRASES IN A SERIES: Kathy spoke to me before breakfast, during lunch, and after dinner.

(Each phrase in the series contains a preposition and its object—all of which modify *spoke*.)

PHRASES IN A SERIES: Floyd learned to give as well as to receive.

(Two *infinitives*—*to* + a verb—are used in this sentence.)

PARALLEL CLAUSES: They not only applauded him, but they also bought his book.

(The correlatives *not only . . . but also* join two independent clauses. *Correlatives* are coordinating conjunctions that function in pairs. *Independent clauses* express a complete thought.)

                                                    indep. cl.   indep. cl.
PARALLEL CLAUSES: Either write a research paper or do a project.

(The correlatives *either . . . or* join two independent clauses.)

                                                      dep. cl.   dep. cl.
PARALLEL CLAUSES: When you have completed your chores and when you
feel like having guests, call me.

(Two dependent clauses are used in this sentence. Recall that dependent clauses are clauses that do not make sense when they stand alone; they are dependent on the rest of the sentence for meaning.)

                                          indep.   indep.   indep.
                                            cl.   cl.   cl.
PARALLEL CLAUSES: We work; we play; we study.

(Three independent clauses are used in this sentence.)
     Before doing the exercises that follow, look at these reminders:

1. Conjunctions (especially *and*) join parallel items.

                        n.   n.   n.   conj.   n.
I have invited Curtis, Mary, Edward, and Tony.

2. All of the items in a series must be the same types of words, phrases, or clauses. (For example, if the first word in a series is an adjective, the other words in the series must also be adjectives.)

                  adj.   adj.   adj.
Dorothy is kind, mature, and sensitive.

Note: The word *to*, the sign of the infinitive, does not have to appear before every verb in a series of infinitive phrases. If the infinitives are widely spaced, however, repeating the *to* may clarify the structure of the sentence.

                  inf.   v.   v.   v.
Gene wants to swim, fish, and relax.

                  inf.   v.
Tony plans to wash dishes eight hours a day in a cafeteria in the south part of
        inf.   v.
Toledo, to work three hours each night in a warehouse near his apartment,
      inf.   v.
and to spend any spare time practicing the piano at the music institute.

3. Do not use *and which, and who (whom)*, or *and that* unless the preceding clause contains *who (whom), which*, or *that*.

Fran believes <u>that</u> this college is growing <u>and that</u> it has potential.

Note: No comma comes before *and* because the clause that follows is *dependent*—not a complete thought.

Review the material in this unit; then begin Exercise 1.

Identifying Parallel Sentences   *Exercise 1*

In each of the spaces provided, write C if the sentence is parallel and W if the sentence is not parallel.

_____ 1. Kalum is considerate, intelligent, and he is pleasant.

_____ 2. I believe that this city is prosperous, and it has a good future.

_____ 3. Mr. Greenberg is a man whom you can trust, and you can respect him.

_____ 4. Either give me two dollars or buy my lunch.

_____ 5. Ms. Rodriguez not only wants to lecture and teach but also she wants to write.

_____ 6. Marilyn Moon has to ride the bus from her apartment to the west side of the city; then she has to ride another bus to her office.

_____ 7. We play baseball, football, and enjoy tennis.

_____ 8. Albert photographed his subject at home, at work, and play.

_____ 9. The children drew pictures, played games, and they saw a movie.

_____ 10. Mr. Morgenstern spoke in Kansas, Utah, and in Washington.

ANSWERS TO EXERCISE 1

1. W		6. C	
2. W		7. W	
3. W		8. W	
4. C		9. W	
5. W		10. W	

If you gave at least nine correct answers, you can begin Exercise 2. Otherwise, you need to review the preceding information.

Exercise 2   Writing Parallel Sentences
Write a correct version for each of the wrong sentences in Exercise 1.

1. _____

_____

2. _____

_____

3. _____

_____

4. C

5. _____

_____

6. C

7. _____

_____

8. _____

_____

9. _____

_____

10. _____

_____

ANSWERS TO EXERCISE 2

Answers will vary and should be checked by your instructor, but here are some possibilities:

1. Kalum is considerate, intelligent, and pleasant.
2. I believe that this city is prosperous and that it has a good future.
   Or: This city is prosperous and has a good future.
3. Frank is a man whom you can trust and whom you can respect.
   Or: You can respect and trust Frank.
4. C
5. Ms. Rodriguez not only wants to lecture and teach, but she also wants to write and speak.
6. C
7. We play baseball, football, and tennis.
8. Albert photographed his subject at home, at work, and at play.
   Or: Albert photographed his subject at home, work, and play.
9. The children drew pictures, played games, and saw a movie.
10. Mr. Morgenstern spoke in Kansas, Utah, and Washington.

A Review of Parallel Sentences   *Exercise 3*

1. Write a sentence containing a series of nouns.

_____

_____

2. Write a sentence containing a series of adjectives.

_____

_____

3. Write a sentence containing a series of verbs.

_____

_____

4. Write a sentence containing a series of phrases (any type).

_____

_____

5. Write a sentence containing a series of dependent clauses.

_____

_____

6. Write a sentence containing a series of independent clauses.

_____

_____

7. Write a sentence containing two infinitives widely separated.

_____

_____

_____

8. Write a sentence containing three infinitives *not* widely separated.

_____

_____

9. Write a sentence containing *and that*.

_____

_____

_____

10. Write a sentence containing *and who*.

_____

_____

_____

11. Write a sentence containing *not only . . . but also*.

_____

_____

12. Write a sentence containing *either . . . or*.

_____

_____

ANSWERS TO EXERCISE 3
Answers will differ; therefore, your instructor should check this exercise.

Postassessment

In each of the spaces provided, write C if the sentence is parallel and W if the sentence is not parallel.

_____ 1. Hazel is not only pleasant, but she is also intelligent.

_____ 2. Either send me a copy of the book or ask your assistant to deliver it to my home.

_____ 3. Allan paints homes, offices, and he paints automobiles.

_____ 4. Mrs. Lassiter told me that I should major in English, and I could possibly get a scholarship.

_____ 5. Mr. Crow is not conceited, temperamental, or sly.

_____ 6. Wren has to type letters, receive patients, make telephone calls.

_____ 7. The Bergfields own cattle, goats, and they have some sheep.

_____ 8. I have to write a research paper for Mr. Ponta in two weeks, and I have to submit an outline by Friday.

_____ 9. Ethel is a friend who always gives me confidence, and she always makes me cheerful.

_____ 10. We toured museums in London, Paris, and in Rome.

ANSWERS TO POSTASSESSMENT

1. C	6. C
2. C	7. W
3. W	8. C
4. W	9. W
5. C	10. W

Study Unit 6□Trite and Wordy Sentences

RATIONALE

Have you ever wished that you could say more in fewer words? Have you caught yourself repeating the expressions of people with whom you talk? Many of these expressions are clichés. Developing a fresh vocabulary instead of always using the same worn-out expressions should really improve your writing style.

OBJECTIVES

After completing this Study Unit 6, you should be able to
1. say more in fewer words
2. avoid using unnecessary words and expressions
3. eliminate clichés
4. develop freshness and originality in your writing style

Preassessment

Underline any overused (trite) words or expressions in these sentences. If a sentence is correct, write C in the space provided.

_____ 1. Terrill's innocence made him look like a newborn babe.

_____ 2. When Don accused Bert of stealing money, that was the last straw.

_____ 3. Bob intervened just in the nick of time.

_____ 4. Like a blundering idiot, Bob took Don's side.

_____ 5. If Bob had it to do over, he would never again interfere.

_____ 6. Now Bert does not speak to Bob.

_____ 7. To retaliate, Bob is cold as ice.

_____ 8. Each and every member of the club wants Bob and Bert to forget the incident.

_____ 9. However, few people in this day and age know how to forgive.

_____ 10. Surprising to note, Don is happy as a lark.

Draw a line through any unnecessary words or phrases in these sentences. Write C if the sentence is correct.

_____ 11. Of all the subjects I take, I hate algebra.

_____ 12. Mr. Giles, my teacher, is the type of man who never smiles.

_____ 13. He is the kind of teacher that always gains momentum toward the end of the semester.

_____ 14. Early in the year, Mr. Giles realized that his job would not be an easy one.

_____ 15. The thing that I wanted to mention is that Mr. Giles will never enjoy teaching.

_____ 16. He is the type of teacher who represents everything that I dislike.

_____ 17. However, Mr. Giles does help his students.

_____ 18. In that way, Mr. Giles is sort of nice.

_____ 19. You know, he changes occasionally.

_____ 20. In my opinion, Mr. Giles needs to enjoy teaching.

ANSWERS TO PREASSESSMENT

You should have underlined or drawn a line through the following expressions:

1. like a newborn babe
2. the last straw
3. the nick of time
4. like a blundering idiot
5. had it to do over
6. C
7. cold as ice
8. Each and every
9. in this day and age
10. Surprising to note, happy as a lark
11. Of all the subjects I take
12. is the type of man who
13. is the kind of teacher that
14. that . . . an . . . one.
15. The thing that I wanted to mention is that
16. is the type of teacher who . . . that
17. C
18. sort of
19. You know
20. In my opinion

Learning Activities

TRITENESS

Triteness is a term for words or expressions that are stale because of overuse. Some trite expressions occur in _similes_ (comparisons using _like_ or _as_).

blind as a bat
brave as a lion
busy as a bee
clear as crystal
clear as mud
cold as ice
cried like a baby
cunning as a fox
cute as a bug

dry as cotton
fat as a pig
fight like a tiger
free as the air
gentle as a lamb
good as gold
green as grass
happy as a lark
happy as the day is long

hard as nails   poor as a church mouse
high as a kite   pretty as a picture
hot as hell   red as a beet
like a blundering idiot   red as a rose
like a duck out of water   scared as a rabbit
like a newborn babe   sharp as a tack
mad as a wet hen   strong as an ox
nervous as a cat   stubborn as a mule
old as the hills   thin as a rail
packed like sardines   tough as leather

Stop at this point and check your ability to locate trite similes in sentences by completing Exercise 1.

Exercise 1 *Trite Expressions*
Underline any trite expressions in these sentences. If a sentence is correct, write C in the space provided.

_____ 1. When I lost my glasses, I was blind as a bat.

_____ 2. To make matters worse, Dr. Valenta assigned a test.

_____ 3. Dr. Valenta is hard as nails.

_____ 4. When I took the test, my head was clear as mud.

_____ 5. However, Maria was sharp as a tack.

_____ 6. Dr. Valenta told me I was as slow as Christmas in finishing the test.

_____ 7. I gave him a look that was cold as ice.

_____ 8. Because I am stubborn as a mule, I waited until bell time to give Dr. Valenta my paper.

_____ 9. I can be gentle as a lamb; however, if someone provokes me, I fight like a tiger.

_____ 10. By the way, Dr. Valenta was mad as a wet hen.

ANSWERS TO EXERCISE 1

You should have underlined the following expressions:

1. blind as a bat
2. To make matters worse
3. hard as nails
4. clear as mud
5. sharp as a tack
6. slow as Christmas
7. cold as ice
8. stubborn as a mule
9. gentle as a lamb, fight like a tiger
10. mad as a wet hen

MORE TRITE PHRASES

Here are some more trite words and phrases that you should try to avoid:

a must
all boils down to
all hours of
all in all
along the line
and all that
and things like that
any manner or means
as a matter of fact
as already indicated
battle of life
beating around the bush
believe me
bigger and better things
bitter end
bright and early
brings to mind
butterflies in my stomach
by and large
by leaps and bounds
center of attraction
chills (shivers) up and down my spine
college career
come to life
comes into the picture
comfortable living
conspicuous by its absence
days gone by
dear old (college, etc.)
deeply grateful
depths of despair
doomed to disappointment
dull thud
each and every
every walk of life

fabulous (time, etc.)

fair land of ours

few and far between

fill the shoes of

fine

first and foremost

fond memories

force of circumstances

get our wires crossed

getting in orbit

give it a try

give out (up)

God-given

goes without saying

good old . . .

grand and glorious

great guy (job, thrill)

green with envy

hang one on

hapless victim

headed for home

honest to goodness

if I had it to do over

important day (time, year) rolled around

in a fix (jam)

After reading this list, are you surprised that you have used many of these words and expressions without reservation? Most students, in fact, read it with amazement.

in dire straits

in glowing terms

in my opinion (estimation)

in the best of health

in the final analysis

in the long run

in this day and age

interesting to note

intestinal fortitude

irony of fate

just around the corner

last but not least

last straw

leaves little to be desired

level (high school, college, etc.)

live it up

lost (his, her) marbles

lost (his, her) shirt

mad dash for

main underlying

make the world a better place

many and varied

meets the eye

modern world today (our)

more than pleased

Mother Nature

much appreciated

Nature in all her splendor

Nature's wonderland (play-ground)

necessary evil

never a dull moment

nick of time

nipped in the bud

no fooling

no respecter of persons

no thinking man

none the worse for wear

Determine how well you have mastered this list by completing Exercise 2.

Underline any trite words or phrases in these sentences. If a sentence is correct, write C in the space provided.

_____ 1. The high-school-level student is often difficult to teach.

_____ 2. In this day and age, high school students want courses to be relevant to their lives.

_____ 3. They want to make the world a better place.

_____ 4. High school students also believe they should live it up in this modern world today.

_____ 5. They often see school as a necessary evil.

_____ 6. It goes without saying that many students see school as a waste of time.

_____ 7. It is interesting to note that they change their attitudes in later years.

_____ 8. As a matter of fact, they preach the value of an education to their children.

_____ 9. The once-reluctant students look back on their high school years with fond memories.

_____ 10. And they say, "If I had it to do over, I would try harder in school."

ANSWERS TO EXERCISE 2

You should have underlined the following expressions:

1. level
2. In this day and age
3. make the world a better place

4. live it up, in this modern world today
5. necessary evil
6. It goes without saying that

7. It is interesting to note that
8. As a matter of fact

9. with fond memories
10. If I had it to do over

STILL MORE TRITE PHRASES

Before doing another exercise, you need to look at one more list.

off his rocker
out of this world
outstanding achievement
played with violence
poor show
pounding like a hammer
proud possessor
psychological moment
raining cats and dogs
real challenge
really a thrill
remains a problem
rise majestically
sadder but wiser
sad to relate
safe to say
salt of the earth
setting the scene
sheer beauty
shout it from the housetops
sign of relief
sight to see (behold)
sit up and take notice
something on the mind
start anew
suffice it to say
surprising to note
take a back seat
take pen in hand

takes shape
terrible (terribly)
that good old
that's another story
the best of everything
the fact is
the time of my life
thing of the past
this day and age
this old world of ours
through thick and thin
tired but happy
to make a long story short
to make matters worse
top it off
true sense of the word
underdog
wait with bated breath
wealth of fond memories
wee small hours of the morning
wends his way
wide open spaces
with a bang
with fear and trembling
wonderful (time, day, meal)
wonders of Nature
words fail to express
you can't take it with you
you know

If you had some difficulty with Exercises 1 and 2, review the material; then try this exercise. Underline any trite word or expressions in these sentences. Write C in the space provided if the sentence is correct.

_____ 1. In the good old days, life was simple.

_____ 2. Mother Nature's beauty had not witnessed progress.

_____ 3. Believe me; people enjoyed life without modern conveniences.

_____ 4. They were happy as the days were long.

_____ 5. Most men were strong as an ox and wild as a March hare.

_____ 6. Yes, Nature in all her splendor left never a dull moment.

_____ 7. And people wanted to make the world a better place.

_____ 8. They marched on through thick and thin—tired but happy.

_____ 9. Words fail to express what I feel for the days gone by.

_____ 10. Of course, I have a wealth of fond memories.

ANSWERS TO EXERCISE 3

You should have underlined the following expressions:

1. In the good old days
2. Mother Nature's beauty
3. Believe me
4. happy as the days were long
5. strong as an ox, wild as a March hare
6. Nature in all her splendor, never a dull moment
7. make the world a better place
8. through thick and thin, tired but happy

9. Words fail to express, days gone by
10. wealth of fond memories

WORDY SENTENCES

Since you are living in an age that makes a virtue of economy, you might as well practice economy in writing. Economy in writing saves time and effort for you and your readers. In the examples that follow, notice that omitting the words in parentheses actually improves the clarity and liveliness of the sentences.

Mayor Horne (is the type of man who) appeals to middle-class people.

The Exorcist (is the kind of movie that) keeps viewers on the edge of their seats.

The owl (is one sort of bird that) has become a novelty in recent years.

Notice that each of the preceding wordy phrases contains one of these pronouns: *who, which,* and *that.* Any time you use one of these pronouns, be sure it is really necessary in the sentence. Some other troublesome words are *all, area, aspect, factor, kind, phase, situation, sort, state, type,* and *what.*

(All I want to say is) Larry is a fair person.

Crime (is one factor that) begins in childhood.

Dave (is the kind of person who) always gets what he wants.

Tommy (is going through that phase of life in which he) is asking, "Who am I?"

The mood of the play (presents a situation that) is depressing.

Lin Yee told me (that) you are staying in a village (that is) near the mountains.

Herta is (in a sort of) excited (state).

Kevin (is the type of friend who) never fails to be a friend.

(What I want to say is that) I enjoy this course.

Avoid using in a sentence two or more words that express the same idea.

The book is <u>sad</u> and <u>depressing</u>.

The <u>moving van truck</u> delivered the furniture.

Olga is <u>brilliant</u> and <u>extremely intelligent</u>.

Ted and Alice left on their <u>honeymoon</u> tr<u>ip</u>.

We <u>cried</u> and <u>wept</u> throughout the movie.

    Caution: Avoid the common expression "you know." This expression is annoying in both oral and written communication.

The Dallas Cowboys, you know, were in the play-offs in 1975.

*Wordy Sentences**Exercise 4*

Improve any wordy sentence by placing parentheses around unnecessary words and phrases or by rewriting the sentence on another piece of paper. Write C in the space provided if the sentence is correct.

_____ 1. Christopher Cimaglia is the type of coach who believes in strict rules for his players.

_____ 2. The coach that I would like to tell you about is Mario Paez.

_____ 3. All I wish is that he would have another successful year.

_____ 4. What I mean to say is that his team should win all of its games.

_____ 5. One thing I cannot stand is the way football fans quit attending games when a team has a few losses.

_____ 6. However, Mario Paez is not the kind of person who allows fans to affect his spirit.

_____ 7. This trait of his personality has won him much admiration.

_____ 8. Mario Paez's reputation is unquestionable.

_____ 9. It is also an enviable one.

_____ 10. Mario Paez coaches with an enthusiasm and a love for the game.

ANSWERS TO EXERCISE 4

1. (is the type of coach who)
2. (The coach that). . .(is)
3. (All). . .(is that)
4. (What I mean to say is that)
5. (One thing) . . . (is)
6. However, Mario Paez does

not allow fans to affect his spirit.

7. (of his personality)
8. C
9. (an) . . . (one)
10. (an) . . . (a)

Exercise 5   **A Review of Wordy Sentences**

If you had difficulty with the preceding exercise, review the information in the learning activity. Then try this exercise, following the same instructions given in Exercise 4.

_____   1. Robert Browning was the type of poet who included art in his poems.

_____   2. One of these poems was a work called "My Last Duchess."

_____   3. The mood of this poem creates a level of suspense.

_____   4. "My Last Duchess" is the kind of poem that has a plot.

_____   5. The one thing that I want to mention about the plot is that the duke is about to remarry.

_____   6. He is talking to a sort of agent sent by the girl's father.

_____   7. The duke and the agent are supposed to discuss the dowry, but the duke spends his time criticizing his last duchess.

_____   8. In the process, he really exposes his own personality, which proves to be a satanic one.

_____   9. And the duchess is actually a kind, warm, and fun-loving lady.

_____ 10. One thing the reader never learns is what happened to the duchess.

1. (was the type of poet who)
2. (a work called)
3. (a level of)
4. (is the kind of poem that)
5. (The one thing that I want to mention about the plot is that)
6. Change *a* to *an* and omit *sort of*
7. C
8. (a) . . . (one)
9. (a) . . . (lady)
10. (One thing) . . . (is)

Postassessment

Underline any trite words or expressions. If a sentence is correct, write C in the space provided.

_____ 1. Matt, honest to goodness, always does a good job.

_____ 2. His high-school-level achievement won him academic and athletic scholarships.

_____ 3. To top it off, Ivy League universities wanted him on their teams.

_____ 4. Many of his former classmates were green with envy.

_____ 5. His parents were more than pleased.

_____ 6. Success was just around the corner for their son.

_____ 7. First and foremost, though, they wanted Matt to have a free education.

_____ 8. You know, Matt's parents wanted him to have the best of everything.

_____ 9. However, Matt and his parents had their wires crossed.

_____ 10. Matt wondered whether he could fill a college athlete's shoes.

Improve any wordy sentence by placing parentheses around any unnecessary words or rewriting the sentence. Write C in the space provided if the sentence is correct.

_____ 11. Matt was not the type of person who was totally committed to sports.

_____ 12. He was also sort of special.

_____ 13. Matt was not one to get plenty of sleep.

_____ 14. He was the kind of person who did not miss a party.

_____ 15. What I mean to say is that Matt enjoyed people.

_____ 16. People, likewise, responded to Matt.

_____ 17. They especially liked his amusing and funny stories.

_____ 18. Matt's social life was one factor that was a consideration.

_____ 19. One thing I must mention is that Matt had a girl friend.

_____ 20. Although I do not remember Matt's decision, I recall that it was a difficult one.

ANSWERS TO POSTASSESSMENT
1. honest to goodness
2. level
3. To top it off
4. green with envy
5. more than pleased
6. just around the corner
7. First and foremost
8. You know . . . the best of everything
9. had their wires crossed

10. fill . . . shoes
11. (the type of person who was)
12. (sort of)
13. Matt did not get plenty of sleep.
14. (was the kind of person who)
15. (What I mean to say is that)
16. C
17. (amusing and)
18. (was one factor that)
19. (One thing I must mention is that)
20. (a) . . . (one)

Study Unit 7□Agreement of Subject and Verb

RATIONALE

Every sentence, spoken or written, contains a *subject* (the noun or pronoun about which something is stated or asked) and a *verb* (the part of speech that shows action, being, or state of being). The subject and verb must be either both *singular* (one) or both *plural* (more than one). This unit gives you some practical suggestions in making subjects and verbs agree, regardless of the structure of the sentence.

OBJECTIVES

After completing Study Unit 7, you should be able to
1. make verbs agree with their subjects
2. improve both writing and speaking skills

Preassessment

Write the correct verbs for these sentences in the spaces provided.

_____ 1. The athlete in this group (is, are) Aaron.

_____ 2. The children (is, are) in the back yard.

_____ 3. Neither Mary nor her friends (is, are) at home.

_____ 4. The table and the sofa (is, are) in storage.

_____ 5. Neither the girls nor Roosevelt (is, are) hungry.

_____ 6. The children as well as their mother (was, were) in the car.

_____ 7. The man in the crowd (was, were) carrying a gun.

_____ 8. The number of emergency cases for today (is, are) more than that of last week.

_____ 9. Physics (is, are) Marsha's favorite subject.

_____ 10. No news (is, are) good news.

_____ 11. Five dollars (is, are) the price of the book.

_____ 12. The band (is, are) on the field.

_____ 13. The jury (has, have) reached a verdict.

_____ 14. There (is, are) two cars in front of the church.

_____ 15. Sidney is one of the persons who (was, were) in the accident.

_____ 16. Mathematics (is, are) a required subject in most schools.

_____ 17. Economics (is, are) interesting this semester.

_____ 18. Everybody (is, are) supposed to attend the meeting.

_____ 19. Someone (is, are) at the door.

_____ 20. The students and their instructors (is, are) voting in this election.

ANSWERS TO PREASSESSMENT

1. is	6. were	11. is	16. is
2. are	7. was	12. is	17. is
3. are	8. is	13. has	18. is
4. are	9. is	14. are	19. is
5. is	10. is	15. were	20. are

Learning Activities

The suggestions that follow cover most of the written and spoken errors involving subject-verb agreement.

1. If a sentence has a *compound subject* (two subjects) joined by *and*, the plural form of the verb is usually necessary.

   subj.   subj.   v.
James and Charles are in California.

     subj.   subj.   v.
The children and their teachers went to the zoo.

2. When two subjects are actually the same person, or when they are two things that can be looked on as a single object, the singular form of the verb is appropriate.

        subj.   pred.
The scholar and lecturer has written his tenth book.

    subj.   v.
Bacon and eggs is my favorite breakfast.

3. Phrases and clauses that separate subjects from verbs do not ordinarily affect the number (singular or plural).

    subj.   phrase   v.
The mother, as well as her children, was in the car.

     subj.   phrase   v.
Mr. Washington, in addition to Mr. Jefferson and Mr. Trotski, is a member of the committee.

subj.   phrase   pred.
One of my friends is visiting me.

    subj.   phrase   v.
The candidate whom most people mention is Betty Jacobson.

4. When *who, whom, which*, and *that* begin a *dependent clause* (a clause that does not make complete sense by itself), they agree in number with the closest *antecedent* (the word to which one of these pronouns

refers). If you have any difficulty, just cover up the pronoun and repeat the closest antecedent along with the verb in the dependent clause.

I met the lady who was our speaker.

David is one of the new members who want to make changes in the club.

Antonio gave me a list of items that are still in the apartment.

5. *There* or *here* can never be the subject of a sentence. If a sentence begins with *there* or *here*, the verb comes before the subject.

There is a man in our garden.

There are twenty students in English 201.

Here is your morning paper.

Here are your slippers.

Check your mastery of these rules by working Exercise 1.

Subject-Verb Agreement   *Exercise 1*

Underline *all* subjects in the following sentences and write the correct verbs in the spaces provided.

_____ 1. Manuel and Jerry (want, wants) to vacation in Europe.

_____ 2. Pork and beans (is, are) Vic's favorite dish.

_____ 3. One of the girls (is, are) leaving tomorrow.

_____ 4. This room, especially the furniture, (remind, reminds) me of my parents' home.

_____ 5. The men, as well as their dates, (is, are) enjoying the party.

_____ 6. I saw the policeman who (was, were) giving the demonstration.

_____ 7. Isabel met the ladies who (live, lives) in Apartment 13.

_____ 8. One of the desks (is, are) beautiful.

_____ 9. Soap is one of the items that (is, are) on Juba's shopping list.

_____ 10. There (is, are) no people in the auditorium.

ANSWERS TO EXERCISE 1

1. <u>Manuel</u>, <u>Jerry</u> want
2. <u>Pork and beans</u> is
3. <u>One</u> is
4. <u>room</u> reminds
5. <u>men</u> are

6. <u>who</u> was
7. <u>who</u> live
8. <u>One</u> is
9. <u>that</u> are
10. <u>people</u> are

If you completed at least eight of the previous sentences without errors, you are ready to proceed to the next set of explanations. If you had more than two errors, you should review the previous suggestions before attempting another set.

MORE RULES FOR SUBJECT-VERB AGREEMENT

1. The verb agrees with the subject, not the complement. (A *complement* renames or describes the subject—it completes the meaning of the verb.)

    subj.   v.   compl.
The best <u>scene</u> in the play <u>was</u> the farewell speeches.

      subj. v.   compl.
The farewell <u>speeches</u> <u>were</u> the best scene in the play.

2. When *either . . . or* or *neither . . . nor* join two subjects (compound subject), the verb agrees with the subject closer to it.

subj.   subj. v.

Either Sergio or his parents are at home.

subj.   subj.   pred.

Either the children or their teacher has decorated the bulletin board.

subj.   subj. v.

Neither the kittens nor their mother is in the box.

subj.   subj. v.

Neither the pen nor the pencils are on my desk.

3. *Anybody, anyone, each, either, every, everyone, neither, no one,* and *someone* are singular and take singular verbs.

subj.   v.

Everyone was at home.

subj.   pred.

No one is going to the movie.

Caution: The word *none* can be either singular or plural.

None of the trees we transplanted has lost its leaves.

None of the trees we transplanted have lost their leaves.

4. *Collective nouns* (nouns that refer to groups) can be either singular or plural, depending on whether the group is thought of as a unit or as separate individuals.

subj.   pred.

The band is playing the "fight" song.

(The whole band is playing as one unit.)

subj.   pred.

The class are giving their answers to the discussion questions.

(The members of the class are giving their own individual answers.) Other examples of collective nouns are *association, audience, club, committee, company, family, federation, jury,* and *team*.

5. Units of money, space, and time are usually singular. For example, in the first of the sentences that follow, five dollars is important as a single amount, not as five individual dollar bills.

subj.   v.
<u>Five dollars</u> <u>is</u> the price of the cup.

COMPARE: He looked at the five bills in his hand. "These five measly <u>dollars</u> <u>represent</u> a lot of work," he said.

subj.   v.
<u>Three miles</u> <u>is</u> a long walk.

subj.   v.
<u>Six hours</u> <u>is</u> a short workday.

(In the first example above, the word *five* is an adjective that modifies *dollars*. We have underlined it as a part of the subject to stress the idea of the single amount rather than the individual bills, but you would be correct in saying that the real subject of the sentence is *dollars* only. The same holds true for *miles* and *hours* in the other examples. The important point is that the verb in all three cases is singular.)

6. Some nouns, including *economics, mathematics, news,* and *physics,* end in *s* but are singular; therefore, they take singular verbs.

subj.   v.
<u>Mathematics</u> <u>is</u> Anna's favorite subject.

subj. v.
The <u>news</u> <u>is</u> good tonight.

Reminder: A good standard dictionary can give you the plural of any noun.

Exercise 2   More Subject-Verb Agreement

For each of the following sentences, write the correct verb in the space provided and underline the subject that governs it.

_____   1. The best part of the party (was, were) the refreshments.

_____   2. The worst entry on the menu (was, were) chocolate frog legs.

_____ 3. Either the man or his pets (has, have) to leave.

_____ 4. Neither the books nor the pen (was, were) on the table.

_____ 5. Each of my friends (hope, hopes) to travel in June.

_____ 6. The jury (was, were) unanimous in opinion.

_____ 7. Some of the guests (is, are) in the other room.

_____ 8. Ten dollars (is, are) my last offer.

_____ 9. Five miles (is, are) the average distance between homes in this area.

_____ 10. Physics (is, are) popular on some campuses.

ANSWERS TO EXERCISE 2

1. <u>part</u> was
2. <u>entry</u> was
3. <u>pets</u> have
4. <u>pen</u> was
5. <u>Each</u> hopes

6. <u>jury</u> was
7. <u>Some</u> are
8. <u>Ten dollars</u> (or <u>dollars</u>) is
9. <u>Five miles</u> (or <u>miles</u>) is
10. <u>Physics</u> is

A Review of Subject-Verb Agreement   *Exercise 3*

For each of the following sentences, write the correct verb in the space provided and underline the subject that governs it.

_____ 1. The cat and dog (is, are) in the back yard.

_____ 2. The poet and lecturer, who uses the pen name of Lou McKernan, (has, have) agreed to visit our campus.

_____ 3. One of the athletes (has, have) broken her arm.

_____ 4. The artist, as well as her major works, (is, are) in the campus center.

_____ 5. I saw the children who (was, were) in the old house.

_____ 6. Ethel Linsky is one of the contestants who (was, were) in Rome.

_____ 7. There (is, are) one of the tickets.

_____ 8. There (is, are) two boys at our door.

_____ 9. Certain people, like Mr. Weiss, (is, are) too kind for their own good.

_____ 10. The best part of the fair (is, are) the exhibits.

_____ 11. Either Julian or his brothers (has, have) to do the chores.

_____ 12. Neither Margaret nor her sisters (is, are) at the party.

_____ 13. No one (is, are) disputing Nino's story.

_____ 14. Everybody (is, are) attending the party.

_____ 15. The team (travel, travels) in one bus.

_____ 16. The Orloff family (is, are) not in agreement about the issue.

_____ 17. The rest of the house (has, have) two fire-places.

_____ 18. Twenty-four hours (make, makes) one complete day.

_____ 19. Ten miles (is, are) the distance from my home to the city limits.

_____ 20. Economics (is, are) Marisa's favorite topic of discussion.

ANSWERS TO EXERCISE 3

1. cat, dog are
2. poet, lecturer has
3. One has
4. artist is
5. who were
6. who were
7. one is
8. boys are
9. people are
10. part is

11. brothers have
12. sisters are
13. No one is
14. Everybody is
15. team travels
16. family are
17. rest has
18. Twenty-four hours (or hours) makes
19. Ten miles (or miles) is
20. Economics is

Postassessment

Write the correct verbs for these sentences in the spaces provided:

_____ 1. The little child in the crowd (is, are) crying.

_____ 2. The kittens (is, are) enjoying the sunshine.

_____ 3. Either Phil or his parents (is, are) at home.

_____ 4. The table, as well as the chairs, (is, are) in the garage.

_____ 5. The woman and her son (is, are) in the restaurant.

_____ 6. The choir, in addition to the minister, (is, are) at the meeting.

_____ 7. The number of students (has, have) increased this semester.

_____ 8. Twelve hours (is, are) a long workday.

_____ 9. Economics (was, were) Mill's major last year.

_____ 10. The news (seems, seem) to dwell on depressing topics.

_____ 11. Fifty dollars (is, are) a good price.

_____ 12. The audience (was, were) generous with applause.

_____ 13. There (is, are) a man in my closet.

_____ 14. Mr. Byrd is one of the persons who (was, were) in Mississippi.

_____ 15. Carlos is the student who (was, were) at the airport.

_____ 16. Neither the cats nor the dog (is, are) in the house.

_____ 17. Here (is, are) the names of my students.

_____ 18. Part of the paper (was, were) missing.

_____ 19. My students, especially the artistic ones, (like, likes) freedom of expression.

_____ 20. Here is one of the items that (was, were) not on the list.

ANSWERS TO POSTASSESSMENT

1. is	6. is	11. is	16. is
2. are	7. has	12. was	17. are
3. are	8. is	13. is	18. was
4. is	9. was	14. were	19. like
5. are	10. seems	15. was	20. were

Study Unit 8□Dangling and Misplaced Modifiers

RATIONALE
Perhaps you occasionally write confusing sentences like this one: "Buying gas, our new car was discovered to only get ten miles to the gallon." This sentence should read, "Buying gas, we discovered that our new car gets only ten miles to the gallon." The improved version eliminates the dangling modifier at the beginning of the sentence as well as the misplaced modifier at the end. The information in this unit can help you to avoid writing dangling and misplaced modifiers and to gain variety and precision in expression.

OBJECTIVES
After completing Study Unit 8, you should be able to
1. write sentences without dangling modifiers
2. write sentences without misplaced modifiers
3. gain variety and precision in expression

Preassessment

In the spaces provided, write M if the sentence has a dangling or misplaced modifier and underline the dangling or misplaced modifier. Write C if the sentence has no dangling or misplaced modifiers.

_____ 1. Julie only bought two suits.

_____ 2. The professor wanted me to quickly answer.

_____ 3. Ms. Ottwell found her dog sitting under a tree.

_____ 4. The policeman nearly gave ten tickets.

_____ 5. We almost saw three movies.

_____ 6. The McDowell family enjoys sports, especially Margaret.

_____ 7. To build a table, good lumber is important.

_____ 8. In painting a home, a good brush is necessary.

_____ 9. When in Europe, the slides were taken by Elizabeth.

_____ 10. Eating my breakfast, the morning air was refreshing.

_____ 11. Herbert Komandaski only presented two reports.

_____ 12. While at the restaurant, the quarrel began.

_____ 13. Ms. Tipton fed the meat to her cat, which she had fried.

_____ 14. When five years old, the watch was given to him.

_____ 15. To support his statement, the question was raised.

ANSWERS TO PREASSESSMENT

You should have underlined the following words or groups of words:

1. only
2. quickly
3. C
4. nearly
5. almost
6. especially Margaret
7. To build a table
8. In painting a home
9. When in Europe
10. Eating my breakfast
11. only
12. While at the restaurant
13. which she had fried
14. When five years old
15. To support his statement

Learning Activities

DANGLING MODIFIERS

A dangling modifier "dangles" because there is no word in the main clause that it can *logically* modify (describe or affect). Through the way it is positioned in the sentence, a dangling modifier does, in fact, modify a word in the main clause, but in doing so it creates an illogical meaning. Consider this sentence: "Falling from the sky, Sarah felt a drop of rain." Because the dangling modifier *falling from the sky* comes right before the word *Sarah,* the structure of the sentence suggests that *Sarah* is the word to which the modifier refers. What the sentence says is that Sarah was falling from the sky.

Look at some additional sentences that contain dangling modifiers.

DANGLING MODIFIER:	Swimming in the lake, the water was refreshing.
CORRECTED:	Swimming in the lake, I found the water to be refreshing.
OR:	When I swam in the lake, the water was refreshing.
DANGLING MODIFIER:	Washing windows, the accident was seen by the children.
CORRECTED:	Washing windows, the children saw the accident.
DANGLING MODIFIER:	Watching the rain, the afternoon was enjoyed.
CORRECTED:	Watching the rain, I enjoyed the afternoon.
DANGLING MODIFIER:	Typing a letter, the lights went off.
CORRECTED:	While I was typing a letter, the lights went off.
DANGLING MODIFIER:	Singing a song, Andy's hands began to shake.
CORRECTED:	While Andy was singing a song, his hands began to shake.

Asking *"Who* was?" before each of the preceding dangling modifiers remedies the problem. *Who* was swimming in the lake? Not the water, but *I.* The word *I,* and not the word *water,* must follow the modifier *swimming in the lake.* Or: *Who* was washing windows? Not the accident, but the *children. Children,* and not *accident*, must follow the modifier.

Note that each of the last two dangling modifiers became a *dependent clause* (a group of words that has a subject and verb but does not make sense by itself).

dep. cl.

While I was typing a letter, the lights went off.

dep. cl.

While Andy was singing a song, his hands began to shake.

This procedure of asking *"Who* was?" is appropriate for correcting other dangling phrases.

DANGLING MODIFIER: In a talkative mood, the book was discussed.

CORRECTED: In a talkative mood, the girls discussed the book.

(*Who* was in a talkative mood? The girls were.)

DANGLING MODIFIER: At work, the letter arrived.

CORRECTED: While Marian was at work, the letter arrived.

(*Who* was at work? Marian was.)

DANGLING MODIFIER: To pass this course, an additional paper must be completed.

CORRECTED: To pass this course, you must complete an additional paper.

(*Who* must pass this course? You must.)

This questioning procedure also applies to elliptical clauses that dangle. (Clauses are *elliptical* when subjects and verbs are understood, or purposely left out.)

ELLIPTICAL CLAUSE: When a child, county fairs were enjoyable.

CORRECTED: When I was a child, county fairs were enjoyable.

(*Who* was a child? I was.)

ELLIPTICAL CLAUSE: Give students a free period when completely bored.

CORRECTED: Give students a free period when they are completely bored.

(*Who* is bored? Students are.)

Before progressing to misplaced modifiers, you should check your mastery of dangling modifiers by working Exercise 1.

Exercise 1 **Sentences without Danglers**

Convert each of the following phrases or clauses into a complete and coherent sentence:

1. reading a book

   _____

   _____

2. smiling with satisfaction

   _____

   _____

3. writing a letter

   _____

   _____

4. while in London

   _____

   _____

5. to build a cabin

   _____

   _____

6. to write an interesting paper

   _____

   _____

7. when in the country

_____

_____

8. winning the prize

_____

9. laughing in the sunshine

_____

_____

10. dangling in the sentence

_____

_____

ANSWERS TO EXERCISE 1

The responses to this exercise will vary, so your instructor needs to check them.

MISPLACED MODIFIERS

Misplaced modifiers are exactly what their name implies: they are modifiers (describing or qualifying words) that are out of place in the sentence. Modifiers should always appear next to or near the words they describe or affect; otherwise, the sentences in which they appear are not clear. Look at these examples:

MISPLACED MODIFIER: Ralph Stonebreaker <u>nearly</u> jumped six feet.

The sentence says that Ralph ran up to the high-jump bar and decided at the last minute not to jump. What the sentence *says* may not be what the writer *meant* it to say.

CORRECTED: Ralph Stonebreaker jumped nearly six feet.

MISPLACED MODIFIER: Alfred Youngblood <u>almost</u> bought one hundred shares of stock.

The sentence says that Alfred was thinking seriously about buying stock, but at the last minute he changed his mind. Again, the sentence may not convey the meaning the writer intended.

CORRECTED: Alfred Youngblood bought almost one hundred shares of stock.

MISPLACED MODIFIER: Sammy Tahoka lifted the roast from the pan, <u>which was tender</u>.

The sentence says that Sammy lifted the roast from a tender pan. This sentence definitely does not say what is meant.

CORRECTED: Sammy Tahoka lifted the tender roast from the pan.

Another very common misplaced modifier is the *split infinitive*. When another word comes between the *to* and the verb that make up an infinitive (as in "to really try hard" or "to carefully observe"), this intervening word "splits" the unit of the infinitive and in this sense is misplaced.

SPLIT INFINITIVE: She told me to never think of selling the farm.
CORRECTED: She told me never to think of selling the farm.

Test your ability to detect and correct misplaced modifiers by working Exercises 2 and 3.

Exercise 2 Misplaced Modifiers
Correct each of the following sentences by writing a better version:

1. Misplaced modifier: I only asked for two dollars.

    Corrected: _____

    _____

2. Misplaced modifier: The child almost ate all of his steak.

Corrected: _____

_____

3. Misplaced modifier: The professor nearly lectured the whole class period.

Corrected: _____

_____

4. Misplaced modifier: Many large cities have slum areas, especially New York.

Corrected: _____

_____

5. Misplaced modifier: Some people never know when to count their blessings, such as Mrs. Washington.

Corrected: _____

_____

_____

6. Misplaced modifier: To speak in public, self-confidence must be gained.

Corrected: _____

_____

7. Misplaced modifier: Mrs. Velasco wanted to always give me a cake.

Corrected: _____

_____

8. Misplaced modifier: Raphael spoke to his instructor in the hall, who teaches biology.

Corrected: _____

_____

9. Misplaced modifier: Ken showed the pen to Mr. Dupres, which he purchased.

Corrected: _____

_____

10. Misplaced modifier: Jethro enjoys discussing books with Mrs. McDougal, that are interesting.

Corrected: _____

_____

ANSWERS TO EXERCISE 2

Answers will vary, so your instructor should check them. Here are some possibilities:

1. I asked for only two dollars.
2. The child ate almost all of his steak.
3. The professor lectured nearly the whole class period.
4. Many large cities, especially New York, have slum areas.
5. Some people, such as Mrs. Washington, never know when to count their blessings.
6. To speak in public, a person must gain self-confidence.

7. Mrs. Velasco always wanted to give me a cake.
8. Raphael spoke to his biology instructor in the hall.
9. Ken showed the pen he purchased to Mr. Dupres.
10. Jethro enjoys discussing interesting books with Mrs. McDougal.

A Review of Dangling and Misplaced Modifiers   *Exercise 3*

Correct each of the following sentences by writing a better version:

1. Misplaced modifier: I wanted to quickly return to my desk.

   Corrected: _____

   _____

2. Misplaced modifier: Rhett served the roast to his guests, which he had burned.

   Corrected: _____

   _____

3. Misplaced modifier: The reporter only asked me one question.

   Corrected: _____

   _____

4. Misplaced modifier: The flooding river nearly rose ten feet.

   Corrected: _____

   _____

5. Misplaced modifier: The three men were very angry, especially Mr. Epstein.

   Corrected: _____

   _____

6. Elliptical clause: When six years old, Herman's mother bought him a bicycle.

   Corrected: _____

   _____

7. Dangling modifier: To get a subscription, a check must be sent to the editor.

   Corrected: _____

   _____

8. Dangling modifier: In preparing a speech, the audience should be considered.

   Corrected: _____

   _____

9. Misplaced modifier: Jessie enjoyed the beach, sitting in the sun.

   Corrected: _____

   _____

10. Misplaced modifier: Mr. McElroy almost bought five hundred acres.

   Corrected: _____

   _____

ANSWERS TO EXERCISE 3
Your instructor should go over your answers. Here are some possibilities for corrected sentences:

1. I wanted to return to my desk quickly.
2. Rhett served the burned roast to his guests.
3. The reporter asked me only one question.
4. The flooding river rose nearly ten feet.
5. The three men, especially Mr. Epstein, were very angry.
6. When Herman was six years old, his mother bought him a bicycle.
7. To get a subscription, you must send a check to the editor.
8. In preparing a speech, you should consider the audience.
9. Sitting in the sun, Jessie enjoyed the beach.
10. Mr. McElroy bought almost five hundred acres.

If you scored at least nine correct answers, you are ready for the postassessment quiz. Otherwise, you need to review the information again.

Postassessment

Correct each of the following sentences by writing a better version.

1. Wrong: Mr. Ling almost typed ten pages.

   Corrected: _____

   _____

2. Wrong: Clara sang the song, standing before the congregation.

   Corrected: _____

   _____

3. Wrong: In preparing for a test, the class notes should be studied.

   Corrected: _____

   _____

4. Wrong: To receive a degree, four years must be completed.

Corrected: _____

_____

5. Wrong: When in California, the ring was bought by Lincoln.

Corrected: _____

_____

6. Wrong: The committee worked many hours, especially Rosita.

Corrected: _____

_____

7. Wrong: The storm nearly destroyed ten trees.

Corrected: _____

_____

8. Wrong: Ms. Onassis only received one letter.

Corrected: _____

_____

9. Wrong: Ethel showed the ring to her aunt that had been lost.

Corrected: _____

_____

10. Wrong: Frank wanted me to quickly decide.

Corrected: _____

_____

ANSWERS TO POSTASSESSMENT

Responses will differ and should be looked over by your instructor.
Here are some possible answers:

1. Mr. Ling typed almost ten pages.
2. Standing before the congregation, Clara sang the song.
3. In preparing for a test, the student should study the class notes.
4. To receive a degree, a student must complete four years.
5. Lincoln bought the ring when he was in California.
6. The committee, especially Rosita, worked many hours.
7. The storm destroyed nearly ten trees.
8. Ms. Onassis received only one letter.
9. Ethel showed her aunt the ring that had been lost.
10. Frank wanted me to decide quickly.

Study Unit 9 □ Pronoun Usage

RATIONALE

Pronoun usage is complicated because it involves gender (sex), person (first, second, or third), and number (singular or plural). A pronoun must agree with its antecedent in gender, person, and number; otherwise, the sentence in which the pronoun appears is incoherent. This unit can help you to write coherent sentences with specific antecedents for all pronouns, and it can also help you to avoid some of the common errors resulting from improper pronoun usage.

OBJECTIVES

After completing Study Unit 9, you should be able to avoid pronoun errors associated with the following:
1. antecedent
2. gender
3. number
4. person

Preassessment

In each of the following sentences, underline the antecedent and select the correct pronoun that agrees with that antecedent.

1. The committee could not agree. (It, They) had varied opinions.

2. Mrs. Sakura has a plan (who, that) might work.

3. Rose has a bird (who, that) sings.

4. If an officer has a problem, (he, they) should talk to his superior.

5. Here is the book (who, that) you wanted.

6. Willard is the writer (who, which) owns a ranch.

7. Some people do not realize how fortunate (they, them) are.

8. Alfonso is the person (who, which) can help you.

9. The average individual dies sometime after (his, their) sixtieth birthday.

10. Alexi is the friend (who, that) wants to study art.

11. Ask someone (who, that) is familiar with the case.

12. Employ anyone (who, that) wants to work.

13. Talk to some children (who, which) live in the neighborhood.

14. In April, Jane cuts some of the flowers (who, that) are in bloom.

15. No one (who, which) lives in Boston has seen the letter.

ANSWERS TO PREASSESSMENT

1. committee (They)	6. writer (who)	11. someone (who)
2. plan (that)	7. people (they)	12. anyone (who)
3. bird (that)	8. person (who)	13. children (who)
4. officer (he)	9. individual (his)	14. flowers (that)
5. book (that)	10. friend (who)	15. No one (who)

Learning Activities

LOOKING AT ANTECEDENTS: GENDER, NUMBER, PERSON

Most of the suggestions in this unit fall under one main principle: *A pronoun should agree with its antecedent in gender, person, and number*. The *antecedent* is the noun or pronoun to which the pronoun refers. *Gender* means sex: female, male, or neuter. *Number* refers to singular or plural. *Person* can be first person (the person speaking), second person (the person being spoken to), or third person (the person being spoken about). Here are some examples of pronouns that agree with their antecedents in gender, number, and person.

Bruce is my supervisor. He is also my best friend.

In this example, *he*, like the antecedent *Bruce*, is masculine (Bruce is a man), singular (there is only one Bruce here), and third person (Bruce is being spoken of).

Kate is typing in this room. She likes the lighting.

Here, *she*, like the antecedent *Kate*, is feminine, singular, and third person.

Some other third-person pronouns are *it, its, they, their*, and *them*. *They, their*, and *them* are plural; *it* and *its* are singular. (Always remember that third person is the person being spoken about.)

Keeping this information in mind, you can begin to examine the various uses of pronouns. Here are some suggestions and examples for your attention.

1. Pronouns like *anybody, anyone, each, either, everyone, everybody, one, somebody,* and *someone* are singular (one) and take singular verbs.

subj.   v.
Anyone is welcome.

subj.   pred.
Everybody is invited.

These singular pronouns should also be the antecedents of singular pronouns.

If you speak to someone, he should speak in return.

If you see somebody in the yard, ask her for directions.

2. Remember that *who* and *whom* refer to people.

Kenneth Brown is the man who addressed the group.

Jill Connolly is the reporter to whom I've been meaning to write.

If you have difficulty deciding whether to use *who* or *whom*, ask yourself this simple question: Does the sentence make sense if I substitute *he* or *she* for *who*, and *him* or *her* for *whom*? Look at the preceding examples, for instance. *"He* addressed the group." (*Who* is correct.) "I've been meaning to write to *her*." (*Whom* is correct.)

3. *Which* and *that* refer to animals, ideas, and objects.

Mr. Guzman's dog, which barks throughout the night, is named Silencio.

A philosophy that appeals to most students is naturalism.

Here is the book that you wanted to borrow.

4. When pronouns have collective nouns (referring to groups) as their antecedents, the pronouns must agree with these collective nouns in gender, in number, and in person.

The team has won five games. It has two more games to play.

(Both *team* and *it* are neuter in gender—no definite sex mentioned; singular in number—one team playing as one unit; and third person—people are being discussed.)

The committee have voiced varied opinions. They have not reached agreement.

(*Committee* and *they* are neuter in gender—no definite sex mentioned; plural in number—having more than one opinion; and third person—people are being discussed.)

Work Exercise 1 to test your understanding of these points before studying any additional suggestions.

Pronouns   *Exercise 1*

In each of the following sentences, underline the antecedent and select the pronoun that agrees with that antecedent.

1. The jury reached a verdict. (It, They) voted "guilty."

2. If you see someone in the café, ask (him, them) about the election results.

3. Everybody should have (his, their) head examined.

4. If you find anybody at the sales counter, ask (her, them) to help you.

5. Lin Yee is the student (who, which) won the contest.

6. Impressionism is a theory (who, that) can be related to a number of plays.

7. Sofia has the information (who, that) I need for my project.

8. Before a student can enroll in this college, (she, they) must pay tuition.

9. Wanda is the woman (who, whom) I met.

10. Mildred Robinson is the kind lady (who, whom) lent me a quarter for the bus.

ANSWERS TO EXERCISE 1

1. jury (It)	6. theory (that)
2. someone (him)	7. information (that)
3. Everybody (his)	8. student (she)
4. anybody (her)	9. woman (whom)
5. student (who)	10. lady (who)

If you completed at least nine of these sentences correctly, you can continue with the next set of aids and examples. If you had several errors, read the preceding material again.

ADDITIONAL RULES FOR USING PRONOUNS

Here are some additional suggestions and examples for your study:

1. Do not use both the noun and the pronoun to refer to one person.

Mario [not Mario he] is at home.

Katherine [not Katherine she] is in San Francisco.

2. Do not mix genders, numbers, and persons in a sentence.

WRONG: If a person is not sure of himself, they usually tell you all their accomplishments.

(*Person* is neuter, third-person singular; *himself* is masculine, third-person singular; *they* is neuter, third-person plural; *you* is neuter, second-person singular or plural; *their* is neuter, third-person plural.)

CORRECTED: If a <u>person</u> is not sure of <u>himself</u>, <u>he</u> usually tells <u>other people</u> all <u>his</u> accomplishments.

Note: Try to avoid *you* and *your* in formal essays. Most writers do not use the second person unless they are giving directions. They avoid taking their readers for granted.

WRONG: He is the kind of teacher whom <u>you</u> immediately dislike.

(How does the writer really know that the reader is going to dislike this man?)

CORRECTED: He is the kind of teacher whom some students immediately dislike.

3. A pronoun must refer clearly to its antecedent.

WRONG: His brother visited him when <u>he</u> was twenty-one.

(*Who* was twenty-one?)

CORRECTED: Andrew's brother visited him when Andrew was twenty-one.

WRONG: In South America, <u>they</u> market cattle, goats, and sheep.

(Who are *they*?)

CORRECTED: In South America, the ranchers market cattle, goats, and sheep.

WRONG: Frieda is a lawyer. <u>That</u> is usually a profitable profession.

(*Lawyer* is not a profession.)

CORRECTED: Frieda practices law. That is usually a profitable profession.

WRONG: In the instructions, <u>it</u> says that the paint should dry in two hours.

(What is *it*?)

CORRECTED: The instructions say that the paint should dry in two hours.

Exercise 2 *More Pronouns*

Underline the noun or pronoun that agrees with the gender, number, and person already established in the sentence.

1. (Sally, Sally she) wants to be an engineer.

2. If a person makes a promise, (he, they) should keep it.

3. Tess Agnew is the kind of person whom (you, some people) would enjoy.

4. Larry's father bought him a watch that (Larry, he) really liked.

5. In Baltimore (they, the police) have problems with crime.

6. (It, The paper) says that the movie begins at eight o'clock.

7. (Mike, Mike he) has completed his research paper.

8. If someone is unhappy with (himself, themselves), he usually reveals tension.

9. (They, The directions) say that only one cup of water is needed.

10. When Pete gave Paul the key, (Paul, he) laughed.

ANSWERS TO EXERCISE 2

You should have underlined the following words:

1. Sally	6. The paper
2. he	7. Mike
3. some people	8. himself
4. Larry	9. The directions
5. the police	10. Paul

Exercise 3 *A Review of Pronouns*

Underline the noun or pronoun that agrees with the gender, number, and person already established in the sentence.

1. (Kathy, Kathy she) is in Vermont.

2. Letty's sister plans to join her when (Letty, she) arrives in Paris.

3. In Florida (they, the people) enjoy fishing.

4. When you see someone cross the bridge, stop (him, them).

5. Lonnie is the student (who, which) won the essay contest.

6. Here is the ring (who, that) Ms. Trueblood lost.

7. Lupe has an idea (who, that) is worth mentioning.

8. If a student wants to keep a bicycle on this campus, (she, they) must have a permit.

9. Lily has a cat (who, that) is very affectionate.

10. The band has played its last song. (It, They) now will march off the field.

ANSWERS TO EXERCISE 3

You should have underlined the following words:

1.	Kathy	6.	that
2.	Letty	7.	that
3.	the people	8.	she
4.	him	9.	that
5.	who	10.	It

Postassessment

Underline the noun or pronoun that agrees with the gender, number, and person already established in the sentence.

1. (Albert, Albert he) drove to the country.

2. (Albert, He) hopes to join Sam just as soon as (Albert, he) arrives.

3. In New Orleans, (the people, they) are aware of history.

4. If you see anybody at the front desk, ask (her, them) for directions.

5. Pauline is the bride (who, which) received an expensive ring.

6. Here are the flowers (who, that) won the prize.

7. I have a plan (who, that) I want to mention.

8. If a teacher has a discipline problem, (he, they) must try to solve it.

9. Mrs. Redstone has a bird (who, that) talks.

10. The committee met for the last time. (It, They) had reached a unanimous decision.

ANSWERS TO POSTASSESSMENT

1. Albert
2. Albert, Albert
3. the people
4. her
5. who
6. that
7. that
8. he
9. that
10. It

Study Unit 10 □ Tense

RATIONALE
The purpose of this unit is not only to help you write more effectively but also to help you solve many of your problems with use of verb tenses. If you can learn to use verbs correctly and to recognize them as the most important words in sentences, your language and your writing should improve.

OBJECTIVES
After completing Study Unit 10, you should be able to
1. recognize the principal parts of verbs
2. use the correct verb tense

Preassessment

The principal parts of verbs are (1) the present, (2) the past, and (3) the past participle. Write in the spaces provided the past and the past participle of each verb.

Present	Past	Past Participle
1. do	_____	_____
2. swim	_____	_____
3. take	_____	_____
4. dive	_____	_____

5. eat   _____   _____

6. write   _____   _____

7. freeze   _____   _____

8. become   _____   _____

9. know   _____   _____

10. see   _____   _____

11. burst   _____   _____

12. hang (execute)   _____   _____

13. lie (tell an untruth)   _____   _____

14. ring   _____   _____

15. sing   _____   _____

In the spaces provided write the proper tenses of the various verbs.

16. Juan _____ himself my friend.
                  present: call

17. Somebody _____ the doorbell.
                  past: ring

18. The children _____ to be good before the holiday.
                  future: try

19. Brent _____ every quotation.
                  present perfect: memorize

20. I _____ the hard work before you came.
                  past perfect: do

21. By the time Eva is sixteen, she _____ everything.
                  future perfect: see

22. I _____ the whistle twice.
    past: *blow*

23. The people _____ by their vote.
    present perfect: *speak*

24. Their parents _____ to the dean.
    past perfect: *write*

25. You _____ famous.
    future: *become*

ANSWERS TO PREASSESSMENT

1. did, done	9. knew, known	18. will try
2. swam, swum	10. saw, seen	19. has memorized
3. took, taken	11. burst, burst	20. had done
4. dived (or dove), dived	12. hanged, hanged	21. will have seen
5. ate, eaten	13. lied, lied	22. blew
6. wrote, written	14. rang, rung	23. have spoken
7. froze, frozen	15. sang, sung	24. had written
8. became, become	16. calls	25. will become
	17. rang	

Learning Activities

PRINCIPAL PARTS OF VERBS

Tense means time; therefore, the tense in a sentence tells the time of the action of the verb. In order to use tense correctly, you need to know the three principal parts of every verb: the *present*, the *past*, and the *past participle*, which always has a helper—*has, had*, or *have*. These three parts are the basis of all tenses.

A mnemonic (memory) device for keeping the three principal parts in mind is to use the verb in these three simple sentences:

I eat today.   (present)

I ate yesterday.   (past)

I have eaten every day this week.   (past participle)

Regular verbs add *ed* or *d* to the present form to make the past and the past participle forms.

Present	Past	Past Participle
walk	walked	walked
talk	talked	talked
hang (execute)	hanged	hanged
prove	proved	proved
drag	dragged	dragged
drown	drowned	drowned
raise	raised	raised
flow	flowed	flowed
stop	stopped	stopped

Irregular verbs do not follow the *ed* or *d* pattern. The verb *to be* is the most common irregular verb. Its present form is *am, are, is*; its past is *was, were*; and its past participle is *been*.

The easiest of all irregular verbs are those that are the same in all three forms.

Present	Past	Past Participle
burst	burst	burst
hurt	hurt	hurt
set	set	set
spread	spread	spread

Those irregular verb forms that are the same in the past and the past participle are also easy to learn.

Present	Past	Past Participle
dive	dove (or dived)	dived
sit	sat	sat
lend	lent	lent
lose	lost	lost

Other irregular verbs that are easy to learn add *n* or *en* to the past to form the past participle.

Present	Past	Past Participle
choose	chose	chosen
tear	tore	torn
beat	beat	beaten
speak	spoke	spoken

There are seven irregular verbs you should know well. They change *i* in the present form to *a* in the past form and to *u* in the past participle form.

Present	Past	Past Participle
begin	began	begun
drink	drank	drunk
ring	rang	rung
sing	sang	sung
sink	sank	sunk
spring	sprang	sprung
swim	swam	swum

Principal Parts of Verbs   *Exercise 1*

Complete each of the following sentences by writing in the space provided the specified principal part of the verb. Remember that the past participle always has a helper—*has, had,* or *have.*

1. The dog _____ that big bone a block.
   past: *drag*

2. Has the murderer been _____?
   past participle: *hang*

3. I am going to _____ the length of the pool.
   present: *swim*

4. Who _____ all of the ice cream?
   past: *eat*

5. He has _____ the test.
   past participle: *take*

6. They _____ into the room crying.
   past: *burst*

7. I have _____ *all right* six times.
   past participle: *write*

8. She _____ to me.
   past: *lie*

9. The college choir _____ four concerts.
   past: *sing*

10. Ms. Angelo has _____ to her family.
    past participle: *write*

11. The champions have _____ the second race.
    past participle: *swim*

12. Emilia _____ into the deepest water.
    past: *dive*

13. The boat _____ soon after it was struck.
    past: *sink*

14. How much water have you _____?
    past participle: *drink*

15. Malcolm _____ work at ten o'clock.
    past: *begin*

ANSWERS TO EXERCISE 1

1. dragged	6. burst	11. swum
2. hanged	7. written	12. dived (or dove)
3. swim	8. lied	13. sank
4. ate	9. sang	14. drunk
5. taken	10. written	15. began

THE SIX TENSES OF VERBS

If you can remember that every verb has three principal parts and that *tense* means *time*, you should have little or no difficulty understanding and using the six tenses. You already know the first two tenses.

1. The *present tense* tells of action in the present time (now) and uses the present form of the verb.

I see	we see
you see	you see
he, she, it sees	they see

EXAMPLES: I <u>see</u> you.

He <u>sees</u> me.

Note: In the present tense, the third-person singular (the person spoken of: he, she, it, Tom, Diana) adds *s* to the present form of the verb.

2. The *past tense* tells of action in the past (ago) and uses the past form of the verb.

I saw	we saw
you saw	you saw
he, she, it saw	they saw

EXAMPLES: I <u>saw</u> him.

He <u>saw</u> me.

3. The *future tense* tells of action that is to take place sometime in the future (later, tomorrow, next year) and uses the present form of the verb plus *shall* or *will*.

I shall (will) see	we shall (will) see
you will see	you will see
he, she, it will see	they will see

EXAMPLES: I <u>shall see</u> you later.

He <u>will see</u> you tomorrow.

Note: If you find it easier to remember, you may use *will* for all persons to express future time.

In addition to the three simple tenses (present tense, past tense, future tense), there are three *compound* tenses (present perfect, past perfect, future perfect). These compound tenses use the past participle of the verb with the helpers *have, has*, or *had*.

4. The *present perfect tense* tells of action at some indefinite time in the past and conveys the sense of stretching back into the past from a current perspective. It uses the past participle form with the helper *have*, except in the third-person singular, when *has* is used.

I have seen	we have seen
you have seen	you have seen
he, she, it has seen	they have seen

EXAMPLES: I <u>have seen</u> the decorations.

He <u>has</u> already <u>seen</u> his Christmas present.

5. The *past perfect tense* tells of an action completed in the past before some other action in the past and uses the past participle with the helper *had*.

I had seen   we had seen
you had seen   you had seen
he, she, it had seen   they had seen

EXAMPLES: I had seen the dress before I bought it.

He had not seen the mistake until I pointed it out.

6. The *future perfect tense* tells of an action to be completed in the future within some time frame and uses the past participle with the helpers *shall have* or *will have*.

I shall (will) have seen   we shall (will) have seen
you will have seen   you will have seen
he, she, it will have seen   they will have seen

Note: If you find it easier to remember, you may use *will* for all persons.

EXAMPLES: Before the holidays end, I will have seen him.

She will have seen everything by the time I arrive.

Exercise 2   Tense
In the spaces provided, write the tense of each *italicized* verb or predicate.

_____ 1. He and I *have known* each other for years.

_____ 2. His car *had run* out of gas.

_____ 3. How *will* her illness *affect* you?

_____ 4. In a week or two, you *will have forgotten*.

_____ 5. They *had seen* all of the best movies.

_____ 6. Who *rang* the bell?

_____ 7. Surely you *will help* him with his spelling.

_____ 8. Ted *has asked* for permission to leave.

_____ 9. All teachers *have heard* that explanation.

_____ 10. We *have lived* in this house all of my life.

_____ 11. *Will* you *have eaten* lunch by twelve o'clock?

_____ 12. I *doubt* the validity of your statement.

_____ 13. Philip *wrote* her a short note of appreciation.

_____ 14. Annabelle *had done* her best to win.

_____ 15. I *do believe* he is correct.

_____ 16. I *want* to sit in that chair.

_____ 17. *Lay* the book on the desk.

_____ 18. *Have* you *laid* the book down?

_____ 19. Yesterday I *lay* in that bed.

_____ 20. I *had lain* down for an hour.

ANSWERS TO EXERCISE 2

1. present perfect
2. past perfect
3. future
4. future perfect
5. past perfect
6. past
7. future

8. present perfect
9. present perfect
10. present prefect
11. future perfect
12. present
13. past
14. past perfect

15. present
16. present
17. present
18. present perfect
19. past
20. past perfect

Exercise 3   Tense

In the following sentences, the present form of the verb is given in parentheses. In each of the spaces provided, write the tense called for.

_____ 1. Has the game (begin)?

_____ 2. Ira had (swim) too far out before we noticed and called him back.

_____ 3. Our team (run) far ahead of the other teams.

_____ 4. The boat exploded and (sink).

_____ 5. Has Betsy ever (sing) with an orchestra before?

_____ 6. Yesterday the sun (begin) to set at six o'clock.

_____ 7. Have you ever (drink) any better cider?

_____ 8. Mr. Ammon had (drive) away in a hurry.

_____ 9. The dog has (eat) all of the cat's food.

_____ 10. The truck (draw) up beside the police car.

_____ 11. The tree has (fall) on the driveway.

_____ 12. By noon we had (do) all of the work.

_____ 13. Kathy (come) running into the house.

_____ 14. Bo and Belita had (ride) the bus all day and all night.

_____ 15. My class has (write) a theme every week this semester.

_____ 16. Have you (sit) here before?

_____ 17. Yesterday he (lay) the package here.

_____ 18. (Lie) down, Fido.

_____ 19. Will you (sit) here beside me?

_____ 20. I have (sit) too long in this chair.

ANSWERS TO EXERCISE 3

1. begun	6. began	11. fallen	16. sat
2. swum	7. drunk	12. done	17. laid
3. ran	8. driven	13. came	18. Lie
4. sank	9. eaten	14. ridden	19. sit
5. sung	10. drew	15. written	20. sat

OTHER VERB FORMS

There are three other verb forms you should be aware of, but it is probable that you do not need to be concerned about them because you already use them correctly.

1. The *present participle form* is made by adding *ing* to the present form.

love — loving
hope — hoping
cry — crying

2. The *progressive form* shows continuing or ongoing action and is made by adding some form of the verb *to be (is, are, am, was, were, be, been)* to the present participle.

Jake is writing a book.

We shall be hoping you win.

They have been crying.

3. The *emphatic form* gives emphasis. Construct this form by adding *do, does,* or *did* to the present form.

She <u>does look</u> lovely in that color.

He <u>did repeat</u> everything I said.

You <u>do know</u> how to cook a delicious roast.

ONE MORE GUIDELINE FOR USING TENSE

One of the most important guidelines for using tense is this one: *Avoid changing tense in main clauses and related sentences.* Use special care not to shift from the present to the past, from the past to the present, and from the historical present to the past. (The *historical present* is the present tense used to narrate events that happened in the past: "Angrily, Mary Wollstonecraft dashes off her *Vindication of the Rights of Woman,* a work that is to become the major feminist statement of the eighteenth century.")

He sav<u>ed</u> every cent. When I ask<u>ed</u> him why he want<u>ed</u> so much money, he look<u>ed</u> at me and smil<u>ed</u>, but he answer<u>ed</u> {not *answers*} not a word.

Postassessment

In the following sentences, the present form of the verb is given in parentheses. In the spaces provided, write the tense called for in each sentence.

_____   1. She has (tear) up all of those old love letters.

_____   2. He has (come) to visit me.

_____   3. She has (prove) her worth.

_____   4. Ophelia (rise) quietly from her chair and left the room.

_____   5. How much did you (bid) for the grandfather clock?

_____ 6. The wind (blow) from the southwest during the storm.

_____ 7. Have you (choose) your partner?

_____ 8. Who (deal) these cards?

_____ 9. She (dive) into the lake to save the child.

_____ 10. Have you already (eat) supper?

_____ 11. Before anybody had (speak), the bell rang.

_____ 12. Has he ever (write) to you?

_____ 13. He (draw) himself up to his full height.

_____ 14. Have you ever (swim) this far before?

_____ 15. She has (take) all the books back to the library.

_____ 16. Did Mr. Jefferson (lie) down?

_____ 17. Why have you (sit) so long in one position?

_____ 18. I know I (lay) my coat on the bed.

_____ 19. Lincoln Jones has (sit) for two hours in the doctor's office.

_____ 20. Mansue has (lie) on her water mattress.

ANSWERS TO POSTASSESSMENT

1. torn
2. wrung
3. proved
4. rose
5. bid
6. blew
7. chosen
8. dealt
9. dived (or dove)
10. eaten
11. spoken
12. written
13. drew
14. swum
15. taken
16. lie
17. sat
18. laid
19. sat
20. lain

Study Unit 11 □ Troublesome Verbs

RATIONALE

The most troublesome verbs are those that form their principal parts irregularly. A large percentage of the errors involving irregular verbs originate with three pairs of verbs: *lay* and *lie, set* and *sit, raise* and *rise*. These verbs are not difficult to learn if one knows what they mean and how they function in a sentence.

OBJECTIVES

After completing Study Unit 11, you should be able to use these verbs correctly in sentences:

1. lay and lie
2. set and sit
3. raise and rise

Preassessment

Underline the correct verb for each sentence.

1. Yesterday I (lay, laid) the book on the desk.

2. Theodore (raised, rose) at five o'clock.

3. (Sit, Set) the table before the guests arrive.

4. (Raise, Rise) the window shade in the kitchen.

5. You can (set, sit) beside me if you want to.

6. We (sat, set) in the park.

7. Calvin (laid, lay) in the sun for two hours.

8. Barbara has also (laid, lain) in the sun for two hours.

9. The baby (laid, lay) on his stomach.

10. He does not like to (lay, lie) on his stomach.

11. I usually (raise, rise) before the other members of my family.

12. Where did you (set, sit) your purse?

13. Are you going to (raise, rise) a question?

14. You can (set, sit) your mind at rest.

15. Did Fred (set, sit) the coin on the counter?

16. Frank (raised, rose) to the occasion.

17. Did the officer (raise, rise) the flag?

18. Who (sat, set) in my chair?

19. Mrs. Alvarez (raised, rose) the hemline of her dress.

20. The letter (laid, lay) on my desk.

ANSWERS TO PREASSESSMENT

You should have underlined the following verbs:

1. laid	6. sat	11. rise	16. rose
2. rose	7. lay	12. set	17. raise
3. Set	8. lain	13. raise	18. sat
4. Raise	9. lay	14. set	19. raised
5. sit	10. lie	15. set	20. lay

Learning Activities

LAY AND LIE, SIT AND SET

Before you concentrate on the meanings of *lay* and *lie*, *sit* and *set*, look at their principal parts.

Present	Past	Past Participle
(Today I) lay.	(Yesterday I) laid.	(Many times I have) laid.
(Today I) lie.	(Yesterday I) lay.	(Many times I have) lain.
(Today I) sit.	(Yesterday I) sat.	(Many times I have) sat.
(Today I) set.	(Yesterday I) set.	(Many times I have) set.

You should have no difficulty using these verbs if you remember that the forms of *set (set, set, set)* and the forms of *lay (lay, laid, laid)* are most commonly used to mean "to put something down." They are *transitive* verbs. In other words, they always take a *direct object* (a word that receives their action). Notice that *clock* and *book* are the direct objects in the sentences that follow.

                               d.o.

Today I <u>set</u> the clock on the mantel.

                               d.o.

Yesterday I <u>set</u> the clock on the mantel.

                               d.o.

Many times I <u>have set</u> the clock on the mantel.

                               d.o.

Today I <u>lay</u> the book on the table.

                               d.o.

Yesterday I <u>laid</u> the book on the table.

                               d.o.

Many times I <u>have laid</u> the book on the table.

The forms of *lie (lie, lay, lain)* most commonly mean "to recline," and the forms of *sit (sit, sat, sat)* most commonly mean "to take a seat." The best way to remember these two sets is to say, "Anything that is not moving is sitting or lying." The forms of *lie* and *sit* never take a direct object: they are *intransitive*. *No* word in any of the sentences that follow receives the action of the verb.

Today I <u>lie</u> on the beach.
Yesterday I <u>lay</u> on the beach.
Many times I <u>have lain</u> on the beach.

Today I <u>sit</u> in the chair.
Yesterday I <u>sat</u> in the chair.
Many times I <u>have sat</u> in the chair.

Now try to write some of your own sentences in Exercise 1.

Exercise 1 *Lay and Lie, Sit and Set*

Apply the definition and direct-object tests and use each of the following verbs in a good sentence.

1. lay (present tense)

_____

_____

2. laid

_____

_____

3. have laid

_____

_____

4. lie

_____

_____

5. lay (past tense)

_____

_____

6. has lain

_____

_____

7. set (present tense)

_____

_____

8. set (past tense)

_____

_____

9. have set

_____

_____

10. sit

_____

_____

11. sat

_____

_____

12. has sat

_____

_____

ANSWERS TO EXERCISE 1
Answers will vary and should be checked by your instructor.

Exercise 2   *Forms of Lay and Lie*

Complete these sentences by filling in the spaces provided with a form of *lay* or *lie*. Use the definition and direct-object tests to check your word choice.

1. The hat has _____ on the sofa for a week.
   past participle

2. The article _____ on the kitchen table.
   past tense

3. Books _____ on Mr. Martinez's desk.
   present tense

4. Viola has already _____ the book on Mrs. Foxe's desk.
   past participle

5. Mary Ellen _____ her head on John's shoulder.
   past tense

6. The baseball _____ on top of the roof.
   past tense

7. Roland did not _____ in bed after eight o'clock.
   present tense

8. Winifred has _____ her tennis shoes on the bench.
   past participle

9. Katherine has never _____ on a water bed.
   past participle

10. The cat _____ in the sun for one hour.
    past tense

ANSWERS TO EXERCISE 2

1.	lain	6.	lay
2.	lay	7.	lie
3.	lie	8.	laid
4.	laid	9.	lain
5.	laid	10.	lay

Exercise 3   *Forms of Sit and Set*

Complete these sentences by filling in the spaces provided with a form of *sit* or *set*. Use the definition and direct-object tests to check your choices.

1. Dorothy did not _____ the table.
   past tense

2. She _____ in the den.
   past tense

3. The clerk _____ the eggs on the top of the tomatoes.
   past tense

4. We must _____ in the shade.
   present tense

5. I can _____ the television in Julio's room.
   present tense

6. Fay has _____ the pieces of china on the shelf.
   past participle

7. Mike has _____ on Karen's steps for three hours.
   past participle

8. Twenty people have _____ at this table.
   past participle

9. Please _____ at my table this morning.
   present tense

10. _____ the books on the large desk.
    present tense

ANSWERS TO EXERCISE 3

1. set	6. set
2. sat	7. sat
3. set	8. sat
4. sit	9. sit
5. set	10. Set

RAISE AND RISE

Also look at the forms of *raise* and *rise*.

Present	Past	Past Participle
(Today I) raise.	(Yesterday I) raised.	(Many times I have) raised.
(Today I) rise.	(Yesterday I) rose.	(Many times I have) risen.

The forms of *raise (raise, raised, raised)* most commonly are used to mean "to elevate something." They always take a direct object.

d.o.

Now I <u>raise</u> the flag.

d.o.

Yesterday I <u>raised</u> the flag.

d.o.

I <u>have raised</u> the flag.

In each of the preceding examples, *flag* is the direct object because it receives the action of the verb.

The primary meaning of the forms of *rise (rise, rose, risen)* is "to assume an upright position." These forms never take a direct object.

Now I <u>rise</u> early.

Yesterday I <u>rose</u> early.

I <u>have risen</u> early.

No word in any of these sentences receives the action of the verb.

Now use the definition and direct-object tests for working Exercise 4.

Exercise 4   ***Raise and Rise***
Use each of the following verbs in a good sentence.

1. raise

_____

_____

2. raised (past tense)

_____

_____

3. has raised

_____

_____

4. rise

_____

_____

5. rose

_____

_____

6. have risen

_____

_____

Complete these sentences by filling in the spaces provided with a form of *raise* or *rise*:

7. Do you _____ early each morning?
   _{present tense}

8. The sun has _____.
   _{past participle}

9. Ms. Penski _____ the blinds in front of her windows.
   _{past tense}

10. The teacher has _____ many questions.
    _{past participle}

11. All club members _____ early to be at the meeting.
    _{past tense}

12. We must _____ at five o'clock tomorrow morning.
    _{present tense}

13. Terry Trawick _____ the blanket covering his car.
    _{past tense}

14. Ethel Lamb has _____ crops on her father's farm.
    past participle

15. _____ the blinds so that you can see the sun.
    present tense

ANSWERS TO EXERCISE 4
Answers for 1–6 will vary; therefore, your instructor should check them.

7. rise	10. raised	13. raised
8. risen	11. rose	14. raised
9. raised	12. rise	15. Raise

Exercise 5 A Review of Troublesome Verbs
Underline the correct verb for each sentence.

1. The test (laid, lay) in front of the instructor.

2. The instructor had (laid, lain) the test on the desk.

3. Guy does not like to (lay, lie) on the beach.

4. The broken flower pot has (laid, lain) on my porch for two days.

5. The gentleman (laid, lay) his napkin on the table.

6. Please (set, sit) in my car.

7. Do not (set, sit) the plate on the stove.

8. Ronald (sat, set) in Dr. Parkinson's class for two days.

9. Have you (sat, set) the date?

10. Have you (sat, set) in the park?

11. Did you (raise, rise) when he entered?

12. Ms. Chung (raised, rose) before dawn.

13. She immediately (raised, rose) her window shades.

14. Has anyone (raised, rose) the flag?

15. The Copelands have not (raised, risen).

ANSWERS TO EXERCISE 5

1. lay	6. sit	11. rise
2. laid	7. set	12. rose
3. lie	8. sat	13. raised
4. lain	9. set	14. raised
5. laid	10. sat	15. risen

If you had more than one incorrect answer, a quick review of the unit should help you to score well on the postassessment questions.

Postassessment

Underline the correct verb for each sentence.

1. I would like to (lay, lie) in bed on Saturday mornings.

2. Last Saturday morning, I (laid, lay) in bed for two hours.

3. Have you ever (laid, lain) too long in the sun?

4. Did you (lay, lie) my comb on the counter?

5. Have you (laid, lain) the papers on the floor?

6. Howard (laid, lay) his watch on a large rock.

7. It (sat, set) there for three days.

8. He wondered where he had (sat, set) his watch.

9. The players (set, sit) on the bench.

10. Mr. Acoma has (sat, set) on my glasses.

11. I (sat, set) the glasses there by mistake.

12. Please (set, sit) the glasses on the table.

13. The children always (raise, rise) when the teacher enters the room.

14. The sun (raised, rose) over the mountain.

15. Toko has (raised, risen) too late for her early class.

16. The teacher (raised, rose) the map.

17. Did Aretha (raise, rise) her hand?

18. He has (raised, risen) his hand many times.

19. The breeze has (raised, risen) some dust.

20. Mildred (raised, rose) her window.

ANSWERS TO POSTASSESSMENT

1. lie	6. laid	11. set	16. raised
2. lay	7. sat	12. set	17. raise
3. lain	8. set	13. rise	18. raised
4. lay	9. sit	14. rose	19. raised
5. laid	10. sat	15. risen	20. raised

Study Unit 12 □ Adjectives and Adverbs

RATIONALE
Adjectives and adverbs are modifiers. Both may be a single word, a phrase, or a clause. Modifiers describe or limit or qualify a meaning to express a point of view, to make a meaning clear and definite, and to increase liveliness of expression and effectiveness in communication. Therefore, a knowledge of adjectives and adverbs is essential to understanding and using the English language well.

OBJECTIVES
After completing Study Unit 12, you should be able to recognize and use correctly adjectives and adverbs.

Preassessment

In the following sentences, underline the adjective (or adjectives), and, in the spaces provided, write the noun or pronoun it modifies. Ignore the articles (a, an, the).

_____ 1. I wish I were beautiful and talented.

_____ 2. The French bread is in the oven.

_____ 3. Charlotte looks beautiful.

_____ 4. I feel bad.

_____ 5. We saw many trees.

_____ 6. Allan won the first race.

_____ 7. The flowers smell sweet.

_____ 8. Which house do you want?

_____ 9. She is the tallest person in the class.

_____ 10. He is the younger child.

In the following sentences, underline the adverb, and, in the spaces provided, write the verb, adverb, or adjective it modifies.

_____ 11. Ms. Longstreet writes well.

_____ 12. Mr. Jacoby arrived early.

_____ 13. Mrs. Higgins spoke loudly.

_____ 14. Miss Rainwater is here.

_____ 15. Dr. Stansky left quickly.

_____ 16. Professor Bodycomb is really intelligent.

_____ 17. Reverend Melkus called twice.

_____ 18. Sergeant Troutman served his country faithfully.

_____ 19. Senator Jakubik is very tall.

_____ 20. Captain Munoz landed the airplane smoothly.

ANSWERS TO PREASSESSMENT

1. I, <u>beautiful</u>, <u>talented</u>
2. bread, <u>French</u>
3. Charlotte, <u>beautiful</u>
4. I, <u>bad</u>
5. trees, <u>many</u>
6. race, <u>first</u>
7. flowers, <u>sweet</u>
8. house, <u>which</u>
9. person, <u>tallest</u>
10. child, <u>younger</u>
11. writes, <u>well</u>
12. arrived, <u>early</u>
13. spoke, <u>loudly</u>
14. is, <u>here</u>
15. left, <u>quickly</u>
16. intelligent, <u>really</u>
17. called, <u>twice</u>
18. served, <u>faithfully</u>
19. tall, <u>very</u>
20. landed, <u>smoothly</u>

Learning Activities

ADJECTIVES

The guidelines and examples that follow illustrate the forms, uses, and kinds of adjectives. As you study this section, keep in mind the definition of *adjective* (a word that modifies a noun or pronoun). Also remember that an adjective can appear in one of these forms: word, phrase, or clause.

1. An adjective can be a word, a phrase, or a clause.

WORD: I wore a <u>new</u> suit.

PHRASE: The suit <u>on the hanger</u> is mine.

CLAUSE: The suit <u>that I bought yesterday</u> is blue.

2. In general, adjectives tell how much, how many, what kind, and which one.

HOW MUCH?   more, enough

HOW MANY?   few, six

WHAT KIND?   big, beautiful

WHICH ONE?   this, that, these, those

3. Adjectives may serve as direct modifiers, appositive modifiers, and predicate modifiers. *Direct modifiers* come before the noun or pronoun.

Ernesto has a keen mind.

Appositive modifiers follow the noun or pronoun and are set off with commas.

The man , <u>old and tired</u> , sat down.

Predicate modifiers complete the predicate and modify the subject. (See pages 131–132.)

This test is <u>difficult</u>.

4. Adjectives may be descriptive, limiting, or in the form of numerals, articles, pronouns, or words based on proper nouns. *Descriptive* adjectives express a quality. They answer the question "what kind?"

<u>delicious</u> apple, <u>friendly</u> dog

Proper adjectives are formed from proper nouns (nouns that name particular persons, places, or things) and are always capitalized. Because they tell what kind, they are a category of descriptive adjectives.

<u>French</u> class, <u>Venetian</u> glass

Limiting adjectives often are pronouns.

<u>this</u> year, <u>that</u> fire

Articles—a, an, the—are a form of limiting adjectives. Rather than describing, they limit, individualize, or give definiteness (*the* house) or indefiniteness (*a* house) to the noun they modify. *Pronominal* adjectives are pronouns that come before nouns.

<u>this</u> year, <u>her</u> book

Numeral adjectives tell how many or in what order.

<u>ten</u> dollars, <u>first</u> choice

5. Adjectives are used to describe three degrees of comparison. The *positive degree* names a quality without comparing it to anything.

Rose Marie is <u>pretty</u>.

The *comparative degree* specifies a higher or lower degree than the positive and compares two persons or things.

Rose Marie is <u>prettier</u> than Kay.

The *superlative degree* tells the highest or lowest degree when comparing more than two persons or things.

Rose Marie is the <u>prettiest</u> girl in the university.

Comparison adjectives are formed in three ways: (1) by adding the suffix *er* or *est* to the positive degree—

big, bigger, biggest

(2) by using *more* and *most* or *less* and *least*—

beautiful, more beautiful, most beautiful

or (3) by changing the words themselves—

good, better, best
little, less or lesser, least
bad, worse, worst
much, more, most

Adjectives   *Exercise 1*

In the following sentences, underline each adjective and, in the spaces provided, write the noun or pronoun it modifies. Ignore the articles (*a, an, the*).

_____ 1. The new cars used a special kind of gasoline.

_____ 2. My brown shoes are wet and muddy.

_____ 3. The latest edition of the evening paper
carried the sad news.

_____ 4. Next year I shall be a wise sophomore.

_____ 5. His revolutionary ideas won little attention.

_____ 6. That package was heavier than I thought.

_____ 7. This bread tastes fresher than that we bought last week.

_____ 8. Who is the greater poet, Chaucer or Shakespeare?

_____ 9. The last letter she wrote was the longest of all.

_____ 10. Many Europeans make a short trip every holiday.

ANSWERS TO EXERCISE 1

1. car, new
   kind, special
2. shoes, my, brown, wet, muddy
3. edition, latest
   paper, evening
   news, sad
4. year, next
   sophomore, wise
5. ideas, his, revolutionary

   attention, little
6. package, that, heavier
7. bread, this, fresher
   week, last
8. poet, greater
9. letter, last, longest
10. Europeans, many
    trip, short
    holiday, every

ADVERBS

An _adverb_ is a word that modifies a verb, an adjective, or another adverb. Like an adjective, an adverb may appear as a word, phrase, or clause. The following guidelines and examples should help you understand adverbs and their uses.

1. An adverb can be a word, a phrase, or a clause.

WORD: He walked slowly.

PHRASE: He walked with measured steps.

CLAUSE: He limps because he is lame.

2. In general, adverbs tell where, when, how, and to what extent.

WHERE?   Put the dog inside.

WHEN?   We came late.

HOW?   She sang beautifully.

TO WHAT EXTENT?   Stimmel's remarks were most interesting.

3. Adverbs specify the manner, time, place, degree, or number of the action or actions expressed. *Manner* defines *how* the action takes place.

Yolanda spoke loudly.

Time specifies *when* the action takes place.

Julius left yesterday.

Place specifies *where* the action takes place.

All of my friends are here.

Degree tells how much.

Lupe turned rather quickly.

Number specifies how many times the action occurs or the order of the action.

Frederick called twice.

4. Adverbs may be simple or conjunctive. *Simple* adverbs are one-word adverbs that modify verbs, adjectives, or other adverbs.

Bruno danced beautifully.
Alfredo is a really handsome beautician.
Helena very quietly spoke.

Conjunctive adverbs connect two independent clauses. Common conjunctive adverbs include *hence, thus, still, then, yet, however, besides, otherwise, nevertheless*, and *therefore*. When a conjunctive adverb joins two *independent clauses* (a group of words that has a subject and a predicate and makes complete sense), a semicolon (;) precedes it. (See pages 182–183.)

Education is expensive ; <u>yet</u> it is worth the cost.

It rained hard ; <u>however</u> , under the trees it was dry.

Note: Use a comma *after* a long (more than one syllable) conjunctive adverb such as *however, otherwise*, or *nevertheless*.

5. Like adjectives, adverbs suggest comparison in three degrees. The *positive degree* names a quality without comparing it to anything.

Mickey tries hard to be <u>good</u>.

The *comparative degree* compares two persons or things and adds *er* to the positive degree of adverbs of one syllable.

hard — harder
loud — louder

It also uses *more* with adverbs ending in *ly*.

smoothly — more smoothly
quickly — more quickly

The *superlative degree* compares three or more persons or things and adds *est* to comparative adverbs that end in *er*.

taller — tallest
louder — loudest

It also adds *most* to comparative adverbs that use *more*.

more politely — most politely
more happily — most happily

6. A few adverbs are responsible for many of the adverb problems that student writers have. Learning the rules that follow will help you to avoid misusing these frequently troublesome adverbs.

Use adjectives instead of adverbs after verbs of the senses, such as *look, taste, feel, smell,* and *sound.*

This flower smells <u>sweet</u>.
I feel <u>bad</u> today.

Use adjectives instead of adverbs after *linking verbs* (verbs that join the subject and the subject complement), such as *appear, remain, seem, become.*

The weather seems <u>cold</u>.
The leaves become <u>red</u> in the fall.

Use *from* (not *than*) after *different* and *differently.*

Your book is different <u>from</u> his.

Use *somewhat* (not *some*) as an adverb.

Jody is <u>somewhat</u> better today.

Remember that *real* is an adjective and, therefore, modifies nouns and pronouns.

n.
She is a <u>real</u> friend.

pro.
Will the <u>real</u> you please stand?

Remember that *really* is an adverb that modifies verbs, adjectives, and other adverbs.

v.
Carmine <u>really</u> tries to do her best.

adj.
Lew is <u>really</u> tall.

adv.
The burglar entered the house <u>really</u> quietly.

Adverbs   *Exercise 2*
In each of the following sentences, select the correct adjective or adverb and write it in the space provided.

_____ 1. I felt very (bad, badly) when our team lost.

_____ 2. Come (quick, quickly) or we will miss the plane.

_____ 3. His playing has improved (considerably, considerable) since his last concert.

_____ 4. This pen never writes very (good, well).

_____ 5. Archibald is (real, really) happy about winning.

_____ 6. Your ticket is different (from, than) mine.

_____ 7. Emily Waters is a (real, really) good counselor.

_____ 8. Arthur is a (real, really) friend.

_____ 9. My grandfather worked (faithful, faithfully) until he was a success.

_____ 10. He was (most, almost) out of sight when I called.

ANSWERS TO EXERCISE 2

1. bad
2. quickly
3. considerably
4. well
5. really
6. from
7. really
8. real
9. faithfully
10. almost

Postassessment

In the first space provided, indicate whether the *italicized* word in each of the following sentences is an adjective (adj.) or an adverb (adv.). In the second space provided, write the word that the adjective or adverb modifies.

_____ _____ 1. Terry Bradshaw feels *good*.

_____ _____ 2. Ron Perez is a *nice* person.

_____ _____ 3. Fay Enoch called *early*.

_____ _____ 4. Sal Winfrey is *late*.

_____ _____ 5. Mel Vaughn won *twice*.

_____ _____ 6. Mae Whitehurst sings *loudly*.

_____ _____ 7. Paul Elkin worked *here*.

_____ _____ 8. Ty Duncan spoke *quickly*.

_____ _____ 9. Lee Kirkendall is *very* brave.

_____ _____ 10. Sue Ling has *pretty* eyes.

_____ _____ 11. Lupe Munoz is *rather* bright.

_____ _____ 12. Lynn Pedigo came *yesterday*.

_____ _____ 13. Pat Myers stayed *inside*.

_____ _____ 14. Lil Jacobs talked *slowly*.

_____ _____ 15. Sam Wong is *taller* than I.

—— ———————————— 16. Maria Luciano is *really* happy.

—— ———————————— 17. Roy Harper's coat is *different*.

—— ———————————— 18. Will Singley's ideas are *fresh*.

—— ———————————— 19. Beryl Ming enjoys *fresh* bread.

—— ———————————— 20. Paula House types *well*.

ANSWERS TO POSTASSESSMENT

1. adj., Terry Bradshaw
2. adj., person
3. adv., called
4. adj., Sal Winfrey
5. adv., won
6. adv., sings
7. adv., worked
8. adv., spoke
9. adv., brave
10. adj., eyes

11. adv., bright
12. adv., came
13. adv., stayed
14. adv., talked
15. adj., Sam Wong
16. adv., happy
17. adj., coat
18. adj., ideas
19. adj., bread
20. adv., types

Study Unit 13 □ Semicolons and Colons

RATIONALE

Although similar in name, the colon and semicolon differ in use. The colon (:), which follows a statement or main clause, is a formal introducer, calling attention to something that is to follow. The colon usually means "as follows." The semicolon (;), which separates the main clauses, is a strong separator, almost equal to the period. The next few pages contain some important rules and exercises that can help you distinguish between the colon and semicolon.

OBJECTIVES

After completing Study Unit 13, you should be able to

1. use semicolons effectively in sentences
2. use colons effectively in sentences

Preassessment

Insert semicolons and colons where they belong in the following sentences. Write C beside each sentence that is correct.

_____ 1. The girls had no money; therefore, a movie was out of the question.

_____ 2. The buyer asked for three items cheese, candy, and milk.

_____ 3. Larry and Jack had to return to their jobs the strike was settled.

_____ 4. Goldman was a generous person: he gave money to many charities.

_____ 5. The train arrived at 5:30; it was twenty minutes late.

_____ 6. Belia invited three people Carlos, a childhood friend; Fidelia, a friend from New York; and Faustina, a close relative.

_____ 7. The speaker challenged the audience "I challenge you to do something for your country."

_____ 8. The children did not, therefore, give all of their time.

_____ 9. Mrs. Savalas has expressed many thoughts; she has released many emotions.

_____ 10. Joe finished his examination before the 10:50 bell rang consequently, he was allowed to leave class early.

ANSWERS TO PREASSESSMENT
1. C
2. items: cheese
3. jobs: the
4. C
5. C
6. people: Carlos
7. audience: "I
8. C
9. C
10. rang; consequently, he

Learning Activities

USING SEMICOLONS

The semicolon functions as a "semi-period," signaling a less definite break than the period but often appearing in positions where a period is also possible. Here are some simple guidelines to follow in using the semicolon:

1. Use a semicolon to separate two or more _independent clauses_ (those that contain a subject and a verb and make complete sense) when the

coordinating conjunction (*and, but, or, for, nor*—conjunctions that join words, phrases, or clauses of equal rank), is omitted. Such clauses should be similar in thought.

```
┌──────────indep. cl.──────────┐  ┌────indep. cl.────┐
Walter is a dependable worker ; he is never late.
```

```
┌──────────indep. cl.──────────┐  ┌────indep. cl.────┐
The children did not join us ; they had to go home.
```

Independent clauses can also be joined to other independent clauses with the help of conjunctive adverbs like *accordingly, consequently, furthermore, hence, however, moreover, nevertheless, still, therefore,* and *yet*. If one of these conjunctive adverbs joins two independent clauses, place a semicolon before the conjunctive adverb and a comma after the adverb if it is more than one syllable (*however, nevertheless, furthermore*).

```
┌──── indep. cl. ────┐  conj. adv.  ┌──────────indep. cl.──────────┐
Jane has problems ; however , she maintains a pleasant disposition.
```

If a one-syllable conjunctive adverb joins two independent clauses, place only a semicolon before it.

```
                            conj.
┌──── indep. cl. ────┐      adv. ┌──────────indep. cl.──────────┐
Dick is very intelligent ; yet he lacks a winning personality.
```

The use of a comma instead of a semicolon in these sentences is called a *comma splice*. (A comma splice is the use of only a comma to separate two or more independent clauses; see pages 182–186.) Here are some examples of comma splices.

COMMA SPLICE: Troy wanted to do well in the course, therefore, he did his assignments every day.

CORRECTED: Troy wanted to do well in the course; therefore, he did his assignments every day.

COMMA SPLICE: The movie has already begun, still I want to see it.

CORRECTED: The movie has already begun; still I want to see it.

In some sentences, the presence of other commas necessitates the use of a stronger mark to indicate the main divisions. Semicolons are necessary for this purpose. Look at the second and third guidelines.

2. Use a semicolon to separate two closely related independent clauses joined by a coordinating conjunction if either of the clauses is long and contains other commas;

```
                     ┌──────────────── indep. cl. ────────────────────────────┐  conj. ┌─
Larry Sacul, a polite, courteous young man, was the best applicant ; but he
indep. cl.┌────────────────────────┐
was not given a definite offer.
```

```
                  ┌─────────────────────────────indep. cl.────────────────────────────┐
Julia Rosenberg's charming, intelligent, vivacious, and witty personality is a
┌──────────┐  conj. ┌─────────────indep. cl.──────────────┐
real asset ; and she knows how to make good use of it.
```

3. Use semicolons in a series between items that have internal punctuation.

Four people were in the room: Brad, a college student ; Charles, a high school teacher ; David, a bank teller ; and Frank, a football coach.

Three people attended the dinner party: Judy, my best friend ; Sally, a childhood friend ; and Lucille, an acquaintance from school.

The preceding guidelines cover the various uses of the semicolon. There are three more guidelines about the semicolon that point out when it should *not* be used.

4. A semicolon should *not* separate a single *dependent clause* (a group of words that contains a subject and verb but cannot stand alone) from a single independent clause.

WRONG: When I saw Ramon ; he waved to me.

CORRECTED: When I saw Ramon , he waved to me.

WRONG: Since the course is free ; Lori plans to take it.

CORRECTED: Since the course is free , Lori plans to take it.

5. A semicolon should never separate an introductory participial phrase (a *participial phrase* is a group of words with a verb form, usually ending in *ing*, functioning as an *adjective*—a word that describes a person, place, or thing) from the rest of the sentence.

WRONG: Wearing large name tags ; the Wrenskys greeted their guests.

CORRECTED: Wearing large name tags , the Wrenskys greeted their guests.

WRONG: Appearing very happy ; the couple left the church.

CORRECTED: Appearing very happy , the couple left the church.

6. A semicolon should not set off a conjunctive adverb (*accordingly,*
consequently, furthermore, hence, however, moreover, nevertheless, still,
therefore, and *yet*) that serves as an interrupter in a sentence. Commas
set off such an interrupter.

                           conj. adv.
WRONG: We are going ; however , to return the visit.

                           conj. adv.
CORRECTED: We are going , however , to return the visit.

                      conj. adv.
WRONG: Lucita ; nevertheless ; plans to enter the contest.

                      conj. adv.
CORRECTED: Lucita , nevertheless , plans to enter the contest.

Remember: You must have a subject and a verb on each side of the
conjunctive adverb before you can use a semicolon.

Now that you have completed your study of the procedures for
using the semicolon, you should be ready to try Exercise 1. If you still
feel that you are not ready, review the material.

Using Semicolons   *Exercise 1*

Test your understanding of semicolons by inserting all necessary
semicolons in the following sentences. Write C in the space provided
before each sentence that is correct and does not need additional
punctuation.

_____ 1. Myra did not vote for John; however, she intends to sup-
           port his platform.

_____ 2. Jeannette is very kind she even gives generously to chari-
           ties.

_____ 3. Dick appointed the following people: Betty, my best
           friend; Anna, the new class member and Sue, my sorority
           sister.

_____ 4. After the girls delivered the letter, they went to the movies.

_____ 5. Mac did not however attend the performance.

_____ 6. Pauline did not go to Europe however she did travel to New York.

_____ 7. Juan is my close friend; moreover, he is also my business partner.

_____ 8. The girls gave a beach party no boys were invited.

_____ 9. Consequently, no dues will be collected, at least not this year.

_____ 10. The message arrived too late the couple had left.

_____ 11. The beautiful, charming, intelligent, and somewhat mysterious lady said that she was from Denver; but I was not ready to believe her.

_____ 12. Driving her new sports car, Margarita felt proud and happy.

_____ 13. While Aaron was in Alaska, his parents bought a new home.

_____ 14. The fresh, fragrant, wet grass lay on the coarse, cracked, and stained sidewalk; and only I seemed to appreciate the beauty of it.

_____ 15. My guests for this weekend are Raul Martinez, a fireman; Nelda, his friend, who is a lawyer; Linda Elkins, a professor at Eastern Kentucky University; and Bill Simmons, an architect from Cleveland, Ohio.

1. C	6. Europe; however, she	11. C
2. kind: she	7. C	12. C
3. member; and	8. party; no	13. C
4. C	9. C	14. C
5. not, however, attend	10. late: the	15. C

USING COLONS

A mark of punctuation that often becomes the mark of anticipation or expectancy is the colon. Here are some guidelines for the uses of the colon.

1. Use a colon after an introductory remark that contains *these, this, the following, as follows*, or a number when a list follows.

Uncas gave <u>this</u> statement : I choose not to run.

<u>These</u> persons were enrolled : Mary Hopkins, Bob Jenkins, and Sam Appolos.

Mr. Chalone bought <u>the following</u> items : bread, cheese, sausage, and wine.

<u>Three</u> cities were cited : Boston, Detroit, and San Francisco.

Note: A complete statement must come before the colon. A colon should never separate the predicate (verb) from the predicate complement or direct object.

WRONG:	My favorite fruits are: apples, pears, and peaches.
CORRECTED:	My favorite fruits are as follows : apples, pears, and peaches.
OR:	My favorite fruits are apples, pears, and peaches.
WRONG:	We saw: Jake Whiteside, Paul Greathouse, and Troy Quanah.
CORRECTED:	We saw the following people : Jake Whiteside, Paul Greathouse, and Troy Quanah.
OR:	We saw Jake Whiteside, Paul Greathouse, and Troy Quanah.

2. Use a colon instead of a comma after an introductory remark before a long or a formal quotation (a significant statement, one that is important enough to be separated by more than a comma from the rest of the sentence).

One of President John F. Kennedy's statements has become a famous quotation. Kennedy said : "Ask not what your country can do for you, but what you can do for your country."

3. Use a colon to separate two independent clauses if the second independent clause explains or illustrates the first.

```
                        ———— indep. cl. ————————         ————————— indep. cl.
The solution to the school problem is simple : more teachers need to be

————————
employed.
```

4. Use the colon after the salutation in a business letter (Dear Sir :) and between the hour and minutes in time (5 : 30 P.M.).

Exercise 2 *Using Colons*
Stop at this point in your lesson and check your understanding of colons by examining these sentences. Insert all necessary colons or write C in the space provided before each sentence that is correct and does not need additional punctuation.

_____ 1. My speech will cover these issues: war, taxes, and crime.

_____ 2. We gathered at 5:30 P.M. on Friday.

_____ 3. The professor introduced his lecture with a serious question "What are you doing for your country?"

_____ 4. Mr. Svatek was more than a teacher; he was also a friend.

_____ 5. Please repeat these words *dog, cat, bird*, and *cow.*

_____ 6. Judy sold her diamond wedding ring she was desperate for money.

_____ 7. Tellman repeated his statement: "I am resigning my position."

_____ 8. Mr. Sachtleben gave invitations to Delores, Pete, and Max.

_____ 9. The Parallel Studies Department has three new directors Herman Stein, Emil Trotski, and May Wentworth.

_____ 10. Give the tape to Imogene, Dora, and Shane.

ANSWERS TO EXERCISE 2

1. C   6. ring: she
2. C   7. C
3. question: "What   8. C
4. teacher: he   9. directors: Herman
5. words: *dog*   10. C

A Review of Colons and Semicolons   *Exercise 3*

Follow the directions for each item. Be sure to use whatever punctuation is necessary. Refer to the usage guidelines for colons and semicolons as necessary.

1. Use a semicolon to separate two or more independent clauses when the coordinating conjunction is missing. These clauses should be similar in thought.

   _____

   _____

2. Use a semicolon and a conjunctive adverb to join two independent clauses when the coordinating conjunction is missing. These clauses should be similar in thought.

   _____

   _____

3. Use a colon before a quotation.

   _____

   _____

4. Use a semicolon in a series between items that have internal punctuation.

_____

_____

5. Use a colon before a statement.

_____

_____

6. Use a colon before a series of items or the names of persons.

_____

_____

7. Use a colon before a statement that explains a preceding statement.

_____

_____

8. Use *therefore* to join two independent clauses.

_____

_____

9. Use a colon after the salutation in a business letter.

_____

_____

10. Use a colon between the hour and minutes in time. Write a complete sentence.

_____

_____

Postassessment

1. Compose three sentences to illustrate three *different* uses of the semicolon.

  a._____

  _____

  _____

  _____

  b. _____

  _____

  _____

  _____

  c._____

  _____

  _____

2. Compose five sentences to illustrate five *different* uses of the colon.

a. _____

_____

_____

_____

b. _____

_____

_____

_____

c. _____

_____

_____

_____

d. _____

_____

_____

_____

e._____

_____

_____

_____

ANSWERS TO POSTASSESSMENT

Answers will vary, so your instructor will need to check them.

Study Unit 14□Commas

RATIONALE

Commas (,) act as signposts along the highway of written conversation and thoughts. By pointing out pauses, stresses, and changes of pitch, they allow readers to motor without confusion through a piece of writing. In other words, commas eliminate communication barriers between the writer and the reader. Therefore, they can improve communication.

OBJECTIVES

After completing Study Unit 14, you should be able to

1. use a comma to separate coordinate (equal) elements from each other
2. use a comma to separate certain introductory subordinate (less important) elements from the rest of the sentence
3. use commas to enclose words that interrupt the main thought
4. use commas to separate dates, addresses, titles after names, rows of figures, informal salutations, complimentary closings, and echoing questions
5. eliminate unnecessary commas
6. improve communication with your readers

Preassessment

Supply commas where they are needed in these sentences. If a sentence is correct, write C in the space provided.

_____ 1. I saw John in town but he did not see me.

_____ 2. Ms. Hernandez is a kind considerate lawyer.

_____ 3. Tracy ordered five pencils two tablets and nine folders.

_____ 4. No Mr. Pelsky has moved.

_____ 5. The children liked the animals but the animals did not like them.

_____ 6. Lloyd plans to visit his cousin in April and he hopes to find a job during his visit.

_____ 7. Alta wore a lovely scarlet dress.

_____ 8. Rosie is my cousin not my sister.

_____ 9. If you want to see the book ask Mr. Henry for a copy.

_____ 10. The ring belongs to the man who rode in my car.

_____ 11. Because the afternoon sun is too hot I plan to stay in my home.

_____ 12. You are my friend aren't you?

_____ 13. As you probably heard my new automobile arrived yesterday.

_____ 14. On the other hand the guests had a good time.

_____ 15. Dr. Samuel Jenkins Ph.D. will speak at the banquet.

_____ 16. You were in the room weren't you?

_____ 17. The students tired and disappointed left the building.

_____ 18. Susan lives at 5 Reese Drive Phoenix Arizona 83205.

_____ 19. The guests having left I cleaned the den.

_____ 20. Jerry who doesn't like parties plans to visit here in June.

ANSWERS TO PREASSESSMENT

1. town, but
2. kind, considerate
3. pencils, two tablets, and
4. No, Mr.
5. animals, but
6. April, and
7. C
8. cousin, not
9. book, ask
10. C
11. hot, I

12. friend, aren't
13. heard, my
14. hand, the
15. Jenkins, Ph.D., will
16. room, weren't
17. students, tired and disap-
    pointed, left
18. Drive, Pheonix, Arizona
19. left, I
20. Jerry, who ... parties,
    plans

Learning Activities

USING COMMAS

The best way to master commas is to learn when to use them.

1. Use a comma to separate two *independent clauses* (groups of words having a subject and verb and making complete sense) joined by a *coordinating conjunction* (*and, but, or, for, nor*, all of which join words, phrases, or clauses of equal rank).

```
                             coor.
  ┌────── indep. cl. ──────┐  conj.  ┌───── indep. cl. ─────┐
```
Peggy prepared the meat , and Ken baked the bread.

```
                         coor.
  ┌──── indep. cl. ────┐  conj.  ┌────── indep. cl. ──────┐
```
The door was open,   but nothing had been taken.

Caution: An independent clause must be on *each* side of the coordinating conjunction before a comma can be used.

2. Use a comma to separate the items of a series of words, phrases, or

short clauses from each other. (A *series* of words consists of three or more equal words; a *phrase* is a group of words *without* a subject or verb; and a *clause* is a group of words *with* a subject and verb.)

WORDS IN SERIES: Kate bought paper , pencils , and folders.

PHRASES IN SERIES: Margaret looked behind the dresser , in the closet , and under the couch.

CLAUSES IN SERIES: Elizabeth did her homework , Sandra wrote a letter , and Tammy watched a movie.

3. Use a comma to separate coordinate (equal) *adjectives* (words that describe persons, places, or things) from each other.

       adj.   adj.
Terry is a kind , sincere person.

Caution: Insert a comma between two adjectives only if they are equal. Use these two tests to determine whether adjectives are equal:

(a) Reverse their order in the sentence. If the sentence still makes good sense, insert the comma between the two adjectives.

Terry is a sincere, kind person.

(This sentence makes good sense.)
(b) Place the conjunction *and* between the adjectives. If the sentence makes good sense, use a comma between the two adjectives.

Terry is a kind and sincere person.

Here is an example of some adjectives that should not be separated by commas because they are not equal.

      adj. adj.
Jill wore a bright red shirt.

Commas are not necessary because the sentence would not make sense if the adjectives were in reverse order or if the conjunction *and* were to come between them.

WRONG: Jill wore a red bright shirt.

(*Bright* describes *red*: it tells how bright. Therefore, *bright* must come before *red*.)

WRONG: Jill wore a bright and red shirt.

(The sentence does not make good sense.)

4. Use a comma to separate contrasted words or phrases.

WORDS: Jackie is president , not secretary.

PHRASES: Sally was born in Detroit , not in New York.

5. Use a comma to set off *dependent clauses* (clauses that do not make complete sense) at the beginning of a sentence. (Some of the key words that indicate these dependent clauses are *after, as, because, if, since, when,* and *while*.)

```
 ┌──────────dep. cl.──────────┐  ┌──────────indep. cl.──────────┐
```
Since the weather is cold , we cannot have our picnic.

(*Since the weather is cold* explains *cannot have* in the independent clause.)

```
 ┌──────────dep. cl.──────────┐  ┌──── indep. cl. ────┐
```
Because the table is a valuable antique , I want to keep it.

(*Because the table is a valuable antique* explains *want* in the independent clause.)

Note: If the dependent clause comes at the end of the sentence, the comma is not necessary: I want to keep the table because it is a valuable antique.

6. Use commas to set off introductory words and phrases.

No , I have not voted.

Oh , you are Sally's brother.

First of all , you must define the problem more clearly.

7. Use commas to set off introductory phrases containing verbals. (A *verbal* is a verb form that functions as another part of speech: *-ed, -en,* and *-ing* forms used as adjectives; *-ing* forms used as nouns; *to* plus the verb used as an adjective, an adverb, or a noun.)

```
 ┌──── verbal used as adj. ────┐
```
Talking the whole time , Freda never noticed us.

```
┌────── verbal used as adv. ──────┐
```
To establish these criteria , we <u>must act</u> soon.

8. Use commas to set off (and indicate a pause before or after) prepositional phrases that should receive emphasis.

```
┌──prep. phrase──┐
```
With these words , I give you my solemn promise.

```
┌─prep. phrase─┐
```
For example , the population of this city has doubled in the last ten years.

9. Use commas to set off a series of introductory prepositional phrases.

```
┌prep. phrase┐ ┌── prep. phrase ──┐
```
At the end of this time period , we asked for a delay.

```
┌────── prep. phrase ──────┐ ┌── prep. phrase ──┐
```
Without the consent of his supporters , the politician withdrew from the race.

Note: If the phrases come at the end of the sentence, the comma is not necessary: *The politician withdrew from the race without the consent of his supporters.*

10. Place a comma after a long (more than one syllable) conjunctive adverb that connects two independent clauses.

```
┌──────────indep. cl.──────────┐  conj. adv.  ┌──────────indep. cl.─────────┐
```
My television is in the repair shop; therefore , I am going to the movies.

```
┌──────indep. cl.──────┐  conj. adv.  ┌──────── indep. cl. ────────┐
```
Professor Perez is ill; consequently , he cannot give this lecture.

Commas

Exercise 1

Supply commas where they are needed in these sentences. If a sentence is correct, write C in the space provided.

_____ 1. The trip provided many interesting experiences and it also made us aware of the beauty of America.

_____ 2. Mrs. Breedlove is an honest kind person.

_____ 3. Mr. Wolfe bought apples corn and peas.

_____ 4. Yes I have seen her at the office but I do not know her name.

_____ 5. The repairman needs to look on top of the roof down the chimney and under the house.

_____ 6. Oh Alberto offered me coffee cookies and cake.

_____ 7. The children watched television the women talked and the men played cards.

_____ 8. Fernando wore a light blue shirt.

_____ 9. As soon as I can afford an airplane I plan to take flying lessons.

_____ 10. Returning from work Rudolpho saw Tom not Mark.

_____ 11. Elsie is wise not conceited.

_____ 12. On the other hand we do not have time to call a meeting.

_____ 13. Before we moved to Dayton we lived in Flagstaff.

_____ 14. The wet fragrant grass lay in the street.

_____ 15. You can be my friend or you can be my enemy.

_____ 16. Reading his newspaper the man never looked up.

_____ 17. To secure good homes for these children this committee must act now.

_____ 18. For example the streets are either muddy or dusty during a good part of the year.

_____ 19. With the promise of additional support from his community the mayor signed the contract.

_____ 20. If you can give me an estimate I can give you an answer within one week.

ANSWERS TO EXERCISE 1

1. experiences, and
2. honest, kind
3. apples, corn, and
4. Yes, I . . . office, but
5. roof, down the chimney, and
6. Oh, Alberto . . . coffee, cookies, and
7. television, the women talked, and
8. C
9. airplane, I
10. work, Rudolpho saw Tom, not
11. wise, not
12. hand, we
13. Dayton, we
14. wet, fragrant
15. friend, or
16. newspaper, the
17. children, this
18. example, the
19. community, the
20. estimate, I

OTHER USES OF COMMAS

Now look at some additional uses of commas.

1. Use commas to set off *nonrestrictive* clauses (clauses that do not restrict, or affect, the main idea of the sentence). Note: Nonrestrictive clauses are always in one of two places: (1) after proper nouns, (2) after nouns that have been identified. (Articles—*a, an,* and *the*—do not identify.)

nonrest. cl.
⌐——after proper n.——⌐
Erica Love , who likes apple fritters , won a scholarship.

(*Who likes apple fritters* is not important to the main idea of the sentence: *Erica Love won a scholarship*. Therefore, this nonrestrictive clause is set off from the rest of the sentence by commas.)

nonrest. cl.
⌐————after proper n. ————⌐
Jeffrey Lewis , who is the worst gossip in town , plans to enroll in college.

(*Who is the worst gossip in town* does not affect the main idea of the sentence: *Jeffrey Lewis plans to enroll in college*. Consequently, the nonrestrictive clause is set off by commas.)

```
                    nonrest. cl.
               ┌──after identified n. ──┐
My feet , which are still cold , hurt.
```

(*Which are still cold* follows *feet*, which have been identified by *my*. The dependent clause does not affect the main idea of the sentence: *My feet hurt*.)

If a clause restricts (is important to) the main idea of the sentence, it is a *restrictive* clause. Restrictive clauses are so important to the meaning of a sentence that they are not set off by commas.

```
               ┌────────rest. cl.─────────┐
He is the man who gave me the watch.
```

(*Who gave me the watch* is important in identifying *man*.)

```
              ┌──────rest. cl.──────┐
Students who have an "A" average do not have to take the final.
```

(*Who have an "A" average* is important in identifying who is exempted.)
2. Use commas to set off nonrestrictive appositives. (*Appositives* rename the words that they follow.)

```
                    nonrest. appos.
               ┌──after proper n.──┐
Larry Chicasa , a very pleasant person , is the new scoutmaster.
```

(*A very pleasant person* renames the subject but is not important to the main idea—that Larry is the new scoutmaster.)

```
           ┌── nonrest. appos. after n. ──────┐
The hit , a powerful line drive into right field , won us the game.
```

(*A powerful line drive into right field* renames the subject but is not crucial to the main idea—that the hit won us the game.)

Here are some examples of *restrictive appositives* (words that rename the subjects they follow and are so important to the meaning of the sentence that they are not set off with commas).

rest.
appos.

Lillian met my cousin Sam.

(*Sam* names a definite cousin that Lillian met.)

rest. appos.

Rupert read the novel *Great Expectations*.

(*Great Expectations* tells what novel Rupert read.)

3. Use commas to set off other nonrestrictive words and phrases.

nonrest.
words

The little boy , rather shy and thin , sang his song.

(*Shy* and *thin* are an afterthought; consequently, they do not affect the main idea: *The little boy sang his song.*)

nonrest. phrase

Anita , dressed in casual clothes , listened to Marie Nicole's speech.

(*Dressed in casual clothes* is extra information and does not affect the meaning of the sentence.)

4. Use commas to set off absolute phrases from the rest of the sentence. An *absolute phrase* contains a noun or pronoun and a participle (a verb, usually ending in *ing*, that describes persons, places, or things) and has no grammatical relationship with the rest of the sentence.

abs. phrase

The customers having left , we closed the restaurant.

abs. phrase

The lady sold the mansion , her husband having died three years ago.

5. Use commas to set off such expressions as "she said" from a direct quotation.

"I want to retire ," *he* said.

Sue said , "I love my home."

Note: If the direct quotation is an exclamation or a question, do not use the comma plus the question mark or exclamation mark.

"What on earth are you doing here?" was all she could say.

6. Use commas to set off words in direct address.

Estelle , will you give me a pen?
What is your address , Lou?

7. Use commas to set off parenthetical expressions (interrupters).

The matter , however , is not simple.
The people , on the other hand , are not free.
Patty , as everyone knows , is an artist.

8. Use commas to separate items in dates and addresses.

On January 8 , 1975 , the case closed.
Twin Forks , Minnesota , gets extremely cold in the winter.
Marilyn's address is 500 Ridge Street , Belvedere , California 94920.

Note that there is no comma between the state and the zip code.

9. Use commas to set off titles after names.

Barbara Brunner , Ph.D. , was named president.
Gerald Sharp , M.D. , was elected secretary.

10. Use a comma after an informal salutation in a personal letter.

Dear Eduardo ,

11. Use a comma after the complimentary closing in personal and business letters.

Sincerely yours ,

12. Use a comma before an echoing question.

You *are* my friend , aren't you?
You plan to help me , don't you?

13. Use a comma to prevent misreading.

WRONG: When Jean moved Anna's apartment was not the same.
CORRECTED: When Jean moved , Anna's apartment was not the same.

WRONG: As the fire burned the children slept.
CORRECTED: As the fire burned , the children slept.

Now try Exercise 2.

Supply commas where they are needed in these sentences. If a sentence is correct, write C in the space provided.

_____ 1. Randa who hardly ever wears shoes is leaving school.

_____ 2. Fire fighters who go to college receive merit pay raises.

_____ 3. Jake spoke to my cousin Molly.

_____ 4. Carrie's home which smells dusty is for sale.

_____ 5. Mr. Peltier employs people who have college degrees.

_____ 6. Mrs. Cayuga however employs people without degrees.

_____ 7. Lawrence Wolverine Ph.D. is the new president isn't he?

_____ 8. Helen as you know is in Las Vegas.

_____ 9. She left on April 1 1975 at three o'clock.

_____ 10. Winifred's address is 799 Quail Lane Wanganui New Zealand.

_____ 11. Did you feed the goat Marilyn?

_____ 12. Whatever you do Scott please do not wreck this car.

_____ 13. The rain having stopped we went to sleep.

_____ 14. The little boy afraid and lonely sat on the empty bench.

_____ 15. Maynard saw Tom painting the family home.

_____ 16. Martha said "There isn't room for both of us."

_____ 17. I plan to leave tomorrow regardless of what anyone says.

_____ 18. Denver as I have remarked is a busy city.

_____ 19. She is the lady who gave me the book.

_____ 20. I visited my aunt Erna.

ANSWERS TO EXERCISE 2

1. Randa, who . . . shoes, is
2. C
3. C
4. home, which smells dusty, is
5. C
6. Cayuga, however, employs
7. Wolverine, Ph.D., is . . . president, isn't
8. Helen, as you know, is
9. April 1, 1975, at
10. 799 Quail Lane, Wanganui, New

11. goat, Marilyn?
12. do, Scott, please
13. stopped, we
14. boy, afraid and lonely, sat
15. C
16. said, "There
17. tomorrow, regardless
18. Denver, as I have remarked, is
19. C
20. C

Exercise 3 A Review of Commas

Supply commas where they are needed in these sentences. If a sentence is correct, write C in the space provided.

_____ 1. The wife spoke to her husband in a solemn tone and he responded with loud ridicule.

_____ 2. Lorraine is a clever witty politician.

_____ 3. Mike bought bolts nails and tacks.

_____ 4. No Peter is my brother.

_____ 5. Curtis did a dance sang a song and told a joke.

_____ 6. Gloria is in Elmira Martel is in Cleveland and Shirley is in Philadelphia.

_____ 7. Ethel's costume was a bright orange box.

_____ 8. If you have no objections we can go in my car.

_____ 9. Patricia is Jim's sister not cousin.

_____ 10. First give me your name and address.

_____ 11. Lucy who used to call me all the time lost her diamond ring.

_____ 12. Teachers who care about their students succeed.

_____ 13. Give the book to Alice, my wife.

_____ 14. Martin F. Altahms Ph.D. will be the speaker.

_____ 15. Frank as you might have expected lost his job.

_____ 16. Arlon left his home on December 6 1974

_____ 17. Beth's address is 1910 College Boulevard, Boise, Idaho 83725.

_____ 18. Did you see the train Mary?

_____ 19. The concert having ended we went home.

_____ 20. The clerk somewhat angry and tired dropped my change.

_____ 21. Clayton give me that watch!

_____ 22. Hilda said "Life is too much for me."

_____ 23. At the beginning of each semester Dr. Murata gives the students an outline of the course.

_____ 24. The examination is today isn't it?

_____ 25. Sam is the man who saved my life.

ANSWERS TO EXERCISE 3

1. tone, and
2. clever, witty
3. bolts, nails, and
4. No, Peter
5. dance, sang a song, and
6. Elmira, Martel is in Cleveland, and
7. C
8. objections, we
9. sister, not
10. First, give
11. Lucy, who . . . time, lost
12. C
13. C
14. Altahms, Ph.D., will
15. Frank, as . . . expected, lost
16. December 6, 1974.
17. C
18. train, Mary?
19. ended, we
20. clerk, somewhat . . . tired, dropped
21. Clayton, give
22. said, "Life
23. semester, Dr.
24. today, isn't
25. C

Postassessment

Supply commas where they are needed in these sentences. If a sentence is correct, write C in the space provided.

_____ 1. The guests had arrived for John's party but no one greeted them at the door.

_____ 2. John is usually a dependable thoughtful person.

_____ 3. The guests had brought cake cookies and punch.

_____ 4. Yes they were surprised.

_____ 5. They knocked on his door called his name and tapped on his window.

_____ 6. Bill drove to the nearest telephone Rose sat on the steps and Adolph walked across the street.

_____ 7. Willard admired Rose's sense of humor.

_____ 8. Because Willard liked Rose he commented about her laugh.

_____ 9. Adolph is Bill's brother not cousin.

_____ 10. Yes Bill has no cousins.

_____ 11. John who is my friend did not know that guests had arrived at his home.

_____ 12. Bill telephoned the neighbor who lived across the street.

_____ 13. I said that she helped not criticized him.

_____ 14. She is Martha H. Brunson Ph.D.

_____ 15. As you might have guessed John was not expecting guests that night.

_____ 16. Not expecting his guests until the following week John had driven to Hopkinsville Kentucky on December 2 1974.

_____ 17. You can't blame him can you?

_____ 18. The guests rather disappointed and puzzled went home.

_____ 19. The party having flopped they really had no other choice.

_____ 20. In spite of what happened they still like John.

ANSWERS TO POSTASSESSMENT

1. party, but
2. dependable, thoughtful
3. cake, cookies, and
4. Yes, they
5. door, called his name, and
6. telephone, Rose ... steps, and
7. C
8. Rose, he
9. brother, not
10. Yes, Bill
11. John, who is my friend, did
12. C
13. helped, not criticized, him.
14. Brunson, Ph.D.
15. guessed, John
16. week, John ... Hopkinsville, Kentucky, on December 2, 1974
17. him, can
18. guests, rather ... puzzled, went
19. flopped, they
20. happened, they

Study Unit 15 □ Other Punctuation and Capitalization

RATIONALE

Because this unit covers a wide range of punctuation and capitalization rules, you can become a more relaxed writer after completing it. A sound knowledge of proper punctuation and capitalization should erase many of the frustrations and problems usually associated with writing. With a knowledge of how to punctuate and capitalize correctly comes a self-confidence that allows concentration on content and style.

OBJECTIVES

After completing Study Unit 15, you should be able to use effectively
1. periods
2. question marks
3. exclamation points
4. quotation marks
5. hyphens
6. apostrophes
7. dashes
8. parentheses
9. brackets
10. italics
11. capitals

Preassessment

Supply all necessary punctuation and capitalization. If a sentence is correct, write C in the space provided.

_____ 1. Natchez, Mississippi, is a charming, historical town

_____ 2. Return the folder to me when you have a chance she said

_____ 3. I wonder if Nito will be at the meeting

_____ 4. Will you please send me a copy of *Economy in Living*

_____ 5. Hiro hiyamas brothers gave the party

_____ 6. NBC has four new programs

_____ 7. Chico asked When do you plan to leave

_____ 8. Fire he yelled.

_____ 9. "Many teachers use teaching aids audio-visual aids," he said.

_____ 10. Arthur is a self sufficient person.

_____ 11. At age twenty one, John Goldwater is co-author of a new book

_____ 12. Ms Wray has twenty four students

_____ 13. Charles watch is expensive.

_____ 14. Does your name have two ls

_____ 15. Martha told me all well, almost all of her secrets.

_____ 16. The title has two nouns the names of persons, places, or things

_____ 17. Ms. Nardi is reading The Great Gatsby

_____ 18. My street address has three 2s.

_____ 19. At home is a prepositional phrase.

_____ 20. Lori is a well mannered child.

1. town.
2. "Return . . . chance," she said.
3. meeting.
4. *Living*.
5. Hiyama's . . . party.
6. programs.
7. asked, "When . . . leave?"
8. "Fire!" he yelled.
9. [audio-visual aids],"
10. self-sufficient
11. twenty-one . . . book.
12. Ms. Wray . . . twenty-four students.
13. Charles's (or Charles')
14. l's?
15. all—well, almost all—
16. (the names . . . things).
17. The Great Gatsby.
18. 2's.
19. At home
20. well-mannered

Learning Activities

USING PERIODS

The uses of periods (.) are simple.

1. Use a period after a sentence that makes a statement.

Miami is an interesting city .

My name is Melody .

2. Use a period after a sentence that makes a demand.

Give me the book .

Check my oil and tires .

3. Use a period after indirect questions.

I wonder if Steve ever arrived in Atlanta .

He asked whether Jill had resigned .

4. Use a period after requests phrased politely as questions.

Will you please send me a copy of your book .
Will you kindly send me a prompt reply .

5. Use a period after certain abbreviations.

Mr . Mrs . Ms . Dr . M .D . Ph .D .

These abbreviations are always acceptable in formal writing. However, in formal writing do not use abbreviations for chemical elements (for example, H_2O for water), contractions (for example, I've, you're, won't), or nicknames (for example, Liz, Walt). Also note that some organizations are so well known by their abbreviations that they are not followed by periods.

CBS (Columbia Broadcasting Service)
UNESCO (United Nations Educational, Scientific, and Cultural Organization)
WAVES (Women Accepted for Volunteer Emergency Service)

USING QUESTION MARKS

Question marks (?) have one main function: They follow a direct question.

"Why did you do that ?" he questioned.
Why is this happening to me ?

Caution: Do not use question marks after indirect questions.

He wanted to know if he could use my notes.
Jo asked me where I had bought my watch.

USING EXCLAMATION POINTS

Exclamation points (!) follow expressions showing very strong feeling.

"Help me !" the child cried.
What an incredible sight !

USING QUOTATION MARKS

1. Place quotation marks before and after the exact words of a speaker or writer.

Samuel Chang said, " I plan to attend the meeting. "

" No, " replied Freda, " my parents are in Florida. "

" You can come back tomorrow, " she said.

Note: Do not set off with quotation marks an *indirect quotation* (when the speaker's meaning is repeated but not the exact words).

Bernadine said that her art project is a secret.

Perry warned customers about parking in front of Mr. Chaney's bakery.

2. Use quotation marks to enclose the names of television shows, short poems, essays, short stories, and chapters from books.

Robert Browning wrote "My Last Duchess."

Felipe Reyes' "The Mexican-American in Texas" won first prize in the essay contest.

Leo Mendelwitz's editorial "Save the City" will appear in the New Braunfels *News*.

3. Use quotation marks sparingly to emphasize sarcasm, irony, or humor. Avoid overuse of this technique; if the irony or humor is obvious, there is usually no need to highlight it with quotation marks.

Thieves no longer steal; they "liberate" a store's stock.

The "furnished" apartment contained a bed, a table, a stool, and a bare light bulb.

Periods, Question Marks, Exclamation Points, and Quotation Marks   *Exercise 1*

Supply all necessary punctuation. If a sentence is correct, write C in the space provided.

_____ 1. Will you please give me a copy of the report.

_____ 2. I wonder if Sam is in Nebraska

—— 3. Take out the trash

—— 4. The geraniums will bloom in two months

—— 5. Leroy L. Jones, Ph D, was elected president

—— 6. Mr. and Ms Chingachgook will be at the banquet

—— 7. Carmine has joined the WAVES

—— 8. CBS has scheduled several new programs for the fall.

—— 9. Margaret asked, "When will you be in New York"

—— 10. No she yelled

—— 11. Freda asked, "Is your mother home"

—— 12. "Stop where you are Karen yelled.

—— 13. Come to see me

—— 14. The wild flowers in the Southwest are beautiful in the spring

—— 15. I wonder if Bob will arrive on time

ANSWERS TO EXERCISE 1

1. C
2. Nebraska.
3. trash.
4. months.
5. Ph.D., . . . president.
6. Ms. Chingachgook . . . banquet.
7. WAVES.
8. C

9. York?"
10. "No!" she yelled.
11. home?"
12. are!"
13. me.
14. spring.
15. time.

USING HYPHENS

1. Use a hyphen to divide a word at a syllable at the end of a line. (If you are in doubt about the syllable division, consult a standard dictionary.)

an - tique

be - tween

con - vene

2. Use a hyphen to join two or more words used as an adjective before a noun when one of the words is a noun.

a second - grade class

three - wheel car

twenty - year contract

3. Use a hyphen with words that have the prefix *self*.

self - centered

self - pity

self - sufficient

Here are some examples of other hyphenated words:

daughter-in-law   non-Caucasian
deaf-mute   time-lag
ex-president   up-to-the-minute
give-and-take   well-known
ill-fated   well-mannered

If you are not sure whether a specific word has a hyphen, consult a dictionary.

4. Use a hyphen to write the compound words in the numbers from twenty-one to ninety-nine. (Numbers over a hundred are usually written as figures—136, for example.)

twenty - six

thirty - one

forty - four

5. Use a hyphen to write fractions.

two - fifths

three - eighths

seven - ninths

USING APOSTROPHES

1. Use an apostrophe and an *s* after *singular nouns* (nouns denoting one object) to show possession.

boy	—	boy's shirt
child	—	child's toy
girl	—	girl's birthday party
man	—	man's poems
sister-in-law	—	sister-in-law's gift

Exception: If a singular noun ends in an *s* or a *z* sound, you may add only the apostrophe to form the possessive.

Bess	—	Bess' apartment (or Bess's)
Keats	—	Keats' poems (or Keats's)

2. Use an apostrophe after all *plural nouns* (nouns denoting more than one object) that end in *s* to show possession.

boys	—	boys' locker room
girls	—	girls' choir

3. Use an apostrophe and an *s* after all possessive plural nouns that do not end in *s*.

children	—	children's toys
men	—	men's cars
sisters-in-law	—	sisters-in-law's gifts
women	—	women's lecture series

4. Use an apostrophe in contractions. Do remember that contractions normally are not acceptable in formal writing.

are not	—	aren't
will not	—	won't

5. Use an apostrophe to indicate the plurals of letters, numbers, and words referred to as words.

Mississippi has four *i*'s.

The students filed in by two's and three's.

Jack's sentences are filled with *and*'s.

USING DASHES

1. Use dashes to show abrupt change in thought in a sentence.

Tom paid all — well, almost all — of his bill.

Be in my office this afternoon — and no later than three o'clock.

2. Use dashes before and after an appositive that is internally punctuated. (An *appositive* is a noun and its modifiers appearing after another noun to explain or identify it.)

All three major networks — ABC, CBS, and NBC — will carry the address.

All three branches — executive, judicial, and legislative — are powerful.

USING PARENTHESES

1. Use parentheses to enclose explanatory information.

Some other verbals (gerunds, infinitives, and participles) are in this sentence.

We sent a check for fifty dollars ($50.00).

2. Use parentheses to enclose numbers in lists.

Mike Zack analyzes four emotions in this discussion: (1) hate, (2) love, (3) joy, and (4) grief.

USING BRACKETS

Use brackets ([,]) to insert an explanation in a quotation.

"When she [Margaret Mead] approached the platform, the audience became serious," wrote the reviewer.

Exercise 2 **Hyphens, Apostrophes, Dashes, Parentheses, and Brackets**
Supply all necessary punctuation. If a sentence is correct, write C in
the space provided.

_____ 1. Monica received another three year contract.

_____ 2. Ira is not a self centered person.

_____ 3. Mabels ten speed bicycle is a beauty.

_____ 4. The minister spoke about self pity.

_____ 5. Ms. Caddoan buys only well known brands.

_____ 6. Jack appreciates his mother in laws kindness.

_____ 7. Two fifths of the students are absent.

_____ 8. The girls baseball team won the trophy.

_____ 9. Jess wife is from the East.

_____ 10. The word *flopped* has two *p*s.

_____ 11. This sentence has too many *but*s.

_____ 12. The dogs ate all well, almost all of their food.

_____ 13. All three candidates Kubala, Talley, and Dorsonia spoke to
the group.

_____ 14. Adjectives (words that describe nouns and pronouns) are
necessary in descriptive writing.

_____ 15. "When he Nixon gave his resignation speech, some Americans cheered," she reported.

ANSWERS TO EXERCISE 2

1. three-year
2. self-centered
3. Mabel's ten-speed
4. self-pity.
5. well-known
6. mother-in-law's
7. Two-fifths
8. girls'
9. Jess's (or Jess')
10. *p*'s.
11. *but*'s.
12. all—well, almost all—of
13. candidates—Kubala, Talley, and Dorsonia—spoke
14. C
15. [Nixon]

USING ITALICS

In handwriting and in typewriting, italics are indicated by underlining. In print, of course, they are indicated by a special typeface: *italic*.

1. Use italics for the titles of books, magazines, newspapers, long plays, long poems, films, ships, airplanes, and trains.

Oliver Twist

Home and Garden

the Cleveland *Plain Dealer* (The full name of many newspapers, such as the *New York Times*, includes the name of the city. However, since many newspaper names do not include the city names, it is often best, for consistency, to use italics for only the shortened name: the Atlanta *Journal*, the New York *Times*. In a sentence, the word *the* in a newspaper name should not be italicized. Unless it is the first word of the sentence, it should not be capitalized, either.)

The Glass Menagerie

Paradise Lost

Queen Mary

Spirit of '76

Orient Express

2. Use italics to refer to a word, phrase, letter, or number.

The word *parallel* has three *l*'s.

In the end is a prepositional phrase.

Mary's street address has no *5*'s.

3. Use italics to indicate a foreign word or phrase not commonly used in English.

Mr. and Mrs. Ronald Struther gave a little *soirée musicale* last week.

They serve a delicious *sopa de ajo* on Wednesday nights.

4. Use italics to give a number, word, or phrase special emphasis.

The examination will be given to *all* students.

Ms. Symes is definitely *not* interviewing more applicants at the present time.

USING CAPITALS
1. Capitalize the first word of a sentence.
2. Capitalize the first word of a conventional line of poetry.
3. Capitalize words referring to the Deity: God, Lord, Our Father.
4. Capitalize the word *I*.
5. Capitalize the first word in a title. Capitalize all other words in a title except articles (*a, an*, and *the*), short prepositions, and short conjunctions, unless they are the first word in the title or the first word after a colon.

A Tale of Two Cities

Brief Lives: A Biographical Companion to the Arts

6. Capitalize proper nouns. (*Proper nouns* are the names of particular persons, streets, buildings, colleges, organizations, sections of the country, rivers, etc.)

Larry Smith is in New Hampshire.

The accident occurred on Main Street.

Raphael has never been on top of the Empire State Building.

Penn Valley Community College is in Kansas City, Missouri.

Norkia Yorimitsu is from the East.

The students walked along the Mississippi River.

Exercise 3 *Italics and Capitals*

Supply all necessary punctuation and capitalization. (Remember to use underlines to indicate italics.) If the sentence is correct, write C in the space provided.

_____ 1. Janet subscribes to the New York Times.

_____ 2. Carl enjoys reading Newsweek.

_____ 3. Mark Twain's Huckleberry Finn now has a movie version.

_____ 4. Fighting in the Clouds for France is a novel written by Fiske.

_____ 5. Sue's favorite novel is Pickwick Papers.

_____ 6. Oscar refers to his mother as Mutter.

_____ 7. He didn't treat just his friends kindly; he treated everyone kindly.

_____ 8. These knitters, or tricoteuses, served as the model for Madame Defarge in Dickens's A Tale of Two Cities.

_____ 9. Sam attended harvard law school.

_____ 10. Richard Nixon is a republican.

_____ 11. The rio grande river is between Texas and Mexico.

_____ 12. We went to the top of the gulf oil building.

_____ 13. Carolyn lives on pecan street.

_____ 14. Marilyn wants to live in the west.

_____ 15. I know larry adkins.

ANSWERS TO EXERCISE 3
1. the New York _Times_
2. _Newsweek_
3. _Huckleberry Finn_
4. _Fighting in the Clouds for France_
5. _Pickwick Papers_

6. *Mutter* (a German word)

7. *everyone* (for special emphasis)

8. *tricoteuses, A Tale of Two Cities.*

9. Harvard Law School

10. Republican

11. Rio Grande River

12. Gulf Oil Building

13. Pecan Street

14. West

15. Larry Adkins

Exercise 4   *A Review of Punctuation*

Supply all necessary punctuation and capitalization, using underlines to indicate italics. If a sentence is correct, write C in the space provided.

_____ 1. Billy J. Wu is the ex president

_____ 2. Thackeray wrote The Newcomes

_____ 3. call me in the morning

_____ 4. I wonder if Salvador ever moved

_____ 5. Will you please mow my grass this week

_____ 6. Tony Jiles, ph d, is the new faculty member

_____ 7. NBC is Larry's favorite network.

_____ 8. "Did you read your assignment patty asked.

_____ 9. Ritas new novel is very interesting.

_____ 10. Twenty five people are in that class.

_____ 11. Mr. Chimakuan is Margarets father in law.

_____ 12. Sylvia is my best well, almost best friend.

_____ 13. In the beginning is a prepositional phrase.

_____ 14. The word committee has two ms, two ts, and two es.

_____ 15. Robert Burns is a well known Scottish poet.

_____ 16. Ouch she yelled.

_____ 17. Fire he screamed.

_____ 18. Eustachio asked me if he could use my car

_____ 19. Joel was born in the north.

_____ 20. The word kind is an adjective adjectives describe nouns and pronouns.

ANSWERS TO EXERCISE 4

1. ex-president.
2. *The Newcomes*.
3. Call . . . morning.
4. moved.
5. week.
6. Ph.D., . . . member.
7. C
8. assignment?" Patty asked.
9. Rita's
10. Twenty-five
11. Margaret's father-in-law.
12. best—well, almost best— friend.
13. *In the beginning*
14. *committee* has two *m*'s, two *t*'s, and two *e*'s.
15. well-known
16. "Ouch!" she yelled.
17. "Fire!" he screamed.
18. car.
19. North.
20. *kind* . . . adjective (adjectives describe nouns and pronouns).

Postassessment

Supply all necessary punctuation and capitalization, using underlines to indicate italics. If a sentence is correct, write C in the space provided.

_____ 1. Robert Redford is a well known actor.

_____ 2. F. Scott Fitzgerald wrote the novel Tender Is the Night

_____ 3. Send me a copy of that letter

_____ 4. I wonder if Helen is at home

_____ 5. Will you please call me as soon as possible

_____ 6. Wilson Schor, M D, will be the speaker

_____ 7. ABC has an experienced news team.

_____ 8. Patricia asked Has the mail arrived

_____ 9. James poem won first prize.

_____ 10. Forty five people attended the party

_____ 11. Mrs Liveman loves her son in law

_____ 12. Alfred spoke to all well almost all of his former teachers

_____ 13. "A person who believes in it capital punishment has to defend his position to many people," she said.

_____ 14. The word personnel has two ns.

_____ 15. Alex Haley wrote _Roots_.

_____ 16. Help the child screamed

_____ 17. Tales of the Uncanny and Supernatural is Joe's most prized book.

_____ 18. Norman asked me if he could work at the store.

_____ 19. We crossed the mississippi river.

_____ 20. The sentence has two adverbs words that explain verbs, adjectives, or other adverbs.

ANSWERS TO POSTASSESSMENT

1. well-known
2. *Tender Is the Night.*
3. letter.
4. home.
5. possible.
6. M.D., . . . speaker.
7. C
8. asked, "Has . . . arrived?"
9. James's . . . prize. (or James')
10. Forty-five . . . party.
11. Mrs. . . . son-in-law.
12. all—well, almost all—of . . . teachers.
13. [capital punishment]
14. *personnel* has two *n*'s.
15. C
16. "Help!" the child screamed.
17. *Tales of the Uncanny and Supernatural* . . . most-prized
18. C
19. Mississippi River.
20. (words that . . . adverbs).

Study Unit 16□Plurals and Possessives

RATIONALE

Perhaps you sometimes wonder whether to write *passers-by* or *passer-bys*, *deer* or *deers, potatoes* or *potatos*. As you work through this unit on plurals and possessives, you will learn some simple aids that will solve most of your problems with troublemakers like these.

OBJECTIVES

After completing Study Unit 16, you should be able to construct nouns in these forms:

1. singular
2. singular possessive
3. plural
4. plural possessive

Preassessment

Complete this chart by giving the singular possessive, plural, and plural possessive of each of the following singular nouns. The first noun is done for you as an example.

	Singular	Singular Possessive	Plural	Plural Possessive
1.	American	American's	Americans	Americans'
2.	author	_____	_____	_____
3.	bandit	_____	_____	_____
4.	Charles	_____	_____	_____

	Singular	Singular Possessive	Plural	Plural Possessive
5.	class	_____	_____	_____
6.	deer	_____	_____	_____
7.	fish	_____	_____	_____
8.	fly	_____	_____	_____
9.	fox	_____	_____	_____
10.	ghost	_____	_____	_____
11.	Keats	_____	_____	_____
12.	Methodist	_____	_____	_____
13.	monkey	_____	_____	_____
14.	ox	_____	_____	_____
15.	passenger	_____	_____	_____
16.	passer-by	_____	_____	_____
17.	policeman	_____	_____	_____
18.	potato	_____	_____	_____
19.	sheep	_____	_____	_____
20.	woman	_____	_____	_____

ANSWERS TO PREASSESSMENT

	Singular	Singular Possessive	Plural	Plural Possessive
1.	American	American's	Americans	Americans'
2.	author	author's	authors	authors'
3.	bandit	bandit's	bandits	bandits'
4.	Charles	Charles's (or Charles')	Charleses (a family)	Charleses'

Singular	Singular Possessive	Plural	Plural Possessive
5. class	class's	classes	classes'
6. deer	deer's	deer	deer's
7. fish	fish's	fish (or fishes)	fishes' (or fish's)
8. fly	fly's	flies	flies'
9. fox	fox's	foxes	foxes'
10. ghost	ghost's	ghosts	ghosts'
11. Keats	Keats's (or Keats')	Keatses	Keatses'
12. Methodist	Methodist's	Methodists	Methodists'
13. monkey	monkey's	monkeys	monkeys'
14. ox	ox's	oxen	oxen's
15. passenger	passenger's	passengers	passengers'
16. passer-by	passer-by's	passers-by	passers-by's
17. policeman	policeman's	policemen	policemen's
18. potato	potato's	potatoes	potatoes'
19. sheep	sheep's	sheep	sheep's
20. woman	woman's	women	women's

Learning Activities

PLURALS

If you have had difficulty with the singulars and plurals of nouns (the names of persons, places, or things), you might ask yourself what these terms mean. If a noun is *singular*, it names only one person, one place, or one thing.

Only <u>Bill</u> could jump that high.

One <u>person</u> responded.

One <u>city</u> was particularly hard hit.

A *plural* noun indicates two or more persons, places, or things.

Twenty <u>men</u> attended.

Many <u>people</u> voted twice.

Several states have agreed to participate.

The twelve missing books must be accounted for.

Study the following guidelines and examples very carefully.

1. Most nouns are made plural by adding *s*.

cat — cats
dog — dogs

2. Nouns ending in *sh, ch, s,* or *x* are made plural by adding *es*.

bush — bushes
church — churches
class — classes
box — boxes

An odd exception to this rule is animal names, which may be the same in the singular and the plural. Fishermen are likely to say they caught several fish (not fishes); hunters might note that the woods are full of fox (not foxes). Still, you would not be incorrect if you used *fishes* or *foxes*.

3. Nouns ending in *y* preceded by a *vowel (a, e, i, o, u,* and sometimes *w* and *y*) are made plural by adding *s*.

monkey — monkeys
key — keys

4. Nouns ending in *y* preceded by a *consonant* (any letter not a vowel) are made plural by changing the *y* to *i* and adding *es*.

baby — babies
lady — ladies

5. Many nouns ending in *f* or *fe* are made plural by changing *f* or *fe* to *ves*.

knife — knives
scarf — scarves

Before reading any additional suggestions, stop and check yourself by writing the plurals of these words.

1. ax _____

2. birch _____

3. box _____

4. cherry _____

5. cow _____

6. donkey _____

7. life _____

8. summary _____

9. turkey _____

10. wife _____

ANSWERS TO EXERCISE 1

1. axes		6. donkeys
2. birches		7. lives
3. boxes		8. summaries
4. cherries		9. turkeys
5. cows		10. wives

If you did at least nine of the ten words correctly, you are ready for the following set of suggestions; otherwise, review the previous pages.

MORE RULES ABOUT FORMING PLURALS

1. Nouns ending in *o* preceded by a vowel are made plural by adding *s*.

rodeo — rodeos

radio — radios

2. Some nouns ending in *o* preceded by a consonant become plural by adding *es*.

potato — potatoes

tomato — tomatoes

3. Many two-word and three-word compound nouns are made plural by adding *s* to the more important noun.

daughter-in-law — daughters-in-law

passer-by — passers-by

4. Certain nouns change the vowel or add *en*.

foot — feet

ox — oxen

5. A few nouns are the same in both singular and plural.

deer — deer

sheep — sheep

6. Some nouns have no singular form.

pants — pants

scissors — scissors

7. Letters used as letters (as in "the letter *b*"), figures used as figures, signs, or words used as words (as in "the word *orange*") are made plural by adding an apostrophe plus *s*.

m — two *m*'s in this word

or — three *or*'s in this sentence

Before trying Exercise 2, you may wish to review the principles that you have just read.

More Plurals   *Exercise 2*

Form the plurals of these words.

1. bear _____   2. calf _____

3. child _____   9. horse _____

4. daughter-in-law   10. radio _____

_____   11. sheep _____

5. farmer _____   12. tax _____

6. fish _____   13. tomato _____

7. fly _____   14. view _____

8. goose _____   15. woman _____

ANSWERS TO EXERCISE 2

1. bears   6. fish or fishes   11. sheep
2. calves   7. flies   12. taxes
3. children   8. geese   13. tomatoes
4. daughters-in-law   9. horses   14. views
5. farmers   10. radios   15. women

POSSESSIVES

As you recall, a singular noun names only one person, place, or thing; a plural noun names two or more persons, places, or things. To write the possessives of singular and plural nouns, you need to learn two additional terms: (1) *singular possessive*, which means that only one person owns something, and (2) *plural possessive*, which means that two or more persons own something.

SINGULAR POSSESSIVE: Bill's car, the boy's shirt, Mother's letter

PLURAL POSSESSIVE: two students' desks, three girls' dresses, children's toys

Notice that the possessive form is shown in these examples by the apostrophe (') and the letter *s*. In this learning activity, you will be investigating the correct placement of the apostrophe and *s* to show possession. But you should be aware that another way to show owner-ship—especially ownership by inanimate objects that cannot, of course, literally own anything—is to use a prepositional phrase.

POSSESSIVE FORM:	the book's cover
PREPOSITIONAL PHRASE:	the cover of the book
POSSESSIVE FORM:	the country's people
PREPOSITIONAL PHRASE:	the people of the country.

Now that you have mastered these ideas, you are ready to learn some additional aids that will help you in writing possessive nouns.

1. The possessive of singular nouns is formed by adding an apostrophe plus *s*.

boy	—	boy's timidity
Mary	—	Mary's speech
mother-in-law	—	mother-in-law's advice

Exception: A singular noun that ends in an *s* or a *z* sound can be made possessive with the addition of an apostrophe only.

Bess	—	Bess' dance class (or Bess's)
Keats	—	Keats' poems (or Keats's)

The sound of the possessive noun can be your guide. You might naturally say what sounds like "Keatses poems." If so, you could use the apostrophe-plus-*s* form: Keats's. But you probably would not say "Euripideses plays," so here the form without the *s* might be better: Euripides' plays. The *s* at the end of the word suggests the pronunciation of an extra syllable.

2. The possessive of plural nouns ending in *s* is formed by adding only an apostrophe.

dentists	—	dentists' implements
students	—	students' essays

3. The possessive of plural nouns that do not end in *s* is formed by adding an apostrophe and *s*.

deer	—	deer's
men	—	men's
sisters-in-law	—	sisters-in-law's

4. When two or more persons own something together, you can show possession by adding an apostrophe and *s* to the last name.

the experience had by Sam and Joe — Sam and Joe's experience

the store run by Sue and Jane — Sue and Jane's store

5. Individual possession by two or more persons is shown by the adding of an apostrophe and an *s* to each name.

reports Bill makes and reports Ann makes — Bill's and Ann's reports

ideas Jean has and ideas Mary has — Jean's and Mary's ideas

Exercise 3 *Possessives and Plurals*

As a review of possessives, fill in the following chart to show the singular, singular possessive, plural, and plural possessive forms for each of the following nouns. Use the first completed example as your guide.

	Singular	Singular Possessive	Plural	Plural Possessive
1.	baby	baby's	babies	babies'
2.	buffalo			
3.	child			
4.	class			
5.	donkey			
6.	man			
7.	ox			
8.	secretary			
9.	sheep			
10.	speaker			
11.	turkey			
12.	wife			

	Singular	Singular Possessive	Plural	Plural Possessive
13.	witch	_____	_____	_____
14.	woman	_____	_____	_____
15.	Yankee	_____	_____	_____

ANSWERS TO EXERCISE 3

	Singular	Singular Possessive	Plural	Plural Possessive
1.	baby	baby's	babies	babies'
2.	buffalo	buffalo's	buffaloes	buffaloes'
3.	child	child's	children	children's
4.	class	class's	classes	classes'
5.	donkey	donkey's	donkeys	donkeys'
6.	man	man's	men	men's
7.	ox	ox's	oxen	oxen's
8.	secretary	secretary's	secretaries	secretaries'
9.	sheep	sheep's	sheep	sheep's
10.	speaker	speaker's	speakers	speakers'
11.	turkey	turkey's	turkeys	turkeys'
12.	wife	wife's	wives	wives'
13.	witch	witch's	witches	witches'
14.	woman	woman's	women	women's
15.	Yankee	Yankee's	Yankees	Yankees'

Punctuating Possessives   *Exercise 4*
Provide apostrophes where they are needed in the following sentences.

1. Katy Bull enjoys her mothers visits.
2. Roland played in the mens baseball tournament.
3. Leon listened to the ladies comments.
4. One monkeys expression was comical.
5. The sheeps wool was long.
6. My mother-in-laws meal was delicious.
7. The two fathers-in-laws conversation was serious.
8. Ashley studied the English teachers notations.

9. The two girls hands were warm.
10. The babys dress was too large.
11. The childs face was clean.
12. The judges selected my two friends drawings.
13. One farmers pond was beautiful.
14. The flys wings were strong.
15. The womans clothes dryer was broken.

ANSWERS TO EXERCISE 4

1. mother's	6. mother-in-law's	11. child's
2. men's	7. fathers-in-law's	12. friends'
3. ladies'	8. teacher's	13. farmer's
4. monkey's	9. girls'	14. fly's
5. sheep's	10. baby's	15. woman's

Exercise 5 *Possibly Puzzling Plurals and Possessives*

Solve the crossword puzzle by applying the rules you have learned concerning plurals and possessives. Note: Apostrophes and hyphens take a square of their own.

ACROSS

4. Plural of *mother-in-law*
6. Singular of *Huns*
7. Plural of *mouse*
8. Singular of *towns*
10. Plural of *goose*
11. Singular possessive of *classes*
14. Jack___ (show possession)
15. Plural of *lady*
17. Plural of *hand*
18. Form of *Mary* in the phrase *Jack and Mary house* when the phrase is rewritten to show that Jack and Mary own the house together
19. Plural of *ox*
21. Plural of *foot*
22. Singular of *sheep*

DOWN

1. Singular of *mosquitoes*
2. Plural of *witch*
3. Singular of *ends*
4. Plural of *mountain*
5. Plural possessive of *woman*
9. Plural possessive of *wife's*
10. Singular possessive of *girls*
12. Singular possessive of *son*
13. Plural of *potato*
16. Plural possessive of *donkey*
17. Plural of *horse*
20. Singular of *news*

ANSWERS TO EXERCISE 5

If you had at least twenty-three correct answers, continue to the postassessment. If you had difficulty, review this unit and consult with your instructor.

Postassessment

Complete this chart by showing the singular, singular possessive, plural, and plural possessive form for each of the following nouns.

	Singular	Singular Possessive	Plural	Plural Possessive
1.	author			
2.	brute			
3.	buffalo			
4.	choir			
5.	deer			
6.	doctor			
7.	donkey			
8.	European			
9.	fairy			
10.	giraffe			
11.	goat			
12.	lady			
13.	kitten			
14.	mosquito			
15.	wolf			

Supply punctuation where it is needed in the following sentences.

16. The one donkeys stable was small.

17. The class comments were on record.

18. The three boys assignment was difficult.

19. Mens views are different.

20. The two mothers-in-laws gifts arrived.

21. The speakers comment went unnoticed.

22. The babys toys were in his room.

23. The ladies watches were from Paris.

24. The mens faces were red.

25. The salesmans voice was loud.

ANSWERS TO POSTASSESSMENT

	Singular	Singular Possessive	Plural	Plural Possessive
1.	author	author's	authors	authors'
2.	brute	brute's	brutes	brutes'
3.	buffalo	buffalo's	buffaloes	buffaloes'
4.	choir	choir's	choirs	choirs'
5.	deer	deer's	deer	deer's
6.	doctor	doctor's	doctors	doctors'
7.	donkey	donkey's	donkeys	donkeys'
8.	European	European's	Europeans	Europeans'
9.	fairy	fairy's	fairies	fairies'
10.	giraffe	giraffe's	giraffes	giraffes'
11.	goat	goat's	goats	goats'
12.	lady	lady's	ladies	ladies'
13.	kitten	kitten's	kittens	kittens'
14.	mosquito	mosquito's	mosquitoes	mosquitoes'
15.	wolf	wolf's	wolves	wolves'

16. donkey's
17. class's
18. boys'
19. men's
20. mothers-in-law's

21. speaker's
22. baby's
23. ladies'
24. men's
25. salesman's

Study Unit 17 □ Spelling Guidelines

RATIONALE

The most frequent error in writing—and the one most likely to convey an impression of carelessness or laziness on the writer's part—is incorrect spelling. You should strive to become a proficient speller in order to begin in a very basic way to communicate effectively with your readers. The suggestions and guidelines in this unit should help you spell correctly and communicate effectively.

OBJECTIVES

After completing Study Unit 17, you should be able to
1. Add prefixes and suffixes correctly
2. double, omit, and retain various consonants and vowels
3. determine whether to use *ie* or *ei*
4. spell all of the words in the list at the end of the unit

Preassessment

Examine each line of words. If one of the words is spelled incorrectly, write its letter in the space provided. If all of the words are spelled correctly, place a check mark (✓) in the space.

——— 1. a. achieve   b. believe   c. deceive   d. releave

——— 2. a. buried   b. occured   c. varieties   d. vegetables

——— 3. a. controled   b. equipped   c. occurrence   d. swimming

——— 4. a. concurred   b. dining   c. omiting   d. stopped

——— 5. a. across   b. conquer   c. loseing   d. seized

_____ 6. a. alleys   b. historys   c. preference   d. reference

_____ 7. a. flies   b. studying   c. turkies   d. valleys

_____ 8. a. brief   b. chief   c. vetoes   d. watchfull

_____ 9. a. boyish   b. effective   c. quizz   d. solo

_____ 10. a. arrival   b. lovable   c. retiring   d. writeing

_____ 11. a. foreign   b. gost   d. perceive   c. shield

_____ 12. a. describing   b. servicable   c. spicy   d. trying

_____ 13. a. inuendoes   b. reprieve   c. weigh   d. yield

_____ 14. a. bareness   b. icy   c. ninty   d. referred

_____ 15. a. acquire   b. proving   c. rekonize   d. strive

_____ 16. a. fortunately   b. interfere   c. parallel   d. reciept

_____ 17. a. especially   b. paid   c. reguard   d. undoubtedly

_____ 18. a. happiest   b. helpfull   c. panicky   d. villain

_____ 19. a. desirable   b. courteous   c. sleigh   d. transmited

_____ 20. a. angryest   b. beautiful   c. picnicking   d. superstitious

ANSWERS TO PREASSESSMENT

1. d	6. b	11. b	16. d
2. b	7. c	12. b	17. c
3. a	8. d	13. a	18. b
4. c	9. c	14. c	19. d
5. c	10. d	15. c	20. a

Learning Activities

The suggestions that follow are valuable hints for learning to spell. Accept them as a personal challenge and check your achievement regularly and often.

1. Keep a list of your own "spelling demons," those simple words that you habitually misspell. Learn to spell your "demons" correctly as soon as you discover them by spelling them correctly so many times you break the bad habit of misspelling them.

2. Study the list of the commonly accepted "spelling demons" at the end of this unit until you are sure you can spell each word correctly.

3. When you find a word that is difficult for you to spell, look it up in a dictionary. As you look carefully at the correct spelling, pronounce the word according to syllable and accent. Repeat the correct pronunciation until the sound and the spelling are united in your mind. Continue to look at the correct spelling until you can close your eyes and see the word in your mind's eye.

4. Work out your own mnemonic (memory) device for remembering the correct spelling, such as the following: bu*sin*ess has *sin* in it; sep*arat*e has *a rat* in it; a box of stationery has *e*nvelopes in it; and *fundame*ntal has *fun* and *dame* in it, and they go together. Your mnemonic device may sometimes or often be absurd, but that is all right—good, in fact—if it helps you spell the word correctly.

5. Study all of the spelling guidelines until you are able to apply them. Select carefully and use those guidelines you find most helpful, including the following, which are the most often used: changing *y* to *i*, doubling the final consonant, and *i* before *e*.

PREFIXES AND SUFFIXES

A *prefix* is one or more letters or syllables added to the beginning of a word. A *suffix* is one or more letters or syllables added to the end of a word. The main part of the word is the *root*.

One of the easiest of all spelling guidelines to remember is that the root remains the same when the prefix *un, dis*, or *mis* is added.

known — unknown
miss — dismiss
spell — misspell

SUFFIXES FOR NOUNS

Recall that a *noun* is the name of a person, place, or thing.

1. Nouns ending in *y* preceded by a *consonant* (any letter that is not a vowel) are made plural by changing the *y* to *i* and adding *es*.

lady — ladies
baby — babies
city — cities

This rule also applies to spelling the verb that pairs with the third-person singular noun or pronoun. (*Verbs,* as you recall, show action, being, or state of being.)

try — he tries
cry — she cries
fly — it flies

Exceptions: Proper names that end in *y* are made plural by adding *s* only.

the Brady family — the Bradys
Sally — several Sallys
Roy — several Roys

2. Caution: Nouns ending in *y* preceded by a *vowel* (*a, e, i, o, u*, and sometimes *w* or *y*) are made plural by adding only *s*.

donkey — donkeys
turkey — turkeys
joy — joys

3. Nouns ending in a sibilant (hissing) sound (*s, ss, ch, sh, x*, or *z*) are made plural by adding *es*.

bus   —   buses

glass   —   glasses

church   —   churches

dish   —   dishes

box   —   boxes

buzz   —   buzzes

4. Nouns ending in *f* or *fe* are made plural by changing the *f* or *fe* to *v* and adding *es*.

shelf   —   shelves

knife   —   knives

half   —   halves

5. Most nouns ending in *o* preceded by a consonant are made plural by adding *es*.

hero   —   heroes

potato   —   potatoes

cargo   —   cargoes

Caution: There are so many exceptions to this rule that you may want to learn to spell the words that end in *o* individually.

piano   —   pianos

auto   —   autos

zero   —   zeros

6. Nouns ending in *o* preceded by a vowel are made plural by adding only *s*.

radio   —   radios

studio   —   studios

coo   —   coos

Exercise 1   *Suffixes for Nouns*

Add *s* or *es* to these nouns to form their plural.

1. donkey _____   2. ash _____

3. comedy	_____	12. valley	_____
4. church	_____	13. knife	_____
5. baby	_____	14. joy	_____
6. tree	_____	15. tax	_____
7. circus	_____	16. house	_____
8. buffalo	_____	17. potato	_____
9. fox	_____	18. plane	_____
10. James	_____	19. city	_____
11. Dorothy	_____	20. piano	_____

ANSWERS TO EXERCISE 1

1. donkeys	6. trees	11. Dorothys	16. houses
2. ashes	7. circuses	12. valleys	17. potatoes
3. comedies	8. buffaloes	13. knives	18. planes
4. churches	9. foxes	14. joys	19. cities
5. babies	10. Jameses	15. taxes	20. pianos

SUFFIXES FOR VERBS

Many of the spelling guidelines for nouns also apply to verbs functioning with nouns and pronouns in the *third-person singular* (the person spoken of—Irene, Larry, he, she, it).

1. Most verbs take the suffix *s* in the third-person singular.

arrive — arrives

drive — drives

say — says

2. Verbs ending in *s*, *z*, *x*, *sh*, or *ch* take the suffix *es* to form the third-person singular.

fuss	—	fusses
buzz	—	buzzes
relax	—	relaxes
rush	—	rushes
lurch	—	lurches

3. Verbs ending in *o* preceded by a vowel add only *s* to form the third-person singular.

radio	—	radios
moo	—	moos

4. Verbs ending in *y* preceded by a consonant change the *y* to *i*, and add *es* to form the third-person singular.

fly	—	flies
reply	—	replies
try	—	tries

5. Some verbs ending in *o* preceded by a consonant add *es* to form the third-person singular.

do	—	does
echo	—	echoes
veto	—	vetoes

Exercise 2   Suffixes for Verbs
Add *s* or *es* to the following verbs.

1. attract _____
2. boo _____
3. catch _____
4. drench _____
5. establish _____

6. guess _____
7. hope _____
8. joke _____
9. lurch _____
10. moo _____

11. nullify _____	16. solo _____
12. occur _____	17. touch _____
13. pass _____	18. unify _____
14. buzz _____	19. veto _____
15. ratify _____	20. watch _____

ANSWERS TO EXERCISE 2

1. attracts	6. guesses	11. nullifies	16. solos
2. boos	7. hopes	12. occurs	17. touches
3. catches	8. jokes	13. passes	18. unifies
4. drenches	9. lurches	14. buzzes	19. vetoes
5. establishes	10. moos	15. ratifies	20. watches

MORE SUFFIXES

1. When a suffix beginning with a vowel joins a word ending with a consonant, the final consonant doubles if the word has *one* syllable or an accent on the *last* syllable:

fit — fitting

plan — planning

remit — remitted

BUT: benefit — benefited

travel — traveling

2. When a word ending in *e* is preceded by a consonant, the *e* is dropped when a suffix beginning with a vowel follows.

describe — describing

love — lovable

Caution: Some exceptions are changeable, courageous, enforceable, noticeable.

3. When a suffix beginning with a consonant joins a word, keep the *e*.

bare — bareness

love — lovely

sincere — sincerely

Caution: Some exceptions are abrid*gm*ent, acknowled*gm*ent, and judg-*m*ent. These spellings are every bit as correct as abrid*gem*ent, acknowl-ed*gem*ent, and jud*gem*ent.

Exercise 3 *More Suffixes*

In the spaces provided, supply the proper spellings.

1. attend + ance _____

2. begin + ing _____

3. benefit + ed _____

4. bid + ing _____

5. club + ed _____

6. concur + ed _____

7. control + ed _____

8. desire + able _____

9. drop + ed _____

10. effect + ive _____

11. equip + ed _____

12. excel + ed _____

13. heat + ing _____

14. hop + ed   _____

15. ice + y   _____

16. love + ly   _____

17. nap + ing   _____

18. occur + ed   _____

19. sincere + ly   _____

20. take + ing   _____

ANSWERS TO EXERCISE 3

1. attendance	6. concurred	11. equipped	16. lovely
2. beginning	7. controlled	12. excelled	17. napping
3. benefited	8. desirable	13. heating	18. occurred
4. bidding	9. dropped	14. hopped	19. sincerely
5. clubbed	10. effective	15. icy	20. taking

SUFFIXES FOR WORDS ENDING IN Y

1. **Words ending in *y* preceded by a vowel retain the *y* before a suffix.**

alley   —   alleys
monkey   —   monkeyed

2. **Most words ending in *y* preceded by a consonant change the *y* to *i* before a suffix.**

ally   —   allies
cry   —   cries
dry   —   dried

3. **If the suffix begins with *i*, the final *y* remains.**

enjoy   —   enjoying
pay   —   paying

4. Proper nouns keep the final *y* when *s* is added.

the Baileys
the Daleys
three Larrys

Exercise 4   ***Suffixes for Words Ending in Y***
In the spaces provided, supply the correct spellings.

1. alley + s   _____

2. angry + est   _____

3. beauty + ful   _____

4. bold + est   _____

5. care + ful   _____

6. carry + ing   _____

7. cry + ed   _____

8. defy + ing   _____

9. deny + es   _____

10. destiny + es   _____

11. destroy + ed   _____

12. easy + est   _____

13. edify + ed   _____

14. eery + est   _____

15. enjoy + ed   _____

16. fly + ing   _____

17. fry + ed   _____

18. history + es   _____

19. icy + est   _____

20. lucky + er   _____

21. mercy + less   _____

22. pay + ing   _____

23. pity + ful   _____

24. play + ed   _____

25. rely + es   _____

26. reply + ed   _____

27. stay + ing   _____

28. turkey + s   _____

29. unify + ed   _____

30. (the) Barry + s   _____

ANSWERS TO EXERCISE 4

1. alleys	7. cried	13. edified
2. angriest	8. defying	14. eeriest
3. beautiful	9. denies	15. enjoyed
4. boldest	10. destinies	16. flying
5. careful	11. destroyed	17. fried
6. carrying	12. easiest	18. histories

19. iciest	23. pitiful	27. staying
20. luckier	24. played	28. turkeys
21. merciless	25. relies	29. unified
22. paying	26. replies	30. (the) Barrys

IE OR EI?

1. When *ie* or *ei* spell the sound *ee*, put *i* before *e* except after *c*.

believe

relief

thief

Caution: Some exceptions are *ei*ther, *lei*sure, *nei*ther, *sei*ze, *wei*rd.

2. If you should have any difficulty with *ie* and *ei*, remember these jingles:

Use *i* before *e*
Except after *c*
Or when sounded like *a*
As in *neighbor* and *weigh*.

If in a word a *c* you spy,
Put the *e* before the *i*.

Exercise 5   *IE or EI?*

In the spaces provided, supply the proper *ie* or *ei* spelling.

1. ach____ve	11. f____ld	21. repr____ve
2. bel____f	12. gr____f	22. retr____ve
3. bel____ve	13. gr____ve	23. sh____ld
4. br____f	14. n____ce	24. shr____k
5. c____ling	15. p____ce	25. s____ge
6. ch____f	16. perc____ve	26. th____f
7. conc____t	17. pr____st	27. w____ld
8. conc____ve	18. rec____pt	28. y____ld
9. dec____t	19. rel____f	
10. dec____ve	20. rel____ve	

ANSWERS TO EXERCISE 5

1. achieve	8. conceive	15. piece	22. retrieve
2. belief	9. deceit	16. perceive	23. shield
3. believe	10. deceive	17. priest	24. shriek
4. brief	11. field	18. receipt	25. siege
5. ceiling	12. grief	19. relief	26. thief
6. chief	13. grieve	20. relieve	27. wield
7. conceit	14. niece	21. reprieve	28. yield

OTHER SPELLING RULES

1. The letter *u* always follows the letter *q*.

bouquet

quiet

quiz

2. When *full* is added to the end of a noun to form an adjective, the final *l* is dropped.

cheerful

helpful

sorrowful

3. In words ending in *c*, insert *k* before *e, i,* or *y* to retain the hard sound before any suffix.

frolic — frolicked

picnic — picknicking

panic — panicky

Other Rules   *Exercise 6*

In the spaces provided, supply the correct spellings.

1. colic____y
2. frolic____y
3. beautifu____
4. panic____y
5. politi____ing

6. q____een
7. q____stion
8. req____st
9. trustfu____
10. watchfu____

1. colicky   6. queen
2. frolicky   7. question
3. beautiful   8. request
4. panicky   9. trustful
5. politicking   10. watchful

Exercise 7   *A Review of Spelling Guidelines*

In the spaces provided, supply the proper spellings.

1. ach____ve (ie or ei)
2. c____ling (ie or ei)
3. dec____ve (ie or ei)
4. f____ld (ie or ei)
5. for____gn (ie or ei)
6. n____ghbor (ie or ei)
7. n____ce (ie or ei)
8. perc____ve (ie or ei)
9. retr____ve (ie or ei)

10. love + able   _____

11. nine + ty   _____

12. notice + able   _____

13. spice + y   _____

14. true + ly   _____

15. write + ing   _____

Add *s* or *es* to form the plurals of these words:

16. alley   _____

17. ally   _____

18. ray   _____

19. study   _____

20. (the) Talley   _____

Add suffixes as indicated.

21. easy + est   _____

22. enjoy + ing   _____

23. lucky + est   _____

24. mercy + less   _____

25. study + ing   _____

ANSWERS TO EXERCISE 7

1. achieve	14. truly
2. ceiling	15. writing
3. deceive	16. alleys
4. field	17. allies
5. foreign	18. rays
6. neighbor	19. studies
7. niece	20. Talleys
8. perceive	21. easiest
9. retrieve	22. enjoying
10. lovable	23. luckiest
11. ninety	24. merciless
12. noticeable	25. studying
13. spicy	

SPELLING LIST

Studies have proven that the words listed below are among those most frequently misspelled. Their popular name is "spelling demons." You should learn to spell these words correctly so that your communication can be more effective.

advice	conscious	fascinate	parallel
advise	criticism	February	performance
affect, effect	describe	foreign	personal
all right	description	fourth	possession
among	dictionary	government	possible
amount	dining	grammar	precede, proceed
argument	disappear	grievous	prejudice
arrangement	disapprove	height	principal, principle
athlete	disastrous	heroes	privilege
athletic	discipline	hoping	professor
bargain	disease	immediately	quiet, quite
beautiful	dissatisfied	interest	receive
becoming	effect, affect	interesting	receiving
belief	eligible	its, it's	recommend
believe	embarrass	laboratory	referring
benefited	encourage	laid	secretary
business	entertain	lead, led	sense, since
calendar	environment	lose, loose	separate
cemetery	equipment	losing	succeed
changing	everything	marriage	to, too, two
choose	excellence	necessary	truly
chose	existence	occasion	until
coming	existent	occurred	villain
committee	experience	omitted	writing
conscience	explanation	opportunity	written

Postassessment

Supply the proper spellings in the spaces provided.

1. ch____f (ie or ei)
2. conc____t (ie or ei)
3. rec____ve (ie or ei)
4. rel____ve (ie or ei)
5. shr____k (ie or ei)

6. benefit + ed   _____

7. begin + ing   _____

8. buy + s   _____

9. change + able   _____

10. control + ed   _____

11. describe + ing   _____

12. effect + ive   _____

13. fly + ing   _____

14. frequent + ed   _____

15. (the) Kelly + s   _____

16. love + ly   _____

17. mercy + less   _____

18. nine + ty   _____

19. occur + ed   _____

20. omit + ed   _____

21. permit + ing   _____

22. study + ing   _____

23. swim + ing   _____

24. try + ed   _____

25. write + ing   _____

ANSWERS TO POSTASSESSMENT

1. chief	10. controlled	19. occurred
2. conceit	11. describing	20. omitted
3. receive	12. effective	21. permitting
4. relieve	13. flying	22. studying
5. shriek	14. frequented	23. swimming
6. benefited	15. (the) Kellys	24. tried
7. beginning	16. lovely	25. writing
8. buys	17. merciless	
9. changeable	18. ninety	

Study Unit 18 □ Latin Roots and Prefixes

RATIONALE

A good vocabulary will help you to succeed in college as well as in your present or future profession. A wide-ranging vocabulary is important because a knowledge of words allows you to express your ideas clearly and to develop new ideas without difficulty. There is a definite correlation between success in life and size of vocabulary. In addition, the ability to communicate effectively is always important in your interactions with other people. To improve your vocabulary you should check the definitions and pronunciations of any unfamiliar words in the exercises that follow.

OBJECTIVES

After completing this unit, you should be able to
1. analyze the composition of words
2. recognize Latin prefixes and roots
3. derive words from these prefixes and roots
4. use a dictionary fully, not only to check meanings and pronunciation but also to find out where words come from

Preassessment

Write in the space provided the best substitute for the *italicized* word. The first is done for you as an example.

_____give up_____ 1. *abdicate* the throne
abuse, criticize, give up, overthrow

_____ 2. *abhor* a person
forgive, hate, love, praise

_____ 3. *ambiguous* statement
clear, short, vague, vocal

_____ 4. *antebellum* home
before the Civil War, expensive, old,
warm

_____ 5. *bisect* an apple
carry, divide into two parts, examine,
polish

_____ 6. *circumscribe* an object
cut in half, describe, encircle, observe

_____ 7. *countermand* orders
change, revoke, write, yell

_____ 8. *counterpart* in marriage
equal, husband, love, planning

_____ 9. *deviate* from the route
gain, learn, stray, tire

_____ 10. *diabolical* personality
angry, devilish, kind, loving

_____ 11. *extraordinary* performance
long, poor, remarkable, shocking

_____ 12. *interrogative* dialogue
humorous, inquisitive, interrupting,
loud

_____ 13. *intervene* in the matter
come between, question, remain silent, speak

_____ 14. *intrastate* commerce
foreign, governmental, inside the state, outside the state

_____ 15. *malign* the opponent
compete with, debate, praise, slander
speak ill of

_____ 16. *omnipotent* ruler
almighty, dethroned, weak, wise

_____ 17. *retrospective* person
bright, easily angered, tending to survey the past, wise

_____ 18. *semiclassical* music
early classical, not classical, somewhat classical, very classical

_____ 19. *substantiate* charges
deny, state, verify, write

_____ 20. *transcend* problems
discuss, give into, realize, rise above

ANSWERS TO PREASSESSMENT

1. give up
2. hate
3. vague
4. before the Civil War
5. divide into parts
6. encircle
7. revoke
8. equal
9. stray
10. devilish

11. remarkable	16. almighty
12. inquisitive	17. tending to survey the past
13. come between	18. somewhat classical
14. inside the state	19. verify
15. slander	20. rise above

Learning Activities

ROOT, PREFIX, SUFFIX

The best way to discover the meanings of words is to learn the meaning of the roots, prefixes, and suffixes that compose these words. A *root* is a word in its most basic form without prefixes and suffixes. A *prefix* is a syllable added to the beginning of a word. A *suffix* is a syllable added to the end of a word. If you should have difficulty remembering which one comes first, think of the alphabet: p - r - s.

Most of the prefixes, roots, and suffixes found in English words are of Latin, Greek, French, or Anglo-Saxon origin. This study unit deals with the prefixes and roots of Latin origin.

Looking at one word in detail should help you to see how to approach the words from Latin that you will come across in this unit. Let us break up the English adjective *commensurable*. The prefix, *com* (it is listed in the dictionary as *com-*), is from the Latin word *cum*; it means, among other things, "same." The root is from the Latin noun *mensura*, "measure," and the verb *mensurare*, "to measure." (The past participle of this verb, *mensuratus*, gives us the English adjective *commensurate*.) The suffix, *able* (listed in the dictionary as *-able*), is from the Latin ending *abilis*, "capable of," "worthy of," or "inclined to." Combining all this information, you can construct the meaning of *commensurable*: "capable of being measured by the same standard." By the way, tracking down the meaning of *commensurate* also gives you a spelling hint: The word has two *m*'s—one from *cum* and one from *mensura*.

Exercise 1 *Using Latin Roots in Sentences*
This exercise contains Latin roots *italicized* and their meanings (in parentheses). Below them are English words that have developed from

these Latin roots. Write sentences using these words on the lines provided.

Be sure that you understand the definition of every word in the exercise. Always check your answers and pronunciations in a dictionary.

acr, acer (sharp)

1. acerbate_____

_____

2. acerbity_____

_____

3. acrimonious_____

_____

aequs (equal)

4. equality_____

_____

5. equinox_____

_____

6. equity_____

_____

ager, agri (field)

7. agrarian_____

_____

8. agriculture _____

_____

9. peregrination _____

_____

○ *amare* (to love), *amicus* (friend)

10. amiable _____

_____

11. amicable _____

_____

12. amour _____

_____

○ *anima* (life, breath)

13. animated _____

_____

14. animation _____

_____

15. inanimate _____

_____

animus (mind, soul)

16. animadvert _____ make (critical) remarks _____

_____

17. magnanimity _____

_____

18. unanimous _____

_____

annus (year)

19. annuity _____

_____

20. biennial _____

_____

21. perennial _____

_____

aptare (to fit)

22. apt _____

_____

23. aptitude _____

_____

24. inept _____

_____

Exercise 2   Using Latin Roots in Sentences
Continue writing sentences using these words formed from Latin roots.

aqua (water)

1. aquarium _____

_____

2. aquatic _____

_____

3. aqueduct _____

_____

ardere (to burn)

4. ardor _____

_____

5. arduous _ needing and using up much energy
_____ arduous task

6. arson _____

_____

ars, artis (art)

7. artifact_____

_____

8. artificial_____

_____

9. artist _____

_____

ben, bon (good, well)

10. beneficial_____

_____

11. benevolence_____

_____

12. bonus _____

_____

capere, captus, cep (to take)

13. capture _____

_____

14. encephalitis_____

_____

15. precept _____

_____

civis (citizen), *civilis* (civil)

16. civil_____

_____

17. civilian _____

_____

18. civilization _____

_____

claudere, clausus (to close)

19. claustrophobia_____

_____

20. enclose_____

_____

21. exclude _____

_____

cognoscere, cognitus (to know), *notus* (known)

22. cognizant_____

_____

23. incognito _____

_____

24. notorious _____

_____

ANSWERS TO EXERCISE 2
Because answers will vary, your instructor should check this exercise.

Using Latin Roots in Sentences   *Exercise 3*
Continue writing sentences using these words derived from Latin roots.

corpus, corporis (body)

1. corporation _____

_____

2. corpse _____

_____

3. incorporate _____

_____

credere, creditus (to believe)

4. credence _____

_____

5. credible _____

_____

6. incredulous _____

_____

crescere, cretum (to grow)

7. crescent _____

_____

8. decrease _____

_____

9. increase _____

_____

crux, crucis (cross)

10. crucial _____

_____

11. crucible _____

_____

12. crucifix _____

_____

culpare, culpatus (to blame)

13. culpable _____

_____

(14) culprit _____

_____

(15) exculpate _____

_____

currere, cursus (to run)

16. currency _____

_____

17. current _____

_____

18. excursion _____

_____

dicere, dictus (to say)

(19) abdicate _____

_____

20. diction _____

_____

21. predict _____

_____

docere, doctus (to teach)

22. docile _____

_____

23. doctor _____

_____

24. indoctrinate _____

_____

ANSWERS TO EXERCISE 3

Once again, answers will vary and should be checked by your instructor.

Exercise 4   Matching Latin Derivatives

After having studied the Latin roots on the preceding pages, you should be able to match the words in the first column with the definitions in the second column by writing the appropriate letters in the spaces provided. Check your pronunciations in a dictionary.

a. amiable
b. arson
c. benevolence
d. biennial
e. civilian
f. claustrophobia
g. diction
h. docile
i. equity
j. excursion
k. inanimate
l. incognito
m. magnanimity

_____ 1. justice

_____ 2. to foretell

_____ 3. general rule of action

_____ 4. pleasing

_____ 5. expedition

_____ 6. malicious burning

_____ 7. choice of words

n. precept

o. predict

_____ 8. fear of closed or narrow places

_____ 9. easily taught

_____ 10. kindness

_____ 11. not living

_____ 12. lasting for two years

_____ 13. generosity

_____ 14. under an assumed name

_____ 15. not on active duty

ANSWERS TO EXERCISE 4

1. i	6. b	11. k
2. o	7. g	12. d
3. n	8. f	13. m
4. a	9. h	14. l
5. j	10. c	15. e

More Latin Roots   *Exercise 5*

Use the words formed from these Latin roots in sentences. Check the pronunciations of the words in a dictionary.

donare, donatus (to give away)

1. condone_____

_____

2. donor_____

_____

3. pardon _____

_____

ducere, ductus (to lead)

4. aqueduct _____

_____

5. educate _____

_____

6. production _____

_____

facere (fic, fec), factus (to make, do)

7. factory _____

_____

8. fiction _____

_____

9. perfect _____

_____

fidere, fisus (to trust)

10. fiducial _____

_____

11. fidelity _____

_____

12. perfidy _____

_____

ire, itus (to go)

13. ambition _____

_____

14. sedition _____

_____

15. transition _____

_____

lex, legis (law)

16. legal _____

_____

17. legislature _____

_____

18. legitimate _____

_____

lux, lucis; lumen, luminis (light)

19. illuminate _____

_____

20. lucid _____

_____

21. luminous _____

_____

mandare, mandatus (to command)

22. commandment _____

_____

23. mandate _____

_____

24. mandatory _____

_____

migrare, migratus (to move)

25. emigrant _____

_____

26. immigrant _____

_____

27. migrant _____

_____

mille (thousand)

28. millimeter _____

_____

29. milligram _____

_____

30. milliliter _____

_____

ANSWERS TO EXERCISE 5
Because answers will vary, your instructor should check this exercise.

Still More Latin Roots   *Exercise 6*
Use the words derived from these Latin roots in sentences:

mittere, missus (to send)

1. admit _____

_____

2. dismiss _____

_____

3. missile _____

_____

mors, mortis (death)

4. immortal _____

_____

5. moribund _____

_____

6. mortality _____

_____

movere, motus (to move)

7. automobile _____

_____

8. emotion _____

_____

9. movement _____

_____

mutare, mutatus (to change)

10. immutable _____

_____

11. mutability _____

_____

12. mutation _____

_____

negare, negatus (to deny)

13. abnegate _____

_____

14. negative _____

_____

15. negate _____

_____

nihil (nothing)

16. annihilate _____

_____

17. nihilism _____

_____

18. nihility _____

_____

nomen, nominis (name)

19. nomenclature _____

_____

20. nominate _____

_____

21. nomination _____

_____

occidere (to kill)

22. homicide _____

_____

23. insecticide _____

_____

24. suicide _____

_____

pendere, pensus (to hang, weigh)

25. impend _____

_____

26. pendant _____

_____

27. pendulum _____

_____

portare, portatus (to carry, bear)

28. export _____

_____

29. import _____

_____

30. report _____

_____

ANSWERS TO EXERCISE 6
Answers will differ and should be looked over by your instructor.

Continuing with Latin Roots   *Exercise* 7
Use the words derived from these Latin roots in sentences:

quaer, quaesit (to ask, complain)

1. inquest _____

_____

2. inquire _____

_____

3. inquisitive _____

_____

regere, rectus (to rule, direct, manage)

4. rectify _____

_____

5. rector _____

_____

6. regency _____

_____

sequi, secutus (to follow)

7. consecutive _____

_____

8. executive _____

_____

9. sequel _____

_____

spectare, spectatus (to observe)

10. aspect _____

_____

11. respect _____

_____

12. spectator _____

_____

tendere, tensus (to stretch, try)

13. tension _____

_____

14. tensive _____

_____

15. tentative _____

_____

tenere, tentus (to hold)

16. tenable ___that can be defended successfully___

___His theory is hardly tenable.___

17. tenacity _____

_____

18. tenure _____

_____

trahere, tractus (to draw)

19. distract _____

_____

20. retract _____

_____

21. subtract _____

_____

_____

venire, ventum (to come)

22. convention _____

_____

23. intervene _____

_____

24. souvenir _____

_____

vertere, versus (to turn)

25. advert _____

_____

26. conversion _____

_____

27. subversion _____

_____

ANSWERS TO EXERCISE 7
Have your instructor check your answers to this exercise.

In the following exercises, look up in your dictionary the definition of any unfamiliar words used as examples before you fill in the spaces with two additional words having the same prefix. Be sure that you know the definition of every word used in the exercise. Check your answers and pronunciations in a dictionary.

Prefix	Meaning	English Words
1. ab-, abs-	from, away from	abduct, abolish, abstract
2. ad-	to, forward, toward	adjective, admit, adventure
3. ambi-	both	ambidextrous, ambiguous, ambivalent
4. an-	without	anarchy, anemia, anesthesia
5. ante-	before	antebellum, antedate, anteroom
6. arch-	chief, first	archbishop, archeology, archetype
7. bi-	two	bicycle, biennial, bisect

(handwritten annotations throughout:)
lead
kidnap
can use both hands — two meaning → not clear
having either or both or two contrary or similar values
without red blood cells — without feeling sensation
before war — before room a hall
divide two part — every 2 years
bigamist

	Prefix	Meaning	English Words
8.	circum-	around	circumference, circumscribe, circumstance
			_____
9.	co-, com-	together, with	combine, commerce, complete
			_____
10.	counter-	against	counteract, countermand, counterpart
			_____
11.	de-	from	detergent, detriment, deviate
			_____
12.	dia-	across	diabolical, diagram, diameter
			_____
13.	dis-, dif-	away from, apart, not	disjoint, dissipate, distend
			_____
14.	ex-	out of, away from	exhume, exit, extend
			_____
15.	extra-	beyond, outside	extracurricular, extraordinary, extravagant
			_____
16.	in-	within, into	income, inside, intern
			_____

Prefix	Meaning	English Words
17. inter-	among, between	interfere, international, intervene
18. intra-	within, inside of	intrastate, intravenous, intrazonal
19. mal-	bad, evil	maladjusted, malicious, malnutrition
20. milli-	one thousand(th)	milliliter, milligram, millimeter
21. multi-	many	multiphase, multiple, multiplex
22. non-	not	nonchalance, noncommittal, nonentity
23. omni-	all	omnipotent, omniscient, omnivorous
24. post-	after	postdate, postgraduate, postpone
25. pre-	before	preamble, precedent, preview

Handwritten annotations: negative; positive to help; put in veins; within a vein ~ injection; evil; ~ filter; all powerful; know everything; eat everything; prior in time, order; beginning; introduction

	Prefix	Meaning	English Words
26.	retro-	backward	retroactive, retrograde, retrospective
27.	semi-	half	semiclassical, semicolon, semiprecious
28.	sub-	under	sublime, subsequent, substantiate
29.	super-	above	superficial, superfluity, supersede
30.	trans-	across	transfer, transgression, transmute

ANSWERS TO EXERCISE 8

Because answers will differ, your instructor should check them.

Exercise 9 *Still Puzzled about Latin Roots?*

ACROSS

1. Dead body
5. Judicial inquiry; investigation
6. Lead into wrongdoing
10. Unalterable
13. Very important; critical
14. Man-made

DOWN

2. Happen as result
3. Person who migrates
4. Person sent on a mission
7. Banish
8. Feeling; sentiment
9. Compliant; easy to handle

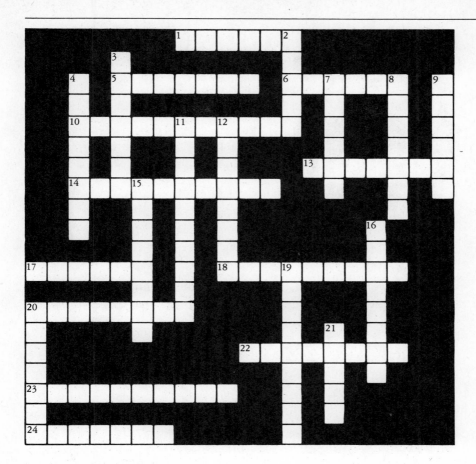

ACROSS (continued)

17. Person licensed to practice medicine
18. Capable of two interpretations
20. Divert attention
22. Pertaining to land
23. That which goes before
24. Leave out

DOWN (continued)

11. All-powerful
12. A substance added in small amounts to another substance
15. Never dying
16. Happening twice a year
19. Meddle; disturb the affairs of others
20. Say or read aloud for others to write down
21. Intentionally setting fire to buildings

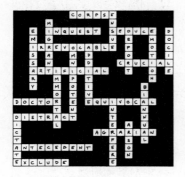

Postassessment

Match the words in the first column with the definitions in the second column by writing the appropriate letters in the spaces provided. Check your pronunciations in a dictionary.

a. ambivalence

b. anemic

c. bisect

d. cognizance

e. countermand

f. diabolical

g. docile

h. exculpate

i. exhume

j. fidelity

k. immigrant

l. inquisitive

m. intervene

n. luminous

o. migrant

p. nihilism

q. perennial

r. rectify

s. sequel

t. tenuous

_____ 1. acquit

_____ 2. persistent

_____ 3. very curious

_____ 4. obedient

_____ 5. faithfulness

_____ 6. lacking vitality

_____ 7. like the devil

_____ 8. revoke

_____ 9. perception

_____ 10. remedy

_____ 11. both attraction and repulsion

_____ 12. one who moves to find work

_____ 13. thin

_____ 14. doctrine that nothing exists

_____ 15. one who settles in a new country

_____ 16. separate

_____ 17. dig up, remove from a grave

_____ 18. come between

_____ 19. consequence

_____ 20. light-giving

ANSWERS TO POSTASSESSMENT

1. h	6. b	11. a	16. c
2. q	7. f	12. o	17. i
3. l	8. e	13. t	18. m
4. g	9. d	14. p	19. s
5. j	10. r	15. k	20. n

Study Unit 19□Greek Roots and Prefixes

RATIONALE

There are not as many Greek roots and prefixes as Latin ones; however, they are equally important, since most of the words common in the English language are combinations of these Latin and Greek derivatives. The Greek roots and prefixes in this unit are especially interesting because they are the sources for many modern scientific terms.

OBJECTIVES

After completing Study Unit 19, you should be able to
1. analyze words composed of Greek derivatives
2. form words by combining Greek derivatives
3. recognize Greek derivatives in English words

Preassessment

Match the words in the first column with the definitions in the second column by writing the appropriate letters in the spaces provided. Check all pronunciations in a dictionary.

a. anemia

b. antithesis

c. asterisk   _____ 1. marriage to one person

d. autobiography

e. bibliography   _____ 2. register events in order

f. biology

g. chroma   _____ 3. color

h. chronicle

i. dichotomy   _____ 4. dissimilar

                         _____ 5. branching in two parts

j. eulogize
k. heterogeneous
l. monogamy
m. pyromania
n. stenography
o. thermal

_____ 6. list of books

_____ 7. study of living things

_____ 8. pertaining to heat

_____ 9. praise

_____ 10. lack of blood

_____ 11. desire to set fires

_____ 12. starlike printing symbol

_____ 13. direct opposite

_____ 14. shorthand

_____ 15. story of a person's life written by himself

ANSWERS TO PREASSESSMENT

1. l	6. e	11. m
2. h	7. f	12. c
3. g	8. o	13. b
4. k	9. j	14. n
5. i	10. a	15. d

Learning Activities

ROOT AND PREFIX

Remember: A *root* is a word in its most basic form; a *prefix* is a syllable added to the beginning of a word.

Greek Roots in English Words

This exercise contains a number of Greek roots common to the English language. On the lines provided, use each root in a word; then compose a sentence using that word. A dictionary should help you. Note that the first root has been completed as an example.

Root	Meaning	English Word with Sentence
1. *aer, aeros*	air	aerate _____ Farmers often aerate the soil. _____
2. *agog*	leader	_____ _____
3. *agonia*	pain	_____ _____
4. *agros, agrios*	open field, wild	_____ _____
5. *amphi*	both, around	_____ _____
6. *anemos*	wind	_____ _____

Root	Meaning	English Word with Sentence

7. *anthrop* man _____ _____

_____

_____

8. *archia* rule _____ _____

_____

_____

9. *archios* primeval _____ _____

_____

_____

10. *aristos* best _____ _____

_____

_____

11. *astron* star _____ _____

_____

_____

12. *auto* self _____ _____

_____

_____

	Root	Meaning	English Word with Sentence
13.	*biblio*	book	_____ _____
			_____
			_____
14.	*bio*	life	_____ _____
			_____
			_____
15.	*chroma, chromatos*	color	_____ _____
			_____
			_____
16.	*chronos*	time	_____ _____
			_____
			_____
17.	*deka*	ten	_____ _____
			_____
			_____
18.	*demos*	people	_____ _____
			_____
			_____

Root	Meaning	English Word with Sentence
19. *derma, dermatos*	skin, hide	_____ _____ _____ _____
20. *doxa*	opinion	_____ _____ _____ _____
21. *dynam*	power, strength	_____ _____ _____ _____
22. *gam*	marriage	_____ _____ _____ _____
23. *gaster, gastros*	stomach	_____ _____ _____ _____
24. *genos*	race, kind, class	_____ _____ _____ _____

Root	Meaning	English Word with Sentence
25. *geo*	earth	_____ _____
		_____
		_____
26. *glotta*	tongue	_____ _____
		_____
		_____
27. *glyphe*	carving	_____ _____
		_____
		_____
28. *gnome*	judgment	_____ _____
		_____
		_____
29. *gonos, gone*	speed, procreation	_____ _____
		_____
		_____
30. *gramma*	letter, weight	_____ _____
		_____
		_____

Since all students who do this exercise will come up with different answers, your instructor should check your work.

More Greek Roots

This exercise contains a number of Greek roots common to the English language. On the lines provided, write at least three words with each root. A dictionary should help you. Note that the first root has been completed to serve as an example.

	Root	Meaning	English Words
1.	*graph, gram*	to write	graph, graphic, graphite
2.	*helio*	sun	_____
			_____
3.	*hemi*	half	_____
			_____
4.	*hieros*	sacred	_____
			_____
5.	*hydro*	water	_____
			_____
6.	*hypnos*	sleep	_____
			_____
7.	*idein*	to see	_____
			_____

Root	Meaning	English Words
8. *kosmos*	order, the world	
9. *kratos*	power	
10. *lithos*	stone	
11. *logos*	word, thought	
12. *lysis*	loosening	
13. *makros*	long	
14. *mania*	madness	
15. *megas,* *megalon*	great, mighty	
16. *metron*	measure	

Root	Meaning	English Words

17. *mikros*   small   _____

                                              _____

18. *monos*   one   _____

                                                _____

19. *morphe*   form   _____

                                                _____

20. *mythos*   fable, speech   _____

                                                _____

21. *neos*   new   _____

                                                _____

22. *neuron*   nerve   _____

                                                _____

23. *nomos*   law, order   _____

                                                _____

24. *octo*   eight   _____

                                                _____

25. *oligos*   small, few   _____

                                                _____

Root	Meaning	English Words
26. *onoma*	name	_____
		_____
27. *orthos*	straight	_____
		_____

ANSWERS TO EXERCISE 2
Answers will vary, so your instructor should check this exercise.

Exercise 3 Additional Greek Roots

Form at least three words using each Greek root.

Root	Meaning	English Words
1. *pan*	all	_____
		_____
2. *pathos*	suffering, disease	_____
		_____
3. *pente*	five	_____
		_____
4. *petro*	stone	_____
		_____
5. *philos*	loving	_____
		_____

Root	Meaning	English Words

6. *phobos*   fear   _____

_____

7. *phone*   voice, sound   _____

_____

8. *phos, photos*   light   _____

_____

9. *physics*   nature   _____

_____

10. *plastos*   formed   _____

_____

11. *ploutos*   wealth   _____

_____

12. *pneumon*   lung   _____

_____

13. *polis*   city   _____

_____

14. *polys*   many   _____

_____

	Root	Meaning	English Words
15.	*pyr, pyros*	fire	_____
			_____
16.	*septikos*	infected	_____
			_____
17.	*skhizein*	to cleave	_____
			_____
18.	*skopein*	to view	_____
			_____
19.	*techne*	art	_____
			_____
20.	*tele*	far, far off	_____
			_____
21.	*theos*	God	_____
			_____
22.	*therme*	heat	_____
			_____
23.	*thesis*	something set down	_____
			_____

Root	Meaning	English Words
24. *tome*	a cutting	_____
		_____
25. *topos*	place	_____
		_____
26. *tri*	three	_____
		_____
27. *typos*	impression	_____
		_____
28. *zoion*	animal	_____
		_____

ANSWERS TO EXERCISE 3
Since your answers will differ, your instructor should check this exercise.

Matching Words of Greek Origin   *Exercise 4*

After having studied the Greek roots in this unit, you should have little difficulty matching the words in the first column with the definitions in the second column by writing the appropriate letters in the spaces provided.

a. demagogue   _____   1. sleep-inducing
b. epidemic
c. epidermis   _____   2. mad person
d. heliotrope
e. hydraulic   _____   3. new convert

f. hypnotic
g. lithology
h. maniac
i. misanthrope
j. neophyte
k. pachyderm
l. pedagogue
m. synagogue
n. topography
o. zoology

_____ 4. study of rocks

_____ 5. false leader of people

_____ 6. hater of mankind

_____ 7. skin

_____ 8. flower that faces the sun

_____ 9. teacher

_____ 10. thick-skinned quadruped

_____ 11. widespread disease

_____ 12. study of animal life

_____ 13. house of worship

_____ 14. operated by water

_____ 15. physical features of a region

ANSWERS TO EXERCISE 4

1. f	6. i	11. b
2. h	7. c	12. o
3. j	8. d	13. m
4. g	9. l	14. e
5. a	10. k	15. n

Exercise 5   Greek Prefixes in English Words

You are now ready to work with Greek prefixes. In this exercise, a definition follows each of the prefixes. On the lines provided, form at least three words using each prefix. You may need a dictionary. The first prefix is completed to serve as an example.

Prefix	Meaning	English Words
1. an-, a-	not, without	anarchy, anemia, anesthesia
2. ana-	up, backward, again, greatly	_____ _____
3. anti-, ant-	against, not, opposite	_____ _____
4. di-	twice, double	_____ _____
5. epi-	upon, beside, among, above	_____ _____
6. eu-	good, well, beautiful	_____ _____
7. hetero-	other, other than the usual	_____ _____
8. hyper-	over, above, beyond the ordinary	_____ _____
9. hypo-	under, down, less than the ordinary	_____ _____
10. iso-	equal, alike	_____ _____

Prefix	Meaning	English Words
11. meta-	along with, after	_____
		_____
12. peri-	around	_____
		_____
13. syl-, syn-, sym-	together, with, at the same time	_____
		_____

ANSWERS TO EXERCISE 5
Since your answers will differ, your instructor should check them.

Exercise 6 *Using Words of Greek Origin in Sentences*
Write a sentence using each of the words that you listed in Exercise 5.
Use one line for each sentence.

1. _____

_____

_____

2. _____

_____

_____

3. _____

_____

_____

4. _____

_____

_____

5. _____

_____

_____

6. _____

_____

_____

7. _____

_____

_____

8. _____

_____

_____

9. _____

_____

_____

10. _____

_____

_____

11. _____

_____

_____

12. _____

_____

_____

13. _____

_____

_____

ANSWERS TO EXERCISE 6

Answers will vary; your instructor should check this exercise.

Exercise 7 *Puzzling Out Greek Derivatives*

ACROSS

2. A nerve cell
4. Abnormal fear of water
9. Regional variety of a language
11. Figure with five sides
14. Science of stars and planets
15. Set of three works, separate yet related

DOWN

1. Summary; brief review
3. Anatomical part that protects the lungs during swallowing
5. Power belonging to a few persons
6. Symbols used by the Egyptians

ACROSS (continued)

16. Ideal representative
18. Persons who are at home in all countries
19. Having to do with the science of correcting bone disorders
21. Short for *automobile*
22. Complete and orderly system
23. Person abnormally concerned about his or her health
24. Device that transmits sound

DOWN (continued)

7. A written account of someone's life
8. Strong dislike
10. Concluding section of a work (plural)
12. Single; one (prefix)
13. Process of producing images by light
14. Sterile; free from infection
17. Instrument for marking time
20. Science of correct reasoning

Postassessment

Match the words in the first column with the definitions in the second column by writing the appropriate letters in the spaces provided.

a. amphitheater

b. anarchy

c. anesthesia

d. antiseptic

e. astronomy

f. autocracy

g. bibliophile

h. bigamy

i. chronology

j. epigram

k. euphemism

l. helium

m. perimeter

n. polygamy

o. theocracy

_____ 1. timetable of events

_____ 2. pleasant way of saying something

_____ 3. many marriage partners

_____ 4. government by religious leaders

_____ 5. free from infection; sterile

_____ 6. distance around

_____ 7. lack of government

_____ 8. element in sun's atmosphere

_____ 9. loss of feeling

_____ 10. a pithy statement

_____ 11. lover of books

_____ 12. rule by self

_____ 13. oval theater

_____ 14. study of stars

_____ 15. marriage to two people at same time

Study Unit 20□Prefixes and Suffixes from Various Origins

RATIONALE

Even though you have completed two units of Latin and Greek derivatives, you still need to review some prefixes and suffixes that are not limited to Latin and Greek origins. This unit should broaden your vocabulary and introduce you to some French and Anglo-Saxon sources.

OBJECTIVES

After completing Study Unit 20, you should be able to
1. analyze the composition of words
2. recognize the sources of most prefixes and suffixes
3. derive words from these prefixes and suffixes

Preassessment

Match the words in the first column with the definitions in the second column by writing the appropriate letters in the spaces provided.

a. centimeter   _____ 1. eliminate

b. delete

c. demigod   _____ 2. official

d. detour

e. fallacy   _____ 3. suspicious

f. leaden

g. magistrate   _____ 4. unpredictable

h. paranoid

i. solitude   _____ 5. deviation

j. wayward

    _____ 6. .01 meter

_____ 7. false idea

_____ 8. minor god

_____ 9. seclusion

_____ 10. made of lead

ANSWERS TO PREASSESSMENT

1. b	6. a
2. g	7. e
3. h	8. c
4. j	9. i
5. d	10. f

Learning Activities

PREFIX AND SUFFIX

In the previous vocabulary studies, you learned that a *prefix* is a syllable added to the beginning of a word and that a *suffix* is a syllable added to the end of a word. You should keep these two points in mind for the following exercises.

Constructing Words with Prefixes   *Exercise 1*

This exercise contains a number of useful prefixes from various sources. On the lines provided, write at least two words that make use of the prefixes listed in the first column. If you are not certain of the correct word, refer to your dictionary. The first prefix is completed to serve as an example.

Prefix	Source	Meaning	English Words
1. centi-	Latin, French	100	centigrade, centimeter
2. de- (dis-)	Latin, French	separation, reversal, down	_____ _____

Prefix	Source	Meaning	English Words
3. dec-	Latin, Greek	ten	_____
			_____
4. demi-	French	half, sub-standard	_____
			_____
5. mis-	Anglo-Saxon, French	wrong	_____
			_____
6. re-	Latin, French	back again	_____
			_____
7. un-	Anglo-Saxon	not	_____
			_____

ANSWERS TO EXERCISE 1

Since your answers will vary, your instructor should check this exercise.

Exercise 2 *Developing Prefixes into Words and Sentences*

Following are prefixes from the previous exercise. On the lines provided, form a word (not used in Exercise 1) with the prefix; then use the word in a sentence.

Prefix	Word Plus Sentence
1. centi-	_____ _____
	_____
	_____

Prefix	Word Plus Sentence

2. de- _____ _____

   _____

   _____

3. dec- _____ _____

   _____

   _____

4. demi- _____ _____

   _____

   _____

5. mis- _____ _____

   _____

   _____

6. re- _____ _____

   _____

   _____

7. un- _____ _____

   _____

   _____

Since your answers will differ, your instructor should check them.

Exercise 3 *Applying Suffixes to Words*

This exercise contains a number of useful suffixes from various sources. On the lines provided, write at least two words that make use of the suffixes listed in the first column. If you are not certain of the correctness of the word formed, refer to your dictionary. In each case, one suffix is completed to serve as an example.

	Suffix	Meaning	English Words
1.	-able	capacity for	comparable, measurable,
			pleasurable
2.	-acious	having, characterized by	gracious,
3.	-acity	the quality of having or being characterized by	capacity,
4.	-acy	state or nature	fallacy,
5.	-al	belonging to	tribal,
6.	-ance	state of	obeyance,

Suffix	Meaning	English Words
7. -ary	one who is	beneficiary, _____ _____
8. -ate	person or thing	magistrate, _____ _____
9. -ation	process	administration, _____ _____
10. -dom	condition of being	freedom, _____ _____
11. -ee	one who is	employee, _____ _____
12. -en	made of	leaden, _____ _____
13. -er	one who acts	teacher, _____ _____
14. -ful	full of	playful, _____ _____

	Suffix	Meaning	English Words
15.	-fy	to make	specify, _____ _____
16.	-hood	state or character of being	brotherhood, _____ _____
17.	-ine	resembling	genuine, _____ _____
18.	-ish	belong to, like, resembling	selfish, _____ _____
19.	-ist	one who does or acts	feminist, _____ _____
20.	-ity	quality	alkalinity, _____ _____
21.	-less	without	colorless, _____ _____

	Suffix	Meaning	English Words
22.	-ly	like	sadly, _____
			_____
23.	-ment	state of	government, _____
			_____
24.	-ness	state or condition of	happiness, _____
			_____
25.	-oid	similar to	paranoid, _____
			_____
26.	-ous	full of	famous, _____
			_____
27.	-ose	having nature or quality of	varicose, _____
			_____
28.	-ship	state of	internship, _____
			_____
29.	-ster	one who acts	monster, _____
			_____

Suffix	Meaning	English Words
30. -tude	state of	solitude, _____
		_____
31. -ure	act, process, being	pleasure, _____
		_____
32. -ward	in direction of	westward, _____
		_____
33. -y	state of, art of, or profession of	dentistry, _____
		_____

ANSWERS TO EXERCISE 3

Since your answers will vary, your instructor should check this exercise.

Exercise 4 *Using Suffixes in Words and Sentences*

Following are suffixes from various sources. On the lines provided, form a word with the suffix; then use the word in a sentence. Do not use the same words you listed in Exercise 3.

Suffix	Word Plus Sentence
1. -able	_____ _____
	_____
	_____

Suffix	Word Plus Sentence

2. -acy   _____   _____

              _____

              _____

3. -ance   _____   _____

              _____

              _____

4. -ary   _____   _____

              _____

              _____

5. -ation   _____   _____

              _____

              _____

6. -en   _____   _____

              _____

              _____

7. -er   _____   _____

              _____

              _____

	Suffix	Word Plus Sentence

8. -ish _____ _____

_____

_____

9. -ity _____ _____

_____

_____

10. -less _____ _____

_____

_____

11. -ous _____ _____

_____

_____

12. -ship _____ _____

_____

_____

13. -tude _____ _____

_____

_____

Suffix	Word Plus Sentence

14. -ure _____ _____

_____

15. -ward _____ _____

_____

ANSWERS TO EXERCISE 4

Since answers will vary, have your instructor check this exercise.

Postassessment

Match the words in the first column with the definitions in the second column by writing the appropriate letters in the spaces provided.

a. alkalinity

b. beneficiary

c. capacity

d. feminist

e. internship

f. misfortune

g. paranoid

h. specify

i. stature

j. villainy

_____ 1. obtaining practical experience

_____ 2. suspicious

_____ 3. state explicitly

_____ 4. adversity

_____ 5. height

_____ 6. vicious acts

_____ 7. one who supports women's rights

_____ 8. salt content

_____ 9. volume

_____ 10. one who receives

ANSWERS TO POSTASSESSMENT

1. e	6. j
2. g	7. d
3. h	8. a
4. f	9. c
5. i	10. b

Glossary

This glossary contains terms often used in reference to matters of grammar and composition. It also gives tips on certain common writing errors. Its main purpose is to explain briefly the grammatical and rhetorical terms and to provide a quick reference in order to help you improve your writing. Other references to the terms in this glossary, as well as other terms not present here, can be found in the index.

abbreviation An abbreviation is the shortened form of a word. Standard abbreviations include Ms., Mrs., Mr., Dr., St., A.M., P.M., ibid., e.g.; most other abbreviations, however, are not acceptable in college and formal writing.

absolute The term *absolute* names a sentence element that has no specific grammatical function in the sentence but clearly belongs.

Yes, I am going.

He is, however, a good friend.

To tell the truth, I am afraid.

active voice, passive voice Verbs have active voice or passive voice. A verb has active voice when the subject of the verb performs the action of the verb.

subj. v.
The ball hit Isadore.

A verb has passive voice when the subject receives the action of the verb or predicate.

sub. pred.
Isadore was hit by the ball.

adjective	An adjective is a part of speech that modifies a noun or pronoun. Descriptive adjectives name a quality or condition of the noun or pronoun they modify. They have three degrees of comparison: positive, comparative, and superlative (*big* dog, *bigger* dog, *biggest* dog). Proper adjectives come from proper names (*French* style, *American* heritage). Limiting adjectives are determiners and have no degrees of comparison (*this* house, *two* days, *some* money, *a, an, the*). Predicate adjectives appear with linking verbs. They complete the predicate and modify the subject. (She is *kind*. All cars are *expensive* today.) Generally speaking, all adjectives, except predicate adjectives, directly precede the nouns they modify.
adjective clause	An adjective clause is a dependent (subordinate) clause that modifies a noun or pronoun. It generally follows the noun or pronoun it modifies and begins with *whose, whom, which,* or *that*.

Students <u>who study</u> nearly always learn.

The house <u>that I want</u> is now for sale. |
| adverb | An adverb is a part of speech that modifies a verb, an adjective, or another adverb. Adverbs generally tell where, when, how, or to what extent. Their specific use is to tell manner, time, place, degree, or number. There are two kinds of adverbs: simple and conjunctive. Like adjectives, adverbs have three degrees of comparison: positive, comparative, and superlative. |
| adverbial clause | An adverbial clause is a dependent (subordinate) clause that generally modifies a verb or a predicate adjective. Sometimes it modifies an adverb.

We waited <u>until we were exhausted</u>.

She is sorry <u>that you are ill</u>. |
| adverbial conjunction | An adverbial conjunction is an adverb that joins independent clauses. Adverbial conjunctions are also conjunctive adverbs (words such as *hence, thus, otherwise, nevertheless, then, yet, however, accordingly, moreover,* and *consequently*). |

advice, advise	*Advice* is a noun and means "information or notice given." *Advise* is a verb and means "to give information or notice."

n.

Jake gave Judy Pavilo some <u>advice</u>.

v.

She did not ask him to <u>advise</u> her.

affect, effect

Because both words are similar in sound and because both words may be used as nouns or verbs, they are often confusing. A good rule to follow is this one: Use *affect* only as a verb and *effect* only as a noun.

v.

Did her speech <u>affect</u> [move, influence, impress] you in any way?

n.

What <u>effect</u> [result] did her lecture have on you?

agree to, agree with

According to idiomatic usage (usage peculiar to the language), the correct forms are

We agree <u>to the plan</u>.

We agree <u>with the person</u>.

agreement

Agreement means that the corresponding forms of sentence elements or parts of speech must match or show accord. A verb must agree in person and number with its subject, and a pronoun must agree in person, number, and gender with its antecedent.

Anna and Irene <u>are</u> going.

Everyone should do <u>her</u> best.

Every member of the team will carry <u>his</u> own suit.

a lot

A lot is an expression that is common in informal speaking and writing, but it is not acceptable in college and formal writing. There is no such word as *alot*.

all right

The two words *all right* should appear as two words. Although *alright* may be in some dictionaries, it is not acceptable standard English and generally has the designation "nonstandard."

allusion	A figure of speech in which something is referred to indirectly, such as *sour grapes* and *kiss of death*.
among	See *between*, *among*.
ampersand	The ampersand (&) is a symbol for the word *and*. The symbol is unacceptable in college and formal writing and is appropriate only when it is a part of a company name.

G. & C. Merriam Company

analogy	Analogy is a kind of writing in which the writer compares two things that are essentially different except in some striking particulars.
antecedent	The antecedent is a word, clause, or sentence to which a pronoun refers.

$\overset{\overbrace{\text{antecedent}}}{\quad}$ $\overset{\text{pro.}}{\quad}$

When T̲a̲n̲a̲ and Z̲o̲r̲n̲ came, they said that we had won the game.

$\overset{\text{antecedent}}{\quad}$ $\overset{\text{pro.}}{\quad}$

Is this the t̲e̲a̲c̲h̲e̲r̲ who gives such long assignments?

apostrophe	The apostrophe (') is a mark of punctuation. Its uses are as follows:

1. to show the possessive case of nouns, as in Andrew's, men's, children's
2. to form contractions, such as he'll, won't, o'clock, they're, I've
3. to form the plural of letters and numbers, of abbreviations, and of words considered as words only (for example, *t*'s, *3*'s, *two*'s, Ph.D's)

appositive	An appositive is a noun and its modifiers that appear after another noun to explain or identify it.

Juanita Yberra, o̲n̲e̲ ̲o̲f̲ ̲m̲y̲ ̲b̲e̲s̲t̲ ̲f̲r̲i̲e̲n̲d̲s̲, is an outstanding lawyer.

argumentative fallacies	Argumentative fallacies are false arguments that distort or oversimplify the truth. The worst common argumentative fallacies are

1. attacking a person instead of an idea
2. begging the question
3. using extension or exaggeration
4. ignoring content
5. name-calling
6. using as red herring
7. making hasty generalizations
8. employing inadequate causal relationships
9. using stereotypes
10. using either-or fallacies
11. making trivial analogies

articles
The articles are *a, an*, and *the*. These adjectives are determiners—they limit the nouns or pronouns they modify.

at
At often incorrectly and needlessly appears at the end of a sentence.

WRONG: Where is it at?

CORRECTED: Where is it?

auxiliary verb
An auxiliary verb is a helping verb that always appears with another verb. The most common auxiliary or helping verbs are *is, are, am, was, were, be, been, shall, will, may, must, can,* and *do*.

basic sentence elements
The basic sentence elements are the subject, the predicate, and the complement.

because of, due to
Because of is the preferred expression.

Mr. Palermo resigned <u>because of</u> his health.

between, among
Between and *among* have a special use. *Between* implies "two" and *among* "more than two."

<u>Between</u> Juan and Pedro there is no bad feeling.

<u>Among</u> the children who ride the bus, there is a strong bond of friendship.

bible
When *bible* refers to the Scriptures, it should begin with a capital. However, do not italicize it, underline it, or put quotation marks around it.

capital letters	The principal uses of capital letters are the following:

1. for the first word in a sentence (Do your work carefully.)
2. for proper names (James, Vermont, February)
3. for words derived from proper names (German, French, Spanish)
4. for titles that come before proper names (President Lincoln, Governor Smith, Princess Grace)
5. for words in titles of books, poems, and compositions, except the articles *a, an,* and *the* and short prepositions and conjunctions unless they are the first word in the title or the first word after a colon (*Life on the Mississippi*)
6. for the first word of a direct quotation
7. for the pronoun *I* and the interjection *O,* but not *oh* (You have my gratitude, O Mother Nature, for sending us this beautiful day. But compare: Bring five eggs, a quart of milk, and . . . oh yes, some lettuce.)

case	Case is the form of a noun or pronoun that shows its use. There are three cases:

1. nominative, the case of the subject

   <u>Cordelia</u> won the award.

   <u>She</u> always wins.

2. objective, the case of the object

   Did she marry <u>Mr. Serur</u>?

   With <u>whom</u> are you going?

3. possessive

   <u>Solvag's</u> mother is a doctor.

   <u>Her</u> estate is large.

causal analysis	Causal analysis is a kind of writing in which the writer breaks down a process into its individual parts and shows how these parts are related to the cause. Causal analysis shows cause to effect (cause = effect + effect + effect) and effect to cause (effect + effect + effect = cause).

classification	Classification is a kind of writing in which the writer groups similar experiences, ideas, persons, or things. It is a way of establishing order in a composition.
clause	A clause is a group of words with a subject (noun or pronoun) and a predicate (or verb). There are two kinds of clauses:

1. An independent clause has a subject and a predicate and makes complete sense.

   <u>Annabel played the piano</u>, and <u>Reban played the drums</u>.

2. A dependent (subordinate) clause does not make complete sense but depends for meaning on the other parts of the sentence.

   <u>If Lincoln comes early enough</u>, he can buy a ticket.

Dependent (subordinate) clauses can function as nouns, adjectives, or adverbs. See *noun clause*; *adjective clause*; *adverbial clause*.

cliché	A cliché is a trite, hackneyed, worn-out phrase or expression that is usually inappropriate in college and formal writing. Examples of clichés include "dark as night," "you know," "picture of health," "crack of dawn."
coherence	In composition, coherence is the logical relationship within and between, and the logical weaving together of, sentences and paragraphs. Coherence in a composition can be achieved by following a pattern in arranging the parts. Some of the methods of organization are

1. chronological (the order of time)
2. spatial (the order of space relationships)
3. inductive reasoning (from the specific to the general)
4. deductive reasoning (from the general to the specific)

collective noun	A collective noun is the name of a group or class of individuals, such as *audience, army, navy, team, family,* and *committee.* A collective noun takes a singular verb when it refers to a group of individuals as a unit and a plural verb when it refers to the individual members in the unit.

The committee is completing the report.

(The committee is working as a unit.)

The committee were divided in their votes.

(Committee members have individual votes.)

colloquial
: Colloquial English is appropriate for familiar conversation but inappropriate for formal speech or writing.

COLLOQUIAL: They haven't got any.

FORMAL: They have none.

comma splice
: A comma splice, also known as a *comma blunder* or *comma fault*, is the use of only a comma to separate two or more independent clauses.

WRONG: The year 1976 is the two-hundredth birthday of our country, we are celebrating in many different ways.

To correct the comma splice,

1. add the appropriate coordinating conjunction (the word *and, or, nor, but,* or *for*) after the comma: ". . . country, and . . ."
2. change the comma to a semicolon: ". . . country; we . . ."
3. change the comma to a semicolon and follow it with an adverbial conjunction: ". . . country; therefore, . . ."
4. change the comma to a period and begin the second independent clause with a capital letter: ". . . country. We . . ."

comparison and contrast
: Comparison and contrast is a kind of writing in which the writer shows the similarities and differences of two or more subjects. Comparison points out likenesses and contrast points out differences. A thing is compared *to* another thing, but is contrasted *with* another thing.

comparison of adjectives and adverbs
: Comparison is the change (inflection) in the form of adjectives and adverbs to indicate degree. There are three degrees of comparison:

1. positive (good, beautiful, bad, fast, quickly)
2. comparative (better, more beautiful, worse, faster, more quickly)
3. superlative (best, most beautiful, worst, fastest, most quickly)

complement	The complement is a word or words that complete the meaning of the predicate (or verb). The complement can be a direct object, a subject complement, or an object complement.

Leon lent <u>Carver</u> his <u>car</u>.

(*Car* is the direct object complement, and *Carver* is the indirect object complement.)

Max is <u>president</u>.

(*President* is the subject complement. It completes the verb and modifies the subject, *Max*.)

The seniors considered the dress <u>code</u> <u>unfair</u>.

(*Unfair* is the object complement. It modifies the direct object, *code*.)

complete predicate	See *predicate*.
complete subject	The complete subject is the simple subject (noun or pronoun) and its modifiers.
complex sentence	A complex sentence is a sentence that has an independent clause and one or more dependent (subordinate) clauses.

┌────dep. cl.────┐
If you know her, please tell me her name.

┌──────────dep. cl.──────────┐
Students who wish to make the honor roll have to study.

compound sentence	A compound sentence contains two or more independent clauses.

┌────indep. cl.────┐   ┌────indep. cl.────┐
Ashley did all the work, but Hilda received all the credit.

compound-complex sentence	A compound-complex sentence contains two or more independent clauses and one or more dependent (subordinate) clauses.

```
        ┌──────── dep. cl. ────────┐   ┌──── indep. cl. ────┐   ┌────
        When the guests left,  Kay made the beds  and  Robin

        ┌── indep. cl. ──────────┐
        worked in the yard.
```

CONJUGATION OF THE VERB *CHOOSE*
(*Principal parts: choose, chose, chosen*)

Active Voice *(Subject performs action of verb)*		Passive Voice *(Subject receives action of verb)*	
Singular *(One)*	Plural *(Two or more)*	Singular *(One)*	Plural *(Two or more)*

INDICATIVE MOOD
(*States a fact or asks a question*)

Present Tense
(*Action happening now*)

I choose	we choose	I am chosen	we are chosen
you choose	you choose	you are chosen	you are chosen
he (she, it) chooses	they choose	he (she, it) is chosen	they are chosen

Past Tense
(*Action happened in the past*)

I chose	we chose	I was chosen	we were chosen
you chose	you chose	you were chosen	you were chosen
he (she, it) chose	they chose	he (she, it) was chosen	they were chosen

Future Tense
(*Action will happen in the future*)

I shall choose	we shall choose	I shall be chosen	we shall be chosen
you will choose	you will choose	you will be chosen	you will be chosen
he (she, it) will choose	they will choose	he (she, it) will be chosen	they will be chosen

conjugation	Conjugation is the arrangement of the inflected (changing) forms of a verb to show the principal parts, voice, mood, and tense.
conjunction	A conjunction is a word that joins words, phrases, or clauses. There are four classes of conjunctions:

1. Coordinating conjunctions join words, phrases, or clauses of equal rank (*and, or, nor, but, for*).

CONJUGATION OF THE VERB *CHOOSE*
(Principal parts: choose, chose, chosen)

Active Voice *(Subject performs action of verb)*		Passive Voice *(Subject receives action of verb)*	
Singular *(One)*	Plural *(Two or more)*	Singular *(One)*	Plural *(Two or more)*

Present Perfect Tense
(Action begun in an indefinite time in the past but still continuing in the present)

I have chosen	we have chosen	I have been chosen	we have been chosen
you have chosen	you have chosen	you have been chosen	you have been chosen
he (she, it) has chosen	they have chosen	he (she, it) has been chosen	they have been chosen

Past Perfect Tense
(Action completed before another action in the past)

I had chosen	we had chosen	I had been chosen	we had been chosen
you had chosen	you had chosen	you had been chosen	you had been chosen
he (she, it) had chosen	they had chosen	he (she, it) had been chosen	they had been chosen

Future Perfect Tense
(Action to be completed in the future before some other action)

I shall have chosen	we shall have chosen	I shall have been chosen	we shall have been chosen
you will have chosen	you will have chosen	you will have been chosen	you will have been chosen
he (she, it) will have chosen	they will have chosen	he (she, it) will have been chosen	they will have been chosen

---

2. Subordinating conjunctions join dependent clauses to independent clauses and also are introductory words (*if, as, when, while, after, since, because, although, whether, where, why, so that*).
3. Correlative conjunctions appear in pairs (*either . . . or; neither . . . nor; not only . . . but also*).
4. Adverbial conjunctions join two independent clauses (*hence, thus, still, yet, nevertheless, however, consequently, therefore, otherwise*).

conjunctive
adverb

Adverbs that connect independent clauses are conjunctive adverbs (or adverbial conjunctions). See *conjunction.*

The vote was large; <u>however</u>, very few young adults voted.

connotation,
denotation

The secondary, suggested, associated, often emotional meaning of a word or expression is the connotation.

Mother—love, understanding, sacrifice

The denotation of a word or expression is the primary, exact, dictionary meaning.

Mother—a person's female parent

contraction

A contraction is a word that results when two words are combined by leaving out a letter or letters and substituting an apostrophe. Contractions are not acceptable in formal speech or writing.

will not	—	won't
it is	—	it's
I will	—	I'll
cannot	—	can't

correlatives

Correlatives are coordinating conjunctions that function in pairs: *not only, but also; neither, nor; either, or.* See *conjunction.*

dangling
modifier

A dangling modifier dangles or hangs in a sentence because, by its position in the sentence, it is made to modify the wrong word. A dangling modifier is often a participial phrase, but it can be a gerund phrase or an infinitive phrase. A dangling modifier can be corrected by placing the word it modifies after it.

WRONG: <u>Taking our seats</u>, the play began.

(The modifier dangles because the play did not take a seat.)

CORRECTED: Taking our seats, we saw the beginning of the play.

WRONG: <u>Reaching sixteen</u>, cars were important to me.

(The cars do not reach sixteen.)

CORRECTED: Reaching sixteen, I found cars more important than anything else.

declarative sentence
A declarative sentence states a fact.

The United States is my native land.

deductive reasoning
Deductive reasoning is a process of thought in which the writer begins with a general statement as a premise known or accepted as true and leads away from it with supporting details to a particular conclusion.

definition
Definition is a kind of writing similar to classification because the writer establishes a word in a particular class before giving more specifically its various aspects, dimensions, or meanings. The writer begins with the most general meaning of the word and then develops within the paper the other definitions associated with the word.

demonstrative
A demonstrative is an adjective or a pronoun that points out something.

<u>This</u> dress I made.

<u>That</u> is mine.

denotation
See *connotation, denotation*.

dependent clause
A dependent clause is a group of words that has a subject and a predicate (or verb) but does not make complete sense.

If you will do your best

different from, different than	*Different from* is the preferred expression, even though *different than* is now recognized as acceptable by standard dictionaries. This schedule is <u>different from</u> the other one.
direct address	Direct address is calling a person or thing by name and directing a remark to that person or thing. <u>Gerda</u>, please make your report. Blow, O Wild West <u>Wind</u>!
direct object	The direct object is the noun or pronoun that receives the action of a transitive verb. To find the direct object ask the verb the question *what*? The car hit the <u>tree</u>. (Hit what? The tree. *Tree* is the direct object.)
direct quotation	A direct quotation means that the words of a speaker have been quoted exactly and enclosed in quotation marks. Any explanation of the speaker's words that a writer includes between the quotation marks must be enclosed in brackets. "I am convinced," Nicole said firmly, "that she [Dr. Blair] is the most competent general practitioner in town."
disinterested	See *uninterested, disinterested*.
due to	See *because of, due to*.
effect	See *affect, effect*.
elliptical construction	An elliptical construction is a word or words that are clearly understood but are not stated. Lydia is taller than I [am tall]. (*I* is the subject of the verb *am* in the elliptical construction.) If [it is] possible, send a check. (The elliptical construction is the clause *it is*.)

emphasis	In composition, emphasis distinguishes the most important from the less important points. The most emphatic position in a sentence, a paragraph, or a composition is at the end; the second most emphatic position is at the beginning. Therefore, in writing, position is important for giving emphasis. Other devices for giving emphasis are these: repeating important ideas in different words (making sure to avoid redundancy), using punctuation, and using proportion—that is, discussing the more important ideas more than the other ideas.
enthuse	*Enthuse* is in colloquial use, but in college and formal writing *be enthusiastic* is more appropriate.
exclamation	An exclamation is a strong or emphatic expression. It should be followed by an exclamation point.
	She's here !
	Ouch !
	Help me !
exclamatory sentence	An exclamatory sentence expresses sudden or strong feeling.
	Call the fire department!
expletive	An expletive is a word or phrase that is used to introduce, fill out, or give emphasis to a sentence. *It* and *there* are expletives when they serve any of these functions. Other expletives are exclamations or oaths, especially profane or obscene ones.
	<u>It</u> is my pleasure to serve as your president.
	<u>There</u> was nobody to comfort the family.
	"<u>Durn</u>!" said Aunt Mary Hayseed. "If that isn't that old bore Solly Stubbs coming up the road."
figure of speech	A figure of speech is a comparison between two things essentially unlike except in some striking particular. In expository writing, figures of speech make the complex simple, make the abstract concrete, and help readers visualize and understand. The five figures of speech most commonly used are simile, metaphor, personification, analogy, and allusion.

gender	Gender is a category (masculine, feminine, or neuter) in which a word is placed according to sex, psychological associations, and other characteristics. In English, the third-person personal pronouns are inflected (altered) to show gender.

MASCULINE: he, him, his

FEMININE: she, her, hers

NEUTER: it, its

In many other languages, every noun has a gender. In Spanish and French, for example, the word for *day* is masculine and the word for *night* is feminine.

general to particular	The general-to-particular composition is one in which the writer begins with a general topic sentence or thesis statement that summarizes the subject of discussion and then adds particulars that support or prove the topic sentence. The general-to-particular method of composition uses deductive reasoning.
gerund	A gerund is an *ing* form of a verb that functions as a noun. The gerund may take an object, a complement, or a modifier.

He won by running faster.

(*Running* is the object of the preposition *by*.)

Seeing is believing.

(*Seeing* is the subject of the verb *is*. *Believing* is the complement.)

Her winning caused great excitement.

(*Her* modifies *winning*.)

illustration	Illustration is a kind of writing in which the writer makes a general statement and supports it with concrete details and examples.
imperative sentence	An imperative sentence states a request or a command.

Please study this assignment carefully.

indefinite pronoun	Such words as *anyone, someone, something, nobody, everybody,* and *everyone* are indefinite pronouns—pronouns that do not indicate specifically the identity of the person or thing to which they refer.
indicative mood	The indicative mood is appropriate for making a statement or asking a question. See *conjugation.*
indirect object	The indirect object is the person or thing to whom the action in a sentence is directed or for whom the action is performed.

They gave <u>me</u> the choice seat.

(Gave what? Seat. *Seat* is the direct object. Who received the seat? The person referred to as *me. Me* is the indirect object.)

Luke's father bought <u>him</u> a new car.

(Bought what? Car. *Car* is the direct object. Who received the car? The person referred to as *him. Him* is the indirect object.)

indirect quotation	An indirect quotation means that the meaning of a speaker's words is repeated, but not the exact words. No quotation marks are used.

She said that she was elated.

I heard him yell that he needed help.

inductive reasoning	Inductive reasoning is a process of thought in which the writer begins with particulars (details) and leads into a general statement or inclusive generalization.
infinitive	An infinitive is a verb form composed of the word *to* plus the present form of the verb (to see, to run, to read). An infinitive often functions as a noun, as in the examples that follow.

He plans <u>to study</u>.   (object of the verb *plan*)

<u>To tell</u> the truth should be our objective.   (subject of the predicate *should be*)

They have a plan <u>to present</u>. (adjective modifying the noun *plan*)

My dream, <u>to be Miss America</u>, never came true. (appositive of *dream*)

inflection

Inflection is the change in the form of a word to show grammatical use. Nouns change to show singular and plural number and possessive case.

SINGULAR POSSESSIVE: man's, child's, dog's

PLURAL POSSESSIVE: men's, children's, dogs'

Some verbs change their form to show the principal parts and tense and mood.

do, did, done, does, doing

play, played, playing

(See *conjugation*.) Most of the personal pronouns change form (are inflected) to show person, number, gender, and case. (See *personal pronoun*.)

interjection

See *parts of speech*.

interpretation

Interpretation is a kind of composition in which the writer tells what a work of literature or a movie means to him or her. The writer takes the elements of a work of literature or a movie (characters, plot, point of view, setting, structure, symbolism, theme, irony, tone) and discusses what they mean and what they have to say about life according to his or her own views and experiences.

interrogative pronoun

The interrogative pronouns are *who, whom, whose, which, what*. They introduce questions.

<u>Who</u> sang the last song?

<u>Whose</u> rings are these?

<u>Which</u> kite do you want?

interrogative sentence

An interrogative sentence asks a question. It must always be followed by a question mark.

<u>What</u> is your favorite song ?

intransitive verb	An intransitive verb does not take an object. The verb *be* is an intransitive verb; it never takes an object. Other intransitive verbs are *lie* (to recline) and *sit* (to take a seat). Lie down, Fido. She sat in that chair for an hour.
irregular verb	An irregular verb does not form its past tense and past participle by adding *d* or *ed*. The verb *be* is the most irregular of all verbs and the most common verb. The present form (*be*) changes to *am, are,* and *is*; the past form to *was* and *were*; and the past participle to *been*. Other irregular verbs include *see, swim, lie, do,* and *take*.
its, it's	*Its* (without the apostrophe) is a pronoun that shows ownership. *It's* (a contraction) means "it is" or "it has." The city lost its [ownership] federal funds. It's [it is] not time to go. It's [it has] been cold all winter.
judgment and evaluation	In a judgment and evaluation composition, the writer gives an overall opinion of the significance of a work of literature or a movie by evaluating it. The content and tone of the composition must indicate not only the judgment and the evaluation of the subject but also the reasons for such judgment and evaluation.
linking verb	A linking verb joins the subject and the subject complement. *Is, are, am, was, were, be, been, become, seem, feel, taste, smell,* and *look* nearly always join a subject and a subject complement. This okra tastes good. (good okra) Reva is beautiful. (beautiful Reva) That expression sounds bad. (bad expression)
metaphor	A figure of speech in which one thing is said to be another thing, either directly (as in "my little girl is a house wren, with all her bustle and happy chatter") or indirectly (as in "the boat ploughed the waves," where *ploughed* implies that the boat is a plough and the waves are a field).

modifier	A modifier is a word or a phrase that describes, qualifies, or restricts another word.

<u>Tired</u>, <u>defeated</u>, <u>discouraged</u>, <u>the</u> team walked <u>slowly</u> <u>from the football field</u> <u>into the dressing room</u>.

mood	Mood is a verb form that names the manner of action. There are three moods:

1. The *indicative* mood states a fact or asks a question.

I know you are glad.

Are you glad?

2. The *imperative* mood states a command or request.

Please come again.

Help me.

3. The *subjunctive* mood states a condition contrary to fact.

If I had your talent, I would enter the contest.

I wish Arne were here.

narrative	A story or a description of a real or fictional incident or series of incidents is a narrative.
nominative absolute	A nominative absolute is a phrase containing a noun or a pronoun followed by a participle.

The <u>work</u> <u>being</u> done, the painters left.

nominative case	The nominative case is the case of the subject. When a noun or pronoun functions as the subject of a verb, the complement of a linking verb, or an appositive of either, it is in the nominative case.

<u>Reg</u> is a loyal friend.   (subject of verb *is*)

Guy is my best <u>friend</u>.   (subject complement)

Rex, my best <u>friend</u>, is loyal.   (appositive)

nonrestrictive modifier	A nonrestrictive modifier describes the thing it modifies but is not crucial to the meaning of the sentence in which it appears; it provides additional, but not necessary, information. Nonrestrictive modifiers are usually found either

after proper nouns or after nouns that are already identified. Always set off nonrestrictive modifiers with commas.

Tom, <u>my brother</u>, is my good friend.

(*Tom* is a proper noun.)

My feet, <u>which are still cold</u>, hurt.

(*My* identifies *feet*.)

noun   A noun is the part of speech that names a person, place, or thing.

noun clause   A noun clause is a dependent (subordinate) clause that functions as a noun.

      subj.
<u>Whatever you do</u> will be news.

          d.o.
Do <u>whatever will make you happiest</u>.

         i.o.
He will give <u>whoever phones first</u> the reward.

       obj. of prep.
Give it to <u>whoever phones first</u>.

     subj. comp.
This is <u>what you saw</u>?

         appos.
He wants the prize, <u>whatever it is</u>.

  direct address
<u>Whoever you are</u>, prepare to do battle!

number   Number is the form of a noun, a personal pronoun, and a verb that indicates how many. There are two numbers: singular, meaning one, and plural, meaning more than one.

woman	—	women
boy	—	boys
city	—	cities
ox	—	oxen

object complement	The object complement comes immediately after the direct object and explains it.

The judges chose Phyllis <u>Miss America</u>.

Did your brother name his baby <u>Albert</u>?

objective case	When a noun or a pronoun is a direct object, an indirect object, the object of a preposition, or the subject or object of an infinitive, it is in the objective case.

She has finished the <u>work</u>.   (direct object of the verb *finished*)

I game <u>him</u> my best wishes.   (indirect object of the verb *gave*)

She came by for <u>Brent</u> and <u>me</u>.   (objects of the preposition *for*)

I wanted <u>her</u> to sing.   (subject of the infinitive *to sing*)

Do you want to tease <u>her</u>?   (object of the infinitive *to tease*)

outline	An outline is a plan, a guide, and a blueprint for constructing a composition. It guides the writer, but it can be changed and improved as it is worked with. Three main divisions of every composition (introduction, body, conclusion) form the skeleton outline. The outline should also include the topic (thesis) sentence and the concluding sentence. There are two major forms of outline: the topic outline and the sentence outline. A writer may use the form best suited to the task at hand; but the sentence and the topic form should not be used in the same outline. The outline form is as follows:

Title of Composition

Introduction and thesis statement:

    I.

       A.

       B.

       C.

          1.

          2.

             a.

             b.

II.

III.

    A.

    B.

Conclusion:

paragraph	A paragraph is a group of related sentences about one central idea. The first line of a paragraph is always indented approximately one inch to the right from the margin (approximately five typewriter spaces). The controlling idea is always in a topic sentence, usually the first sentence. The sentences follow each other in a logical order so that the paragraph has emphasis (stress or force), unity (oneness), and coherence (logical connection).
parallel structure	Parallel structure is the use of the same grammatical form to express closely related ideas.
	The children rushed down the steps, ran out the door, and raced up the hill.
participle	A participle is a verb-based word that ends in *ing, ed, en,* or *t* and functions as an adjective.
	We all tried to comfort the frightened dog.
	Screaming wildly, the child had a temper tantrum.
participial phrase	A participial phrase is a group of related words (without subject or verb) that contains an *ing, ed*, or *en* verb form that functions as an adjective.
	Seeing the fire, I ran for help.
	Being discouraged, Otto cried.
particular to general	The particular-to-general composition includes particular details that lead to a general statement. The particular-to-general method of composition uses inductive reasoning.
parts of speech	The eight parts of speech are as follows:

1. *noun*, the name of a person, place, or thing (Andrea, psychiatrist, Boston, Nile, gravel)
2. *verb*, a word (or words) that shows action, being, or a state of being (*Throw* the ball. She *is* the queen. They *are married*.)

3. *pronoun*, a word used in place of a noun (she, it, they)
4. *adjective*, a word that modifies (describes) a noun or pronoun (*intelligent* woman, *kind* person, *high* tower)
5. *adverb*, a word that modifies an adjective, a verb, or another adverb (*very* intelligent, ran *slowly, more nearly* perfect)
6. *conjunction*, a word that joins words, phrases, or clauses (kind *and* gentle, to study *or* to play)
7. *preposition*, a word that shows the relationship of a noun or pronoun to the sentence (Please call *for* me.)
8. *interjection*, a word expressing sudden or strong feeling (Oh! Help! Fire!)

passive voice	See *active voice, passive voice*.
person	Nouns and pronouns have person to distinguish among the person speaking (first person), the person spoken to (second person), and the person spoken of (third person). Person also has singular and plural number.

We told you about the students who are going to Mexico.

(*We* is first-person plural; persons are speaking. *You* is second-person singular or plural; a person or persons are being spoken to. *Students* is third-person plural; persons are being spoken of.)

personal pronoun — A personal pronoun is a pronoun that indicates the person speaking, the person spoken to, or the person spoken about. The personal pronouns are as follows:

1. nominative case (the case of the subject)

I	we
you	you
he, she, it	they

2. objective case (the case of the object)

me	us
you	you
him, her, it	them

3. possessive case (shows ownership)

my, mine	our, ours
your, yours	your, yours
his, her, hers, its	their, theirs

Note: The apostrophe does not appear with any personal pronoun to show ownership. The possessive personal pronoun form by itself signifies ownership.

personification   A personification is a figure of speech in which human qualities are assigned to inanimate objects.

Springtime skips merrily across the meadow, scattering daffodils and tulips from the basket she carries gracefully over her arm.

persuasion   The persuasive composition is exactly what the word *persuasion* implies: the writer persuades readers to agree with an opinion. The writer uses either deductive or inductive reasoning to give a valid argument that convinces readers to agree with the opinion.

phrase   A phrase is a group of related words with no subject or predicate.

on the hill, going home, doing his work, to whom

point of view   The point of view is the position the writer takes in relation to the composition. These are four points of view:

1. *first* person, the person speaking (I or we)
2. *second* person, the person spoken to (you)
3. *third* person, the person spoken of (he, she, it, they)
4. *omniscient*, the point of view in which the writer has complete, unlimited knowledge

possessive case of nouns   A noun in the possessive case shows ownership. Most nouns with singular number form the possessive by adding an apostrophe and *s* ('s).

girl's, man's, child's, woman's, John's, Irene's

All nouns with plural numbers that end in *s* form the possessive by adding only an apostrophe.

girls', boys', babies', Johns'

All nouns with plurals that do not end in *s* form the possessive by adding an apostrophe and *s* (*'s*).

men's, children's, women's, oxen's

possessive case of pronouns	See *personal pronoun*.

predicate	The predicate (or *simple predicate*) of a sentence consists of the verb or verbs that tell what the subject does or is. The *complete predicate* (one underline in the examples that follow) contains the main verb plus its auxiliaries, complements, and modifiers.

                  v.

He goes to work early.

                      v.

Everyone should do his best.

           v.   v.

She dresses nicely but prefers simple styles.

A *compound predicate* consists of two or more predicate verbs plus their auxiliaries. The predicate in the third example above is compound.

predicate adjective	A predicate adjective is an adjective that follows the predicate and describes the subject, as in "The weather is *cool* today."

predicate noun	A predicate noun is a noun that follows the predicate and renames the subject, as in "Sarah is my cousin."

predicate pronoun	A predicate pronoun is a pronoun that follows the predicate and renames the subject, as in "The person I hoped to talk to was *you*."

prefix	A prefix is a meaningful syllable added to the beginning of a word. In a dictionary a prefix being defined is followed by a hyphen, as in *com-, de-, pre-*.

preposition	A preposition is a word that joins a noun or pronoun that

follows it to another word in the sentence (generally a noun or a verb).

They bought the house <u>on</u> the hill.

(*On* is the preposition; *hill* is the word that follows *on* and is joined to the sentence by *on; on the hill* modifies *house*.) See also *parts of speech*.

process

Process is a method of composition in which the writer discusses a series of actions, operations, or steps that lead to an end result. The writer should know the subject well because the process must be divided into steps, each step described, and the end result stated. Process is used primarily in "how-to-do-it" writing.

pronoun

A pronoun is a word that stands for a noun. There are four kinds of pronouns:

1. *Personal* pronouns stand for nouns that name people. They have gender, number, and case. (See *personal pronoun*.)
2. *Relative* pronouns introduce adjective clauses (who, which, that, what, whoever, whosoever, whichever, whatever).
3. *Demonstrative* pronouns point out (this, these, that, those).
4. *Reflexive* pronouns end in *self* (myself, yourself, herself, ourselves, themselves) and must have a subject on which to reflect.

<u>I</u> did it <u>myself</u>.
<u>They</u> blame <u>themselves</u>.

See also *indefinite pronoun*.

proper noun

A proper noun is the name of a particular person, place, or thing.

James, Maggie, Arizona, the Alamo, December

punctuation

Punctuation is the use of symbols (marks) to separate written words into meaningful units. The most common punctuation symbols are the period, the question mark, the exclamation point, the comma, the semicolon, the colon, the dash, the apostrophe, quotation marks, parentheses, and brackets.

| real, really | *Real* is an adjective that modifies nouns and pronouns. |

A <u>real</u> fireplace

the <u>real</u> me

Really is an adverb that modifies a verb, an adjective, or another adverb.

<u>really</u> sings

<u>really</u> good

<u>really</u> well

| reflexive pronoun | See *pronoun*. |

| regular verb | A regular verb is a verb whose principal parts are formed by adding *ed* or *d* to the present tense and the past participle. |

Present	Past	Past Participle
walk	walked	walked
talk	talked	talked

| relative pronoun | See *pronoun*. |

| restrictive modifier | A restrictive modifier identifies the word it modifies. Because a restrictive modifier is necessary to the meaning of the sentence, no commas come before or after it. |

The girl <u>whose name is Freda</u> is her cousin.

The song <u>that she sang</u> was from an opera.

| root | A root is a word in its most basic form without prefixes and suffixes. |

| run-on sentence | A run-on sentence is a group of words that is punctuated as a single sentence but that actually contains two or more sentences running into each other with no punctuation separating them. |

sentence	A sentence is a group of words having at least one subject and one predicate and expressing one complete thought or one or more closely related thoughts. It begins with a capital letter and ends with a period, a question mark, or an exclamation point. Four types of sentences according to use are declarative, imperative, interrogative, and exclamatory. And three types of sentences according to form are simple, complex, and compound.
sentence fragment	A group of words not having both a subject and a predicate and not making complete sense is a sentence fragment.
simile	A simile is a figure of speech in which two things are compared by using *like* or *as*. Many of the most common clichés (such as "Her cheeks were *as red as roses*" or "Searching for my contact lenses was *like looking for a needle in a haystack*") are similes.
simple sentence	A simple sentence consists of a subject and a predicate—a single independent clause.
subject	The subject (or *simple subject*) of a sentence is the noun or pronoun about which something is stated or asked. The subject generally comes before the predicate or verb. The *complete subject* (one underline in the examples that follow) is the subject plus any modifiers.

          subj.
The <u>house on the hill</u> is brightly painted.

          subj.   subj.
<u>My fat cat and chunky dog</u> prefer my dinner to theirs.

A compound subject consists of two or more nouns that serve as subjects. The subject in the second example above is compound.

subject complement	See *complement*.
subordinate clause	See *clause*.

suffix	A suffix is a meaningful syllable added to the end of a word. In a dictionary a suffix being defined is preceded by a hyphen, as in *-able, -est,* and *-ose.*
technical analysis	Technical analysis is a kind of writing in which the writer explains carefully the presentation of the characters, irony, plot, point of view, setting, structure, symbolism, theme, tone, or other literary elements in a work of literature or a movie. The literary work or movie must be thoroughly analyzed before a technical-analysis composition is attempted.
tense of verbs	Tense means *time.* There are six tenses of verbs: present, past, future, present perfect, past perfect, future perfect. See *conjugation.*
their, there	*Their* is a pronoun that shows ownership. *There* usually indicates "that place or position."
	The Rozelle children wanted their toys.
	Mrs. Romano always sits there.
to, too, two	*To* is a function word that suggests "action or movement toward a person, place, or thing." *Too* means "also, excessively, or very." *Two* indicates the number "two."
	Mr. Capelo drove to Salem.
	Mrs. Cohen will be on the committee, too.
	Miss Luzinski is too kind.
	Mrs. Johnson has two cars.
topic sentence	The topic sentence (thesis statement) is usually the beginning statement of a composition or paragraph. In it, the writer states the main idea of the composition or the paragraph.
transition	A transition is a word or an expression that connects sentences and paragraphs. Common transitions include *furthermore, first, second, third, in the second place, in addition, however, but, yet, at the same time, for this purpose, then, as a result, in other words,* and *for example.*

transitive verb	A transitive verb takes an object. It has the name "transitive" because the action of the verb travels ("transits") from the subject to the object.

v.   d.o.

Joel <u>won</u> the <u>award</u>.

uninterested, disinterested	*Disinterested* means "unbiased"; *uninterested* means "apathetic" or "not interested."

Mr. Stefano is a <u>disinterested</u> reviewer.

Ms. Minot is <u>uninterested</u> about her future.

verb	A verb is a part of speech that shows action, being, or a state of being. Verbs are inflected to show principal parts, number, person, voice, mood, and tense. See *conjugation, predicate*.
verbal	A verbal is a verb form that functions as a noun or an adjective. Three kinds of verbals are

1. the infinitive (to see, to run, to play)
2. the present participle or gerund (seeing, running, playing)
3. the past participle (seen, run, played)

very	*Very* is an adverb that expresses intensity. Avoid overusing this word.
voice	See *active voice, passive voice, conjugation*.
you	Avoid using *you* as an indefinite pronoun in college and formal writing. Use *one*.

Index

Denotation, 48
Dependent clause, 146, 164–166
  punctuation of, 146, 304
Details, in students' essays, 3, 8, 44, 51,
    55, 63, 66, 68, 69, 72, 73, 75, 83,
    101
Diction
  clichés, 199
  denotation and connotation, 48
  similes, 201–202
Direct address, use of comma with, 310
Direct object, 132
  with *lay,* 265
  with *raise,* 269–270
  with *set,* 265
  test for, 132
Direct quotation
  use of comma with, 309
  use of quotation marks with, 321

Each, number of pronoun and verb with,
    242
East, Linda, 115
Effect-to-cause analysis, 61–64
  formula for, 61
ei, spelling errors and, 360
Either, number of pronoun and verb with,
    242
Either-or fallacy, 81
Elements of style, list of, 89–90
Elliptical clause, 229
Elliptical construction, *see* Subject, implied
Emotional appeal
  in persuasion, 77
  of words, 73
Evaluation, *see* Judgment and evaluation
Everybody, number of pronoun and verb
    with, 242
Everyone, number of pronoun and verb with,
    242
Exclamation point, use of, 320
Exclamatory sentence, 148
  use of exclamation point with, 320
Explanation
  use of brackets with, 325
  use of parentheses with, 325

Expletive, sentence introduced by,
    127–128
Extension, fallacy of, 79

Fallacies, 79–81
Figures, *see* Numbers
Foreign words, use of italics to indicate, 328
Formula
  for cause-to-effect analysis, 58–59
  for deductive reasoning, 66
  for effect-to-cause analysis, 61
  for inductive reasoning, 71

Gender, agreement of pronoun and antece-
    dent in, 240–243, 244
Generalization, *see* Hasty generalization
General to particular (as method of composi-
    tion), 65–70
  deductive reasoning in, 65–66
  explanation of, 65
  in students' essays, 66–69
Gerunds, 162
Glass Menagerie, The (Williams), 111–112

Hallman, Robert P., 55
Hanks, Susan, 91
Hasty generalization, 80
Hennig, Debbie, 67
Hyphen, use of, 323–324

I, capitalization of, 328
Ignoring context, fallacy of, 79–80
Illustration (as method of composition),
    3–18
  definition of, 3
  formula for, 3–4
  outline for, 4, 6
  in students' essays, 4–5, 6–7
Imperative sentence, 148
Inadequate causal relationship, fallacy of,
    80–81
Indefinite pronouns
  agreement with antecedent, 242
  agreement with verb, 242
  definition of, 451
  use of in hasty generalization, 80

Truesdell, Judy, 53
Tyler, Tom, 101

Underlining, *see* Italics, use of
Unity of sentence, 143–144
Usage
  colloquial, 67
  formal, 245

Verbals, 304
Verbs
  agreement with subject, 214, 216–220
  emphatic form of, 260
  intransitive, 265
  irregular, 252–253
  linking, 131, 283
  participle, form of, 259
  principal parts of, 251–253
  progressive form of, 259
  regular, 251
  sensory, 131, 283
  tense of, 254–256, 260
  transitive, 132, 265
  troublesome, 263–265, 269–270
  voice, 128–129

Violent Bear It Away, The (O'Connor), 113–114
Vocabulary
  crossword puzzle, Greek derivatives, 419 (fig.)
  crossword puzzle, Latin derivatives, 397 (fig.)
  French and Latin sources, 422–434
  Greek roots and prefixes, 400–421
  Latin roots and prefixes, 367–399
Voice, of verbs
  active, 128
  passive, 128–129
  use of, 129

Walton, Peter, 42
Wartes, Carolynn L., 68
Which, antecedent of, 243
"White Heron, A" (Jewett), 101–103
Who, antecedent of, 242
Whom, antecedent of, 242
Wooten, Thomas A., 56
Wordiness, 208–209
Wray, Sam, 85